GREATEST-EVER
PASTRY
COOKBOOK

GREATEST-EVER
PASTRY
COOKBOOK

HOW TO MAKE PERFECT PIES, TARTS, FLANS, PASTRIES AND STRUDELS:
120 RECIPES SHOWN IN 280 STUNNING PHOTOGRAPHS

CATHERINE ATKINSON

HERMES
HOUSE

This edition is published by Hermes House,
an imprint of Anness Publishing Ltd,
Hermes House,
88–89 Blackfriars Road,
London SE1 8HA
tel. 020 7401 2077; fax 020 7633 9499

www.hermeshouse.com; www.annesspublishing.com

If you like the images in this book and would like to
investigate using them for publishing, promotions or
advertising, please visit our website
www.practicalpictures.com for more information.

Publisher: Joanna Lorenz
Editors: Kath Jewitt and Kate Eddison
Food Styling: Emma Patmore and Annabel Ford
Stylist: Helen Trent
Designer: Shelley Doyle
Additional Recipes: Alex Barker, Angela Boggiano,
Carla Capalbo, Jacqueline Clarke, Carole Clements,
Trish Davies, Roz Denny, Matthew Drennan,
Joanna Farrow, Christine France, Sarah Gates,
Brian Glover, Nicola Graimes, Christine Ingram,
Lucy Knox, Norma MacMillan, Sue Maggs,
Sally Mansfield, Maggie Mayhew, Norma Miller,
Sally Morris, Keith Richmond, Liz Trigg,
Hilaire Walden, Laura Washburn, Steven Wheeler
and Elizabeth Wolf-Cohen
Special Photography: Janine Hosegood
Additional Photography: Karl Adamson, Steve Baxter,
James Duncan, Gus Filgate, Ian Garlick, Michelle Garrett,
Amanda Heywood, Dave Jordan, Dave King,
William Lingwood, Thomas Odulate, Craig Robertson
and Sam Stowell
Copy Editors: Rosie Hankin and Jenni Fleetwood
Production Controller: Mai-Ling Collyer
Indexer: Diana Lecore

Designed and edited for Anness Publishing Ltd by
Brierley Books

ETHICAL TRADING POLICY

At Anness Publishing we believe that business should be
conducted in an ethical and ecologically sustainable way,
with respect for the environment and a proper regard to
the replacement of the natural resources we employ.

As a publisher, we use a lot of wood pulp to make
high-quality paper for printing, and that wood commonly
comes from spruce trees. We are therefore currently
growing more than 750,000 trees in three Scottish forest
plantations: Berrymoss (130 hectares/320 acres), West
Touxhill (125 hectares/305 acres) and Deveron Forest
(75 hectares/185 acres). The forests we manage contain
more than 3.5 times the number of trees employed
each year in making paper for the books we manufacture.

Because of this ongoing ecological investment
programme, you, as our customer, can have the pleasure
and reassurance of knowing that a tree is being
cultivated on your behalf to naturally replace the
materials used to make the book you are holding.

Our forestry programme is run in accordance with the
UK Woodland Assurance Scheme (UKWAS) and will be
certified by the internationally recognized Forest
Stewardship Council (FSC). The FSC is a non-government
organization dedicated to promoting responsible
management of the world's forests. Certification ensures
forests are managed in an environmentally sustainable
and socially responsible way. For further information
about this scheme, go to www.annesspublishing.com/trees

PUBLISHER'S NOTE
Although the advice and information in this book are
believed to be accurate and true at the time of going to
press, neither the authors nor the publisher can accept
any legal responsibility or liability for any errors or
omissions that may be made.

NOTES
Bracketed terms are intended for American
readers.

For all recipes, quantities are given in both
metric and imperial measures and, where
appropriate, in standard cups and spoons.
Follow one set, but not a mixture, because they
are not interchangeable.

Standard spoon and cup measures are level.
1 tsp = 5ml, 1 tbsp = 15ml, 1 cup = 250ml/8fl oz.

Australian standard tablespoons are 20ml.
Australian readers should use 3 tsp in place of
1 tbsp for measuring small quantities of
gelatine, flour, salt, etc.

American pints are 16fl oz/2 cups. American
readers should use 20fl oz/2.5 cups in place of
1 pint when measuring liquids.

Electric oven temperatures in this book are for
conventional ovens. When using a fan oven, the
temperature will probably need to be reduced
by about 10–20°C/20–40°F. Since ovens vary,
you should check with your manufacturer's
instruction book for guidance.

Medium (US large) eggs are used unless
otherwise stated.

Front cover shows Dark Chocolate and
Hazelnut Tart – for recipe see page 138.

Contents

Introduction

Few can resist the display in the window of a good quality pâtisserie, and many of us have fond memories of the savoury pies and rich, fruit-laden tarts served up at family dinnertimes. Be it a humble apple tart or a hearty chicken and mushroom pie, there is something irresistible about well-made pastry that makes it popular with people of all ages.

A BRIEF HISTORY OF PASTRY
Pastry dates back to the 5th century BC. As the ancient Romans and Greeks used oil, not butter, in their cooking, it would not have been possible to shape the pastry. Consequently, pastry was used primarily as a container for a filling, to protect it from the heat of the fire and ensure that juices would not be lost during cooking. It was often simply a mixture of flour and water, which cooked to a leaden covering that was broken off and discarded. As ovens improved, it was possible to explore ways of making pastry a more edible

and appealing part of the dish. In Northern Europe, butter and lard were used in cooking, and it was this addition to the basic recipe that made firmer, more pliable pastries possible.

At first little distinction was made between sweet and savoury pastries – a meat or fish pie could be topped with a sweet pastry with a sugary glaze. In Tudor times, the emphasis was on appearance. Beautifully moulded pies formed the centrepieces at banquets, and had dramatic fillings, such as live animals or performers. Little wonder no one wanted to eat the pastry!

Meanwhile, the poorer classes relied on pastry both for nourishment and to package their food. Pastry parcels often contained two fillings at once – sweet at one end and savoury at the other.

Over the years, pastry became richer and more flavoursome; by the 17th century, butter, eggs and spices were being added to the basic recipe.

The 19th century saw the creation of many classic pastry recipes. One of the greatest pastry chefs of all time,

BELOW: *Chicken and mushroom pie is a classic recipe that has stood the test of time.*

ABOVE: *The Cornish pasty with its meat and vegetable filling was a simple way for miners to eat properly down the mines.*

ABOVE: *The availability of ready-made pastries means recipes such as mille-feuille are within the grasp even of beginners.*

ABOVE: *Easy travel and communication means today we are as likely to serve a Turkish baklava as an English pudding.*

Antonin Carême, is credited with creating the classic vol-au-vent, mille-feuille and croquembouche.

As chefs experimented with different ingredients and various techniques, pastry making became simpler and less time-consuming, and a number of short-cut recipes came into being.

PASTRY MAKING TODAY

Time-saving machines, such as food processors and refrigerators, further simplified the art of pastry making. Trends have come and gone, but at heart, all sweet and savoury pastries still rely on a well-made pastry. Indeed, the rules of pastry making

have hardly changed since the 19th century and still apply to both classic and contemporary recipes.

Easy travel and communication has increased our knowledge of pastries from around the world. Ready-made pastry, such as filo, is as easily available as shortcrust, and modern cooks are as likely to serve a rich Turkish baklava as a tarte tatin. It is interesting to see how certain combinations or uses for pastry constantly reappear. Dishes such as apple pie and blueberry pie are found worldwide, as are layered pastries and turnovers. The potential combinations of pastry and filling are limited only by the cook's imagination.

How to use this book

You do not need to be an experienced pastry cook to make good pastry. This book has all the necessary information to get started, as well as containing many fabulous recipes, from all-time classics to new and contemporary dishes. It will help you to feel confident about every aspect of making good pastry. Once you have mastered the art, you can turn to the recipe chapters for a comprehensive selection of sweet and savoury treats. Whatever the filling, each is a delicious example of the pleasure to be had from pastry making.

Small savoury pastries

Individual pastries brimming with tasty

fillings are ideal for serving as appetizers.

Delicate pastries, such as Cheese Scrolls

and Moroccan Prawn Packages, made from

melt-in-the-mouth filo, are just right to tempt

the tastebuds at the beginning of a meal,

while more substantial first courses, such as

Egg and Salmon Puff Parcels, will please

those with larger appetites. This chapter also

contains numerous recipes that are perfect

for light lunches or snacks.

Cheese scrolls

These traditional East European cheese savouries are eaten in cafés, restaurants and homes at any time of the day and are delicious when eaten both warm and cold.

MAKES 14–16

450g/1lb feta cheese, well drained and finely crumbled
90ml/6 tbsp Greek (US strained plain) yogurt
2 eggs, beaten
14–16 sheets of filo pastry, each measuring 40 x 30cm/
    16 x 12in, thawed if frozen
225g/8oz/1 cup butter, melted
sea salt and chopped spring onions (scallions), to garnish

1 Preheat the oven to 200°C/400°F/Gas 6. Mix together the feta cheese, yogurt and eggs in a large bowl, beating well until the mixture is smooth.

2 Fit a piping (pastry) bag with a large 1cm/½in plain round nozzle and fill with half of the cheese mixture.

3 Fold one sheet of the filo pastry into a 30 x 20cm/12 x 8in rectangle and brush it carefully with a little melted butter. Pipe a strip of feta cheese mixture along one long edge of the filo pastry rectangle, leaving a margin of about 1cm/½in.

4 Fold in each end to prevent the filling from escaping, then roll up the pastry to form a sausage shape. Brush with more melted butter.

5 Gently twist the 'sausage' into an 'S' or a crescent shape. Repeat with the remaining ingredients, refilling the piping bag as necessary.

6 Arrange the filo pastry shapes on a buttered baking sheet and brush with a little melted butter. Sprinkle with sea salt and chopped spring onion. Bake the pastries for 20 minutes until golden brown and crisp. Cool them on a wire rack before serving.

Nutritional information per portion: Energy 212kcal/878kJ; Protein 6.2g; Carbohydrate 5.5g, of which sugars 0.7g; Fat 18.6g, of which saturates 11.7g; Cholesterol 73mg; Calcium 125mg; Fibre 0.2g; Sodium 503mg.

Wild mushroom and Fontina tartlets

The nuttiness of walnut pastry goes beautifully with the creamy flavour of Italian Fontina cheese in these delectable tarts. Serve them as a summer first course.

SERVES 4

25g/1oz/$\frac{1}{2}$ cup dried wild mushrooms
30ml/2 tbsp olive oil
1 red onion, chopped
2 garlic cloves, chopped
30ml/2 tbsp medium-dry sherry
1 egg
120ml/4fl oz/$\frac{1}{2}$ cup single
    (light) cream
25g/1oz Fontina cheese, thinly sliced
salt and ground black pepper
rocket (arugula) leaves, to serve

FOR THE PASTRY

115g/4oz/1 cup wholemeal
    (whole-wheat) flour
50g/2oz/$\frac{1}{4}$ cup butter, diced
25g/1oz/$\frac{1}{4}$ cup walnuts, roasted
    and ground
1 egg, lightly beaten

1 Make the pastry. Sift the flour into a mixing bowl. Tip the bran back in. Rub in the butter, then stir in the ground walnuts. Add the egg and mix to form a soft dough. Wrap the pastry in clear film (plastic wrap). Chill for 30 minutes.

2 Soak the mushrooms in 300ml/$\frac{1}{2}$ pint/1$\frac{1}{4}$ cups boiling water for 30 minutes. Drain, reserving the liquid. Heat the oil in a large frying pan. Fry the chopped onion for 5 minutes until soft, then add the garlic and fry for 2 minutes. Add the mushrooms. Cook for 7 minutes over a high heat. Add the sherry and reserved liquid. Cook until the liquid evaporates. Season and set aside.

3 Preheat the oven to 200°C/400°F/Gas 6. Grease four 10cm/4in tartlet tins (muffin pans). Roll out the pastry on a lightly floured surface and line the tins. Prick the pastry bases all over with a fork, line with foil and baking beans and bake blind for 10 minutes. Remove the foil and beans.

4 Whisk the egg and cream, add to the mushrooms, then season. Spoon into the pastry cases and top with the cheese. Bake for 20 minutes until set. Serve warm.

Nutritional information per portion: Energy 409kcal/1701kJ; Protein 10.2g; Carbohydrate 21.9g, of which sugars 2.3g; Fat 31g, of which saturates 13.4g; Cholesterol 143mg; Calcium 121mg; Fibre 2.3g; Sodium 199mg.

Spinach turnovers

These little pastry parcels have a rich spinach filling spiked with ingredients that give it a strong Spanish influence – pine nuts and raisins.

MAKES 20

25g/1oz/3 tbsp raisins
25ml/1½ tbsp olive oil
450g/1lb fresh spinach, washed
   and chopped
6 canned anchovies, drained and chopped
2 garlic cloves, finely chopped
25g/1oz/⅓ cup pine nuts, chopped
350g/12oz puff pastry
1 egg, beaten
salt and ground black pepper

1 To make the filling, soak the raisins in a little warm water for 10 minutes. Drain, then chop them roughly. Heat the oil in a large pan or wok and add the spinach, stir, then cover and cook over a low heat for about 2 minutes.

2 Remove the lid, slightly raise the heat and let any liquid evaporate. Add the anchovies, garlic, salt and pepper. Cook, stirring continuously, for 1 minute. Remove the pan or wok from the heat, stir in the raisins and pine nuts, and cool.

3 Preheat the oven to 180°C/350°F/Gas 4. Roll out the puff pastry on a lightly floured surface to a thickness of about 3mm/⅛in. Using a 7.5cm/3in plain pastry (cookie) cutter, cut out 20 rounds, re-rolling the dough as necessary. Place two teaspoons of the filling in the middle of each, then brush the edges with a little water.

4 Bring up the sides of the pastry. Press the edges together. Brush with beaten egg. Place on a greased baking sheet and bake for 15 minutes until golden.

Nutritional information per portion: Energy 96kcal/398kJ; Protein 2.4g; Carbohydrate 7.8g, of which sugars 1.5g; Fat 6.5g, of which saturates 0.3g; Cholesterol 10mg; Calcium 53mg; Fibre 0.5g; Sodium 127mg.

Leek, saffron and mussel tarts

Serve these vividly coloured tartlets as a first course, with a few salad leaves, such as watercress, rocket and frisée, or as a light lunch with a more substantial salad.

SERVES 6

large pinch of saffron threads
15ml/1 tbsp hot water
30ml/2 tbsp olive oil
2 large leeks, sliced
2 large yellow (bell) peppers, halved,
    de-seeded, grilled (broiled) and peeled,
    then cut into strips
900g/2lb mussels, scrubbed, beards removed
2 large eggs

300ml/½ pint/1¼ cups single (light) cream
30ml/2 tbsp finely chopped fresh parsley
salad leaves, to serve

FOR THE PASTRY

225g/8oz/2 cups plain (all-purpose) flour
pinch of salt
115g/4oz/½ cup butter, diced
45–60ml/3–4 tbsp chilled water

1 Make the pastry. Sift the flour and salt into a large bowl. Rub in the butter. Sprinkle over 45ml/3 tbsp of the water and mix to a dough, adding a little more water if needed. Wrap and chill for 30 minutes.

2 Preheat the oven to 190°C/375°F/Gas 5. Roll out the pastry on a lightly floured surface. Line six 10cm/4in tartlet tins (muffin pans). Chill the cases for 10 minutes, then prick the bases all over with a fork and line the sides with strips of foil.

3 Bake the cases for 10 minutes. Remove the foil and bake for 5–8 minutes. Remove from the oven. Reduce the oven temperature to 180°C/`350°F/Gas 4.

4 Soak the saffron in the hot water for 15 minutes. Fry the leeks in oil over a medium heat for 6–8 minutes until soft and beginning to brown. Add the pepper strips and cook for 2 minutes.

5 Bring 2.5cm/1in depth of water to a rolling boil in a pan and add 10ml/2 tsp salt. Discard any open mussels that do not shut when tapped. Add the rest to the pan. Cover and cook over a high heat for 3–4 minutes, or until the mussels open. Discard any that do not open. Shell the remaining mussels.

6 Strain the saffron liquid. Add the eggs and cream. Beat well, season and whisk in the parsley.

7 Arrange the leeks, peppers and mussels in the pastry cases, pour the egg mixture over and bake for 20–25 minutes, or until risen and just firm. Serve the tarts at once with salad leaves.

Nutritional information per portion: Energy 338kcal/1408kJ; Protein 11.5g; Carbohydrate 23.4g, of which sugars 4.1g; Fat 22.7g, of which saturates 12.2g; Cholesterol 104mg; Calcium 148mg; Fibre 1.9g; Sodium 182mg.

Moroccan prawn packages

These elegant rolls are traditionally made using a local pastry, but filo is an excellent substitute. The filling is lightly spiced with paprika for a wonderfully tasty appetizer.

MAKES ABOUT 24

175g/6oz filo pastry, thawed if frozen
40g/1¹/₂oz/3 tbsp butter, melted
sunflower oil, for frying
ground cinnamon and icing (confectioners')
    sugar, for dusting (optional)
spring onions (scallions) and coriander
    (cilantro) leaves, to garnish

FOR THE FILLING

15ml/1 tbsp olive oil
15g/¹/₂oz/1 tbsp butter
2–3 spring onions (scallions)
15g/¹/₂oz/2 tbsp plain
    (all-purpose) flour
300ml/¹/₂ pint/1¹/₄ cups milk
2.5ml/¹/₂ tsp paprika
350g/12oz cooked peeled prawns
    (shrimp), chopped
salt and ground white pepper

1 To make the filling, heat the olive oil and butter in a pan. Chop the spring onions finely and add to the pan. Fry over a low heat for 2–3 minutes until soft.

2 Stir in the flour. Slowly pour in the milk, stirring constantly, until it boils and thickens. Season with paprika, salt and white pepper. Stir, then fold in the prawns.

3 Cut a sheet of filo pastry in half widthways to make an 18 x 14cm/ 7 x 5¹/₂in rectangle. Cover the rest of the pastry with a damp dish towel.

4 Brush the pastry with melted butter. Place a heaped teaspoon of filling at one end. Roll it up like a cigar, tucking in the sides as you go. Set aside, covered with clear film (plastic wrap). Make more pastry rolls, using all the pastry and filling.

5 Heat about 1cm/¹/₂in oil in a heavy pan and fry the filo packages, in batches, for 2–3 minutes until golden. Drain on kitchen paper. To serve, dust the pastry with icing sugar or cinnamon, and garnish with spring onions and coriander.

Nutritional information per portion: Energy 80kcal/334kJ; Protein 3.5g; Carbohydrate 4.5g, of which sugars 0.7g; Fat 5.5g, of which saturates 1.8g; Cholesterol 34mg; Calcium 34mg; Fibre 0.2g; Sodium 47mg.

Egg and salmon puff parcels

These attractive parcels hide a mouthwatering mixture of flavours, and make a delicious appetizer or lunch dish. Serve with curry-flavoured mayonnaise or hollandaise sauce.

SERVES 6

75g/3oz/scant ¹/₂ cup long grain rice
300ml/¹/₂ pint/1¹/₄ cups good-quality fish stock
350g/12oz tail pieces of salmon
juice of ¹/₂ lemon
15ml/1 tbsp chopped fresh dill
15ml/1 tbsp chopped fresh parsley
10ml/2 tsp mild curry powder
6 small eggs, soft-boiled and cooled
425g/15oz flaky or puff pastry
1 egg, beaten

1 Cook the rice in a pan following the packet instructions, using fish stock instead of water. Drain and set aside in a bowl. Preheat the oven to 220°C/425°F/Gas 7.

2 Cover the salmon with cold water in a pan. Gently heat until the water is not quite simmering. Cook for 8–10 minutes until it flakes easily.

3 Remove the salmon bones and skin. Flake the fish into the rice, add the lemon juice, herbs, curry powder and seasoning. Mix well.

4 Peel the eggs. Roll out the pastry. Cut the pastry into six 15cm/6in squares. Brush the edges with the beaten egg. Spoon a ball of rice in the middle of each of the squares. Push an egg in the centre and top with more rice. Pull in the pastry corners to the middle to form a parcel and seal the edges.

5 Brush with more beaten egg. Place on a baking sheet and bake for 20 minutes. Reduce the oven to 190°C/375°F/Gas 5. Cook for 10 minutes more until golden.

Nutritional information per portion: Energy 494kcal/2063kJ; Protein 23.4g; Carbohydrate 36.9g, of which sugars 1.1g; Fat 29.7g, of which saturates 2.7g; Cholesterol 219mg; Calcium 112mg; Fibre 0.8g; Sodium 326mg.

Turkey and cranberry purses

These delicious filo pastry parcels are an excellent way of using up small pieces of cooked turkey – a useful idea if you have lots of leftovers from a roast dinner. The addition of Brie and cranberry keeps the purses deliciously moist inside.

SERVES 6

450g/1lb cooked turkey, cut into chunks
115g/4oz/1 cup diced Brie cheese
30ml/2 tbsp cranberry sauce
30ml/2 tbsp chopped fresh parsley
9 sheets of filo pastry, each measuring
    45 x 28cm/18 x 11in, thawed if frozen
50g/2oz/¼ cup butter, melted
salt and ground black pepper

1 Preheat the oven to 200°C/400°F/Gas 6. Place the turkey, Brie, cranberry sauce and chopped parsley in a mixing bowl, mix well and season.

2 Cut the sheets of filo in half widthways and trim to make 18 squares. Keeping the remaining filo covered with clear film (plastic wrap), layer three pieces of pastry together, brushing each layer with a little melted butter.

3 Repeat step 2 with the remaining filo squares to make six filo pastry stacks. Divide the turkey mixture evenly among the stacks, making neat piles in the centre of each.

4 Gather up the pastry to enclose the filling in neat bundles. Brush with melted butter and bake on a baking sheet for 20 minutes until crisp and golden.

VARIATIONS
These little parcels can be made with a variety of fillings and are great for using up left-over cooked meats.
• Replace the turkey with ham and use Cheddar cheese in place of the Brie. A fruit chutney would make a good alternative to the cranberry sauce.
• Use cooked, diced chicken breast portions in place of the turkey and white Stilton cheese instead of the Brie. Replace the cranberry sauce with mango chutney.

Nutritional information per portion: Energy 307kcal/1286kJ; Protein 24.8g; Carbohydrate 23.1g, of which sugars 4g; Fat 13g, of which saturates 8.1g; Cholesterol 78mg; Calcium 99mg; Fibre 1g; Sodium 198mg.

Tunisian brik

You can make these little parcels into any shape you like, but the important thing is to encase the egg completely to prevent it from running out during cooking.

SERVES 6

40g/1½oz/3 tbsp butter
1 small red onion, finely chopped
150g/5oz skinless, boneless chicken or
    turkey, minced (ground)
1 large garlic clove, crushed
juice of ½ lemon
30ml/2 tbsp chopped fresh parsley
12 sheets of filo pastry, each measuring
    25 x 15cm/10 x 6in, thawed if frozen
6 small eggs, such as bantam, pheasant
    or guinea fowl
oil, for deep-frying
salt and ground black pepper

1 Heat half the butter in a pan. Sauté the onion for 3 minutes until soft. Add the minced meat, garlic, lemon juice, parsley and seasoning. Cook (stirring with chopsticks) for 2–3 minutes until the meat is just cooked. Set aside.

2 Melt the remaining butter. Brush a sheet of pastry with butter and top with a second sheet. Brush the edges with butter. Place some filling on the lower left side, 2.5cm/1in from the base. Flatten the filling, making a slight hollow in it.

3 Crack an egg into the hollow. Lift the right-hand edge of the pastry. Fold it to the left edge to enclose the filling. Fold the bottom edge straight up to seal, then fold the bottom left corner across to the right corner, forming a triangle.

4 Make another five parcels in the same way. Heat the oil in a wok until a cube of bread added to it turns golden in about 1½ minutes. Cook the pastries, two at a time until golden, then lift out and drain on kitchen paper.

Nutritional information per portion: Energy 329kcal/1374kJ; Protein 12.4g; Carbohydrate 26.7g, of which sugars 1.1g; Fat 20g, of which saturates 6g; Cholesterol 127mg; Calcium 66mg; Fibre 1.2g; Sodium 92mg.

Smoked chicken filo tartlets

The filling for these chicken tartlets can be prepared a day in advance and chilled, but do not fill the pastry cases until you are ready to serve them or they will become soggy.

MAKES 12

25g/1oz/2 tbsp butter

3 sheets of filo pastry, each measuring
    45 x 28cm/18 x 11in, thawed if frozen

2 skinless, boneless smoked chicken
    breast portions, finely sliced

150ml/ ¼ pint/⅔ cup mayonnaise

grated rind of 1 lime

30ml/2 tbsp lime juice

2 ripe peaches, peeled, stoned (pitted)
    and chopped

fresh tarragon sprigs, lime slices
    and salad leaves, to garnish

1 Preheat the oven to 200°C/400°F/Gas 6. Place the butter in a pan and heat gently until melted. Lightly brush 12 mini flan rings with a little melted butter.

2 Cut each sheet of filo pastry into 12 equal rounds large enough to line the flan rings and stand above the rims. Place a round of pastry in each ring. Brush with a little butter, then add another pastry round, then a third, brushing each with butter.

3 Bake the tartlets for 5 minutes. Leave in the rings for a few moments before transferring to a wire rack to cool.

4 Mix together the chicken, mayonnaise, lime rind and juice, peaches and seasoning. Chill for at least 30 minutes, but preferably overnight. When ready to serve, spoon the chicken mixture into the filo pastry cases and garnish with tarragon sprigs, lime slices and salad leaves.

Nutritional information per portion: Energy 246kcal/1021kJ; Protein 7g; Carbohydrate 6.3g, of which sugars 1.4g; Fat 21.7g, of which saturates 4.5g; Cholesterol 42mg; Calcium 13mg; Fibre 0.4g; Sodium 146mg.

Mini pork and bacon pies

These little pies can be made up to a day ahead of being served. They are a good choice for a summer picnic or special packed lunch for school or the office.

MAKES 12

10ml/2 tsp sunflower oil
1 onion, chopped
225g/8oz pork, coarsely chopped
115g/4oz cooked bacon, finely diced
45ml/3 tbsp chopped fresh herbs, such
    as sage, parsley and oregano
6 eggs, hard-boiled and halved
1 egg yolk, beaten

20g/$^{3}/_{4}$ oz packet powdered aspic
300ml/$^{1}/_{2}$ pint/1$^{1}/_{4}$ cups boiling water

**FOR THE HOT WATER
CRUST PASTRY**
450g/1lb/4 cups plain (all-purpose) flour
115g/4oz/$^{1}/_{2}$ cup white vegetable fat
275ml/9fl oz/generous 1 cup water

1 To make the pastry, sift the flour into a bowl and add a good pinch each of salt and pepper. Gently heat the fat and water in a large pan until the fat has melted. Increase the heat and bring the mixture to the boil. Pour the hot liquid into the flour, stirring constantly. Press the mixture into a ball of dough using a spoon. When the dough is smooth, cover the bowl and set aside.

2 Preheat the oven to 200°C/400°F/Gas 6. Heat the oil in a frying pan, add the onion and cook until soft. Stir in the pork and bacon and cook until just brown. Remove from the heat and stir in the herbs and seasoning.

3 Roll out two-thirds of the pastry. Use a 12cm/4$^{1}/_{2}$in fluted cutter to stamp out rounds and use to line a 12-hole tartlet tin (muffin pan). Place a little meat mixture in each pie , add half an egg and top with the remaining meat mixture.

4 Roll out the remaining pastry and use a 7.5cm/3in fluted cutter to stamp out lids for the pies. Dampen the rim of each base and press a lid in place. Pinch the edges to seal. Brush with egg yolk and make a steam hole in the top of each pie.

5 Bake for 30–35 minutes. Leave to cool for 15 minutes, then place on a wire rack to cool completely.

6 Meanwhile, stir the aspic powder into the boiling water until dissolved. Shape a piece of foil into a small funnel and use this to guide a little aspic through the hole in the top of each pie. Leave to cool and set, then chill the pies for up to 24 hours before serving at room temperature.

Nutritional information per portion: Energy 311kcal/1302kJ; Protein 12.1g; Carbohydrate 30.4g, of which sugars 1.6g; Fat 16.4g, of which saturates 5.5g; Cholesterol 135mg; Calcium 77mg; Fibre 1.5g; Sodium 74mg.

Cornish pasties

These traditional pasties are made with a rich, crumbly shortcrust. The filling is raw when enclosed in the pasty, so they must be cooked thoroughly.

MAKES 6

450g/1lb chuck steak, diced
1 potato, about 175g/6oz, diced
175g/6oz swede (rutabaga), diced
1 onion, chopped
2.5ml/1/2 tsp dried mixed herbs
1 egg, beaten
salad, to garnish

FOR THE PASTRY

350g/12oz/3 cups plain (all-purpose) flour
pinch of salt
115g/4oz/1/2 cup butter, diced
50g/2oz/1/4 cup lard or white
    vegetable fat
75–90ml/5–6 tbsp chilled water

1 To make the pastry, sift the flour and salt into a bowl. Using your fingertips or a pastry blender, lightly rub or cut in the butter and lard or vegetable fat, then sprinkle over most of the chilled water and mix to a soft dough, adding more water if necessary. Knead the pastry on a lightly floured surface for a few seconds until smooth. Wrap in clear film (plastic wrap) and chill for 30 minutes.

2 Preheat the oven to 220°C/425°F/Gas 7. Divide the pastry into six pieces, then roll out each piece on a lightly floured surface to a 20cm/8in round.

3 Mix together the steak, vegetables, herbs and seasoning in a bowl, then spoon an equal amount on to one half of each pastry round.

4 Brush the pastry edges with water, then fold the free half of each round over the filling. Press the edges firmly together to seal, then use your fingertips to crimp the edges.

5 Brush the pasties with the beaten egg. Bake for 15 minutes, then reduce the temperature to 160°C/325°F/Gas 3 and bake for 1 hour more. Serve the pasties hot or cold with a salad garnish.

Nutritional information per portion: Energy 414kcal/1731kJ; Protein 10.4g; Carbohydrate 38.8g, of which sugars 1.4g; Fat 25.3g, of which saturates 9.2g; Cholesterol 51mg; Calcium 93mg; Fibre 1.4g; Sodium 620mg.

Quiches and savoury tarts

This chapter contains an inspirational collection of savoury tarts that taste better than any you can buy, including all-time classics, such as Caramelized Onion Tart, with its deep, rich flavour, and Quiche Lorraine, with its crisp shortcrust pastry and creamy egg filling. Although shortcrust features in many of the recipes, pastries made with potato, walnut and cornmeal are also used, making wonderful cases for all manner of contents.

Cheese and onion quiche

Perfect for summer picnics, parties or family suppers, this tasty quiche celebrates a delicious and timeless taste combination: cheese and onion.

SERVES 6–8

25g/1oz/2 tbsp butter
1 large onion, thinly sliced
4 rindless streaky (fatty) bacon rashers
    (strips), roughly chopped (optional)
3 eggs
300ml/1/2 pint/11/4 cups single (light)
    cream or milk
1.5ml/1/4 tsp freshly grated nutmeg
90g/31/2oz grated hard cheese,
    e.g. Cheddar
salt and ground black pepper

FOR THE PASTRY
200g/7oz/13/4 cups plain (all-purpose) flour
2.5ml/1/2 tsp salt
90g/31/2 oz/scant 1/2 cup butter, diced
about 60ml/4 tbsp chilled water

1 To make the pastry, sift the flour and salt into a bowl. Rub in the butter. Add 45ml/3 tbsp of water and mix to a dough. Knead until smooth, wrap in clear film (plastic wrap) and chill.

2 Roll out the dough and line a 23cm/9in loose-based flan tin (pan). Press the pastry into the sides and base, allowing it to rise above the rim by about 1cm/1/2in. Prick the base. Line the pastry case with foil and some baking beans. Chill in the refrigerator for 15 minutes. Place a baking sheet in the oven.

3 Preheat the oven to 200°C/400°F/Gas 6. Put the flan tin on the baking sheet and bake blind for 15 minutes. Remove the foil and beans. Return it to the oven for 5 minutes, then reduce the temperature to 180°C/350°F/Gas 4.

4 Sauté the onion and bacon in the butter for 10 minutes. Beat the eggs and cream in a bowl. Add grated nutmeg and season. Spoon into the case, sprinkling with cheese. Pour the egg and cream over and bake for 35–40 minutes, until just set. Allow to cool before easing out of the tin.

Nutritional information per portion: Energy 438kcal/1825kJ; Protein 15.8g; Carbohydrate 31.5g, of which sugars 5.2g; Fat 28.2g, of which saturates 15.9g; Cholesterol 165mg; Calcium 246mg; Fibre 1.6g; Sodium 768mg.

Quiche Lorraine

This classic quiche has some delightful characteristics that are often forgotten in modern recipes: namely, very thin pastry, a creamy, light filling and smoked bacon.

SERVES 4–6

6 slices of rindless smoked streaky
    (fatty) bacon
300ml/1/2 pint/11/4 cups double
    (heavy) cream
3 eggs, plus 2 yolks
25g/1oz/2 tbsp butter
salt and ground black pepper

FOR THE PASTRY

175g/6oz/11/2 cups plain
    (all-purpose) flour
pinch of salt
115g/4oz/1/2 cup butter, at room
    temperature, diced
1 egg yolk

1 To make the pastry, place the flour, salt, butter and egg yolk in a food processor and process until blended. Tip out on to a lightly floured surface and bring the mixture together into a ball. Leave to rest for 20 minutes.

2 Lightly flour a deep 20cm/8in round flan tin (pan) and place it on a baking sheet. Roll out the pastry and use to line the flan tin, trimming off any overhanging pieces.

3 Gently press the pastry into the tin. If it breaks, gently push it together again. Chill for 20 minutes.

4 Preheat the oven to 200°C/400°F/ Gas 6. Meanwhile, snip the bacon into small pieces and grill (broil) until the fat runs. Arrange in the pastry case. Beat together the cream, the eggs and yolks and seasoning, and pour into the pastry case.

5 Bake the quiche for 15 minutes, then reduce the oven temperature to 180°C/350°F/Gas 4 and bake for 20 minutes more. When the pastry is crisp and the filling is puffed up and golden, remove the quiche from the oven and top with cubes of butter. Cool for 5 minutes before serving.

Nutritional information per portion: Energy 1006kcal/4164kJ; Protein 19.6g; Carbohydrate 35.5g, of which sugars 2.2g; Fat 88.4g, of which saturates 49.4g; Cholesterol 454mg; Calcium 141mg; Fibre 1.4g; Sodium 917mg.

Smoked salmon quiche with potato pastry

The simple mixture of ingredients in this light but richly flavoured quiche perfectly complements the melt-in-the-mouth pastry, which is, unusually, made with potatoes.

SERVES 6

275g/10oz smoked salmon
6 eggs, beaten
150ml/¼ pint/⅔ cup creamy milk
300ml/½ pint/1¼ cups double
   (heavy) cream
30–45ml/2–3 tbsp chopped fresh dill
30ml/2 tbsp capers, drained and chopped
salt and ground black pepper
salad leaves and fresh dill, to serve

FOR THE PASTRY

1 floury potato, about 115g/4oz, diced
225g/8oz/2 cups plain
   (all-purpose) flour
115g/4oz/½ cup butter, diced
½ egg, beaten
about 10ml/2 tsp chilled water

1 Cook the diced potato in a pan of lightly salted boiling water for 15 minutes. Drain well, return to the pan and mash until smooth. Set aside.

2 To make the pastry, place the flour in a bowl and rub in the butter. Beat in the potatoes and egg. Bring the mixture together, adding chilled water if needed.

3 Roll out the pastry on a lightly floured surface and line a deep 23cm/9in round, loose-based, fluted flan tin (pan). Chill for 1 hour. Preheat the oven to 200°C/400°F/Gas 6.

4 Place a heavy baking sheet in the oven to heat up. Chop the salmon into bitesize pieces and set aside.

5 Beat the eggs, milk and cream in a bowl with a wooden spoon. Stir in the chopped dill and capers and season. Add the salmon and stir.

6 Prick the pastry base with a fork and pour in the salmon mixture. Place on the baking sheet and bake for 35–45 minutes, or until the filling is just set. Serve warm with mixed salad leaves and some dill.

Nutritional information per portion: Energy 679kcal/2825kJ; Protein 23.3g; Carbohydrate 34.1g, of which sugars 2.7g; Fat 51.1g, of which saturates 28.9g; Cholesterol 317mg; Calcium 142mg; Fibre 1.4g; Sodium 1070mg.

Greek picnic pie

Aubergines layered with spinach, feta cheese and rice make a marvellous filling for the perfect picnic pie. It can be served warm or cold and makes a good vegetarian dish for a buffet lunch.

SERVES 6

45–60ml/3–4 tbsp olive oil

1 large aubergine (eggplant), sliced

1 onion, chopped

1 garlic clove, crushed

175g/6oz fresh spinach, washed

4 eggs

75g/3oz/1/2 cup crumbled feta cheese

40g/11/2oz/1/2 cup grated
   Parmesan cheese

60ml/4 tbsp natural (plain) yogurt

90ml/6 tbsp creamy milk

225g/8oz/2 cups cooked long grain rice

FOR THE PASTRY

225g/8oz/2 cups plain (all-purpose) flour

pinch of salt

5ml/1 tsp dried basil

115g/4oz/1/2 cup butter, diced

45–60ml/3–4 tbsp chilled water

1 To make the pastry, sift the flour and salt into a bowl. Stir in the basil. Rub in the butter. Sprinkle over most of the water. Mix to a dough. Cover with clear film (plastic wrap) and chill for 30 minutes. Roll out the pastry thinly and use to line a 25cm/10in flan ring or flan tin (pan). Cover and chill for 30 minutes. Preheat the oven to 180°C/350°F/Gas 4. Prick the base of the pastry case with a fork and bake for 10–12 minutes.

2 Heat 45ml/3 tbsp of the oil in a frying pan. Gently fry the aubergine slices for 6–8 minutes on each side until golden. Remove and drain on kitchen paper. Fry the onion and garlic in the remaining oil over a gentle heat till soft. Chop the spinach finely. Beat the eggs in a large mixing bowl. Add the spinach, feta, Parmesan, yogurt, milk and the onion mixture. Season well and stir thoroughly.

3 Spread a layer of cooked rice over the pastry base. Arrange all but eight slices of aubergine over the rice. Spoon over the spinach and feta mixture and top with the reserved aubergine slices. Bake for 30–40 minutes until lightly browned.

Nutritional information per portion: Energy 554kcal/2309kJ; Protein 16.6g; Carbohydrate 53.3g, of which sugars 4.3g; Fat 31.4g, of which saturates 15.5g; Cholesterol 185mg; Calcium 299mg; Fibre 2.7g; Sodium 473mg.

Tomato and black olive tart

This delicious tart has a fresh, rich Mediterranean flavour and is perfect for picnics. If you are taking this tart on a picnic, keep it in the tin for easy transporting.

SERVES 8

6 firm plum tomatoes
75g/3oz ripe Brie cheese
about 16 pitted black olives
3 eggs, beaten
300ml/½ pint/1¼ cups milk
30ml/2 tbsp chopped fresh herbs
salt and ground black pepper

FOR THE PASTRY

225g/8oz/2 cups plain
    (all-purpose) flour
115g/4oz/½ cup butter, diced
45–60ml/3–4 tbsp chilled water

1 To make the pastry, sift the flour into a bowl. Rub or cut in the butter until it resembles fine breadcrumbs. Sprinkle over the water and mix to a dough. Knead on a floured surface until smooth. Wrap and chill for 30 minutes.

2 Preheat the oven to 190°C/375°F/Gas 5. Roll out the pastry thinly and use to line a greased 28 x 18cm/11 x 7in loose-based rectangular flan tin (pan). Trim the edges. Line the pastry case with some foil and baking beans, and bake blind for 15 minutes. Remove the foil and beans and bake for a further 5 minutes until the base is crisp.

3 Slice the tomatoes, cube the cheese and finely slice the olives. Place the tart case on a baking sheet and arrange the tomatoes, cheese and olives in it. Mix together the eggs, milk, seasoning and chopped herbs. Pour the egg mixture into the case. Bake for about 40 minutes until just firm and turning golden. Slice hot or cool in the tin, then serve.

Nutritional information per portion: Energy 315kcal/1316kJ; Protein 9.3g; Carbohydrate 26.1g, of which sugars 4.6g; Fat 19.9g, of which saturates 7.2g; Cholesterol 90mg; Calcium 151mg; Fibre 1.7g; Sodium 505mg.

Shallot and garlic tarte tatin

Savoury versions of the celebrated apple tarte tatin have been popular for some years. Here, caramelized shallots are baked beneath a layer of Parmesan pastry.

SERVES 4–6

300g/11oz puff pastry
50g/2oz/¼ cup butter, softened
75g/3oz/1 cup freshly grated
    Parmesan cheese
40g/1½oz/3 tbsp butter
500g/1¼ lb shallots

12–16 large whole garlic cloves, peeled
15ml/1 tbsp caster (superfine) sugar
15ml/1 tbsp balsamic or sherry vinegar
45ml/3 tbsp water
5ml/1 tsp chopped fresh thyme
salt and ground black pepper

1 Roll out the pastry to a rectangle on a lightly floured work surface. Spread the butter over it, leaving a 2.5cm/1in border. Sprinkle the grated Parmesan on top.

2 Fold the lower third of the pastry up to cover the middle and fold the top third down over it. Seal the edges well, give the pastry a quarter turn and roll it out to a rectangle, then fold in thirds and seal as before. Wrap in clear film (plastic wrap) and chill in the refrigerator for at least 30 minutes.

3 Preheat the oven to 190°C/375°F/Gas 5. Melt the butter in a 23–25cm/9–10in round, heavy, ovenproof omelette pan. Add the shallots and garlic and cook over a low heat until lightly browned all over.

4 Sprinkle the sugar over and increase the heat a little. Cook until the sugar begins to caramelize, then stir. Add the vinegar, water, thyme and seasoning. Cook, partly covered, for 5–8 minutes until the garlic cloves are just tender. Set aside to cool.

5 Roll out the pastry to a round the same size as the omelette pan. Lay the pastry round over the shallots and garlic. Prick the pastry all over with a fork, then bake for 25–35 minutes until risen and golden. Cool for about 10 minutes, then invert the tart on to a serving platter.

Nutritional information per portion: Energy 618kcal/2567kJ; Protein 12.8g; Carbohydrate 35.5g, of which sugars 9.6g; Fat 48.2g, of which saturates 22.8g; Cholesterol 79mg; Calcium 313mg; Fibre 3g; Sodium 605mg.

Red onion tart with cornmeal crust

The wonderfully mild and sweet taste of red onions when cooked goes perfectly with Fontina cheese and thyme in this tart. Cornmeal gives the pastry a crumbly texture.

SERVES 5–6

60ml/4 tbsp olive oil

1kg/2¼ lb red onions, thinly sliced

2–3 garlic cloves, thinly sliced

**5ml/1 tsp chopped fresh thyme, plus a
few whole sprigs, to garnish**

5ml/1 tsp soft dark brown sugar

10ml/2 tsp sherry vinegar

225g/8oz Fontina cheese, thinly sliced

FOR THE PASTRY

115g/4oz/1 cup plain (all-purpose) flour

75g/3oz/ ¾ cup fine yellow cornmeal

5ml/1 tsp soft dark brown sugar

5ml/1 tsp chopped fresh thyme

90g/3½oz/7 tbsp butter, diced

1 egg yolk

30–45ml/2–3 tbsp chilled water

1 To make the pastry, sift the flour and cornmeal with 5ml/1 tsp salt in a bowl. Season. Stir in the sugar and thyme. Rub in the butter. Beat the egg yolk with 30ml/2 tbsp water and use to bind the pastry. Wrap in clear film (plastic wrap) and chill for 30 minutes.

2 Heat 45ml/3 tbsp of the oil in a frying pan and add the onions. Cover and cook slowly, stirring often, for 20–30 minutes. Add the garlic and thyme and cook, stirring, for 10 minutes. Increase the heat slightly, then add the sugar and vinegar.

3 Cook, uncovered, for a further 5 minutes until the onions start to caramelize slightly. Season and cool.

4 Preheat the oven to 190°C/375°F/ Gas 5. Roll out the pastry and use to line a 25cm/10in loose-based flan tin (pan). Prick all over and support the sides with foil. Bake for 15 minutes.

5 Remove the foil and spread the onions in the base. Add the Fontina, season and drizzle with the remaining oil. Bake for 15–20 minutes, then garnish with thyme sprigs and serve.

Nutritional information per portion: Energy 494kcal/2051kJ; Protein 13.2g; Carbohydrate 38.9g, of which sugars 11.3g; Fat 31.7g, of which saturates 16g; Cholesterol 100mg; Calcium 172mg; Fibre 3.2g; Sodium 307mg.

Caramelized onion tart

The filling for this tart is rich, dark and delicious. The sweet caramelized onions add wonderful depth and flavour to this simple yet classic tart.

SERVES 6

15g/¹/₂oz/1 tbsp butter
15ml/1 tbsp olive oil
500g/1¹/₄ lb onions, sliced
large pinch of grated nutmeg
5ml/1 tsp soft dark brown sugar
2 eggs
150ml/¹/₄ pint/²/₃ cup single
   (light) cream
50g/2oz/¹/₂ cup grated Gruyère cheese

FOR THE PASTRY

75g/3oz/²/₃ cup plain (all-purpose) flour
75g/3oz/²/₃ cup wholemeal
   (whole-wheat) flour
75g/3oz/6 tbsp butter, diced
1 egg yolk

1 Make the pastry. Mix the plain and wholemeal flours in a bowl. Use your fingertips to rub in the butter. Mix in the egg yolk and enough chilled water to form a firm dough. Transfer the dough to a floured work surface.

2 Knead the dough and gather it into a smooth ball. Wrap in clear film (plastic wrap) and chill for 30 minutes.

3 Heat the butter and oil in a frying pan. Cook the onions over a low heat for 30 minutes until soft, stirring. Add the nutmeg, sugar and seasoning.

4 Gently cook for 5 minutes until the onions have caramelized. Cool slightly.

5 Preheat the oven to 220°C/425°F/ Gas 7. Lightly grease a loose-based 35 x 12cm/14 x 4¹/₂in fluted tranche tin (pan). Roll out the pastry and use to line the tin. Chill for 20 minutes. Prick the base. Line with foil and beans. Bake for 10 minutes. Remove the foil and beans and add the onions.

6 Beat the eggs and cream, add the cheese and season. Pour over the onions. Bake for 30 minutes until set.

Nutritional information per portion: Energy 905kcal/3748kJ; Protein 15g; Carbohydrate 36.7g, of which sugars 3g; Fat 78.2g, of which saturates 47.1g; Cholesterol 384mg; Calcium 272mg; Fibre 1.6g; Sodium 383mg.

Vegetarian festive tart

This sophisticated flan is made with a spicy cheese pastry, and can be served as a vegetarian alternative for any celebration or special occasion.

SERVES 8

50g/2oz/4 tbsp butter
1 onion, chopped
1–2 garlic cloves, crushed
350g/12oz/4–5 cups chopped mushrooms
10ml/2 tsp dried mixed herbs
15ml/1 tbsp chopped fresh parsley
50g/2oz/1 cup fresh white breadcrumbs
25g/1oz/2 tbsp plain (all-purpose) flour
300ml/1/2 pint/11/4 cups milk
25g/1oz Parmesan cheese, grated
75g/3oz Cheddar cheese, grated
1.5ml/1/4 tsp English (hot)
    mustard powder
1 egg, separated
15ml/1 tbsp Dijon mustard

FOR THE PASTRY
225g/8oz/2 cups plain (all-purpose) flour
175g/6oz/3/4 cup butter
10ml/2 tsp paprika
115g/4oz Parmesan cheese, grated
1 egg (beaten with 15ml/1 tbsp cold water)

1 Make the pastry. Sift the flour into a bowl and rub in the butter. Stir in the paprika and Parmesan. Bind to a soft dough with the egg and water. Knead until smooth, wrap in clear film (plastic wrap) and chill for 30 minutes.

2 To make the filling, melt 25g/1oz/ 2 tbsp of the butter in a pan, add the onion and cook until tender. Stir in the garlic and mushrooms and cook, uncovered, for 5 minutes, stirring, to evaporate off any liquid.

3 Remove the pan from the heat and stir in the herbs, white breadcrumbs and seasoning. Allow to cool. Put a baking sheet in the oven and preheat to 190°C/375°F/Gas 5.

4 Roll out the pastry and use to line a 23cm/9in loose-based flan tin (pan). Make a thin rim around the top. Chill.

5 Make the cheese topping. Melt the remaining butter in a pan, stir in the flour and cook for 2 minutes. Blend in the milk. Bring to the boil, stirring constantly, and simmer for 2–3 minutes. Off the heat, stir in the cheeses, mustard powder and egg yolk, and season. Beat until smooth.

6 Whisk the egg white to soft peaks, then fold into the cheese mixture. Spread the Dijon mustard over the pastry case. Add the mushrooms, then pour over the topping. Bake on the baking sheet for 35–45 minutes.

Nutritional information per portion: Energy 500kcal/2083kJ; Protein 16.8g; Carbohydrate 31.8g, of which sugars 3.1g; Fat 34.7g, of which saturates 21.2g; Cholesterol 136mg; Calcium 393mg; Fibre 1.7g; Sodium 514mg.

Courgette and dill tart

The subtle flavour of courgettes is lifted dramatically by the addition of fresh dill in this tart.
Take time to arrange the layers of courgette to create an eye-catching dish.

SERVES 4

15ml/1 tbsp sunflower oil
3 courgettes (zucchini), thinly sliced
2 egg yolks
150ml/¼ pint/⅔ cup double
   (heavy) cream
1 garlic clove, crushed
15ml/1 tbsp finely chopped fresh dill

FOR THE PASTRY
115g/4oz/1 cup wholemeal
   (whole-wheat) flour
115g/4oz/1 cup self-raising
   (self-rising) flour
pinch of salt
115g/4oz/½ cup butter, chilled
   and diced
75ml/5 tbsp chilled water

1 To make the pastry, sift the flours into a bowl, tipping the bran into the bowl, then place in a food processor. Add the salt and diced butter and process using the pulse button until the mixture resembles breadcrumbs.

2 With the motor running, gradually add the water until the mixture forms a dough. Do not over-process. Wrap the pastry and chill for 30 minutes.

3 Preheat the oven to 200°C/400°F/ Gas 6 and grease a 20cm/8in flan tin (pan).

4 Roll out the pastry and ease it into the tin. Prick the base, trim the edges and bake blind for 10–15 minutes.

5 Heat the oil in a pan and add the courgettes. Sauté for 2–3 minutes, turning occasionally. Mix the egg yolks, cream, garlic and dill in a small bowl. Season with salt and pepper.

6 Line the pastry case with courgettes and pour over the cream mixture. Return to the oven for 25–30 minutes and bake until firm. Cool the pie in the tin, then remove and serve.

Nutritional information per portion: Energy 666kcal/2767kJ; Protein 11.1g; Carbohydrate 43.6g, of which sugars 4.3g; Fat 50.9g, of which saturates 28.9g; Cholesterol 214mg; Calcium 184mg; Fibre 4.8g; Sodium 293mg.

Roquefort tart with walnut pastry

Mild leeks go exceptionally well with the salty flavour of the Roquefort cheese, and the nuttiness of the pastry complements the ingredients perfectly in this tart.

SERVES 4–6

25g/1oz/2 tbsp butter
450g/1lb leeks (trimmed weight), sliced
175g/6oz Roquefort cheese, sliced
2 large eggs
250ml/8fl oz/1 cup double
   (heavy) cream
10ml/2 tsp chopped fresh tarragon

FOR THE PASTRY

175g/6oz/1½ cups plain (all-purpose) flour
5ml/1 tsp soft dark brown sugar
50g/2oz/¼ cup butter, diced
75g/3oz/¾ cup walnuts, ground
15ml/1 tbsp lemon juice
30ml/2 tbsp chilled water

1 To make the pastry, sift the flour and 2.5ml/½ tsp salt into a bowl. Add some black pepper and the sugar. Rub in the butter until the mixture resembles breadcrumbs, then add the ground walnuts and stir well. Add the lemon juice and chilled water and bind to form a dough. Gather the mixture into a ball, wrap in clear film (plastic wrap) and chill for 30–40 minutes.

2 Preheat the oven to 190°C/375°F/Gas 5. Roll out the pastry and use to line a 21–23cm/8½–9in loose-based flan tin (pan).

3 Protect the sides of the pastry case with a thin strip of foil, prick the base all over with a fork and bake for about 15 minutes. Remove the foil and bake for 10 minutes more until just firm. Reduce the oven to 180°C/350°F/Gas 4.

4 To make the filling, melt the butter in a pan, add the leeks, then cover and cook for 10 minutes. Season and cook for 10 minutes more until soft. Set aside to cool.

5 Spoon the leeks into the pastry case, spreading them evenly, and arrange the slices of Roquefort cheese on top. Beat the eggs with the cream in a small bowl, and season with plenty of black pepper. Beat in the tarragon and carefully pour the mixture into the case, evenly covering the leek filling.

6 Bake the tart on the centre shelf of the oven for 30–40 minutes until the filling has risen and browned and become firm to the touch. Allow to cool for 10 minutes before serving.

Nutritional information per portion: Energy 950kcal/3941kJ; Protein 22.5g; Carbohydrate 40.1g, of which sugars 5.8g; Fat 78.9g, of which saturates 41.2g; Cholesterol 273mg; Calcium 371mg; Fibre 4.5g; Sodium 708mg.

Single- and double-crust pies

Comforting and substantial main-course pies

are always welcome. Winter chills are warded

off with a classic Steak and Kidney Pie with

a contemporary mustard gravy, while summer

specials include a mouthwatering Chicken

and Apricot Filo Pie. At Christmas or

Thanksgiving, either Turkey and Cranberry Pie

or Chestnut, Stilton and Ale Pie would make

a stunning centrepiece, as would a vegetarian

Potato and Leek Filo Pie.

Chestnut, Stilton and ale pie

This hearty winter dish has a rich gravy and a herb pastry top. The Stilton cheese adds a delicious creaminess to the chestnut and mushroom filling.

SERVES 4

30ml/2 tbsp sunflower oil

2 large onions, chopped

500g/1¼ lb/8 cups button
   (white) mushrooms

3 carrots, thickly sliced

1 parsnip, thickly sliced

15ml/1 tbsp chopped fresh thyme

2 bay leaves

250ml/8fl oz/1 cup Guinness (dark ale)

120ml/4fl oz/½ cup vegetable stock

5ml/1 tsp Worcestershire sauce

5ml/1 tsp soft dark brown sugar

350g/12oz/3 cups canned chestnuts

30ml/2 tbsp plain (all-purpose) flour

150g/5oz Stilton cheese, diced

1 egg, beaten

FOR THE PASTRY

115g/4oz/1 cup wholemeal
   (whole-wheat) flour

50g/2oz/¼ cup butter

15ml/1 tbsp fresh thyme

1 To make the pastry, put the flour and a pinch of salt in a mixing bowl and rub in the butter until the mixture resembles fine breadcrumbs. Add the chopped thyme and enough water to form a soft dough. Knead until smooth, then wrap and chill for 30 minutes.

2 Meanwhile, to make the filling, fry the onions until soft. Add the mushrooms and cook for 3 minutes more. Add the carrots, parsnip and herbs and cook for 3 minutes. Pour in the Guinness, vegetable stock and Worcestershire sauce, then add the sugar and season. Simmer, covered, for 5 minutes. Add the chestnuts.

3 Mix the flour with 30ml/2 tbsp water in a bowl to make a paste. Add to the vegetable mixture and cook, stirring constantly, for 5 minutes till the sauce thickens. Stir in the cheese and heat until melted, still stirring constantly, then set aside. Preheat the oven to 220°C/425°F/Gas 7.

4 Roll out the pastry. Spoon the chestnut mixture into a 1.5 litre/ 2½ pint/6¼ cup deep pie dish. Dampen the edges of the dish and cover with the pastry. Seal, trim and crimp the edges.

5 Cut a small slit in the top of the pie and use the pastry trimmings to make pastry leaves, then arrange these on the pie. Lightly brush with egg to glaze, and bake for 30 minutes until the pastry is golden.

Nutritional information per portion: Energy 666kcal/2782kJ; Protein 18.9g; Carbohydrate 70.3g, of which sugars 22.6g; Fat 32.7g, of which saturates 16.6g; Cholesterol 62mg; Calcium 238mg; Fibre 11g; Sodium 415mg.

Chicken charter pie

This is a traditional recipe from Cornwall, in England, an area famous for its cream. It is not surprising, therefore, that the sauce for this pie is cream-based.

SERVES 4

50g/2oz/¼ cup butter
4 chicken legs
1 onion, finely chopped
150ml/¼ pint/⅔ cup milk
150ml/¼ pint/⅔ cup sour cream
4 spring onions (scallions), quartered
20g/¾ oz/¾ cup chopped parsley
225g/8oz puff pastry
2 eggs, beaten, plus extra for glazing
120ml/4fl oz/½ cup double
    (heavy) cream
salt and ground black pepper

1 Melt the butter in a shallow pan, then brown the chicken legs on all sides. Add the chopped onion and cook until just softened. Stir in the milk, sour cream, spring onions, parsley and seasoning. Simmer for 2 minutes. Return the chicken and juices to the pan, cover and cook gently for 30 minutes. Transfer the chicken and sauce to a 1.2 litre/ 2 pint/5 cup pie dish. Leave to cool.

2 Roll out the pastry until just larger than the top of the dish. Leave to relax while the chicken cools. Preheat the oven to 220°C/425°F/Gas 7.

3 Cut off a narrow strip around the edge of the pastry and place it on the edge of the dish. Moisten the strip with water, then cover the dish with the pastry. Press the edges to seal. Trim and neatly crimp the edge. Make a hole in the centre of the pastry. Insert a foil funnel. Brush with egg, then bake for 15–20 minutes.

4 Reduce the oven to 180°C/350°F/ Gas 4. Mix the cream and eggs and pour into the pie through the funnel, gently shaking the dish to distribute it. Return to the oven for 7 minutes more. Cool for 5 minutes, then serve.

Nutritional information per portion: Energy 713kcal/2967kJ; Protein 37.8g; Carbohydrate 25g, of which sugars 4.9g; Fat 52.6g, of which saturates 22.8g; Cholesterol 250mg; Calcium 154mg; Fibre 0.4g; Sodium 426mg.

Hare pot pies

The full, gamey flavour of hare is perfect for this dish; however, boneless venison, rabbit, pheasant or any other game meat can be used instead.

SERVES 4

30ml/2 tbsp olive oil
1 leek, sliced
225g/8oz parsnips, sliced
225g/8oz carrots, sliced
1 fennel bulb, sliced
675g/1¹/₂ lb boneless hare, diced
30ml/2 tbsp plain (all-purpose) flour
60ml/4 tbsp Madeira
300ml/¹/₂ pint/1¹/₄ cups game
   or chicken stock
45ml/3 tbsp chopped fresh parsley
450g/1lb puff pastry
1 egg yolk, beaten
salt and ground black pepper

1 Heat the oil in a casserole, add the leek, parsnips, carrots and fennel and cook for 10 minutes, stirring often. Remove the vegetables and set aside. Add the hare to the casserole in batches. Stir-fry over a high heat for 10 minutes, or until browned.

2 Return all the browned meat to the pan. Sprinkle in the flour, stir, then add the Madeira and stock. Return the vegetables to the casserole with the parsley. Season. Bring to a simmer, increase the heat slightly and cook for 20 minutes, stirring.

3 Preheat the oven to 220°C/425°F/ Gas 7. Spoon the hare mixture into four individual pie dishes. Cut the pastry into quarters. Roll out on a floured surface, making the pieces just larger than the dishes. Trim off the excess pastry and use it to line the rims of the pie dishes.

4 Dampen the rims with water and cover with pastry lids. Pinch the edges together to seal. Glaze each pie with beaten egg yolk and make a steam hole in the top. Bake for 25 minutes until the pastry is risen and golden.

Nutritional information per portion: Energy 911kcal/3810kJ; Protein 60.2g; Carbohydrate 62.2g, of which sugars 11.8g; Fat 47.8g, of which saturates 1g; Cholesterol 0mg; Calcium 172mg; Fibre 6.3g; Sodium 444mg.

Cheese and spinach flan

The decorative pastry topping for this flan is made using a lattice cutter. If you don't have one, cut the pastry into fine strips and weave them into a lattice.

SERVES 8

450g/1lb frozen spinach
1 onion, chopped
pinch of grated nutmeg
225g/8oz/1 cup cottage cheese
2 large eggs plus 1 beaten egg
50g/2oz Parmesan cheese, grated
150ml/¼ pint/⅔ cup single
  (light) cream
salt and ground black pepper

FOR THE PASTRY
225g/8oz/2 cups plain (all-purpose) flour
115g/4oz/½ cup butter
2.5ml/½ tsp English (hot)
  mustard powder
2.5ml/½ tsp paprika
115g/4oz finely grated Cheddar cheese
45–60ml/3–4 tbsp chilled water

1 Make the pastry. Sift the flour into a bowl and rub in the butter until the mixture resembles breadcrumbs. Stir in the mustard powder, paprika, salt and cheese. Bind to a pliable dough with the chilled water. Knead until smooth, wrap in clear film (plastic wrap) and chill for 30 minutes.

2 Cook the spinach and onion in a pan until the onion softens. Evaporate off any liquid. Season with nutmeg, salt and pepper. Transfer to a bowl. Add the cottage cheese, eggs, Parmesan and cream. Preheat the oven to 200°C/400°F/Gas 6.

3 Roll out two-thirds of the pastry and line a 23cm/9in loose-based flan tin (pan). Press the pastry into the edges and make a lip around the top edge. Remove the excess with a rolling pin. Spoon the filling into the case.

4 Roll out the remaining pastry and cut it with a lattice pastry (cookie) cutter. Carefully open the lattice and, using a rolling pin, lay it over the flan. Brush the edges with beaten egg, press together and trim off the excess. Brush the top of the lattice with egg and bake on a hot baking sheet for 35–40 minutes.

Nutritional information per portion: Energy 401kcal/1674kJ; Protein 17.5g; Carbohydrate 24.1g, of which sugars 2.4g; Fat 26.4g, of which saturates 15.6g; Cholesterol 147mg; Calcium 374mg; Fibre 2.2g; Sodium 389mg.

Potato and leek filo pie

This filo pastry pie would make an attractive and unusual centrepiece for a vegetarian buffet. It is best served cold, with a selection of salads.

SERVES 8

800g/1¾ lb new potatoes, sliced
75g/3oz/6 tbsp butter
2 large leeks, trimmed, rinsed and
  thinly sliced
15g/½ oz/½ cup fresh parsley,
  finely chopped
60ml/4 tbsp chopped mixed fresh herbs
12 sheets of filo pastry, thawed
  if frozen
150g/5oz Cheshire or Lancashire
  cheese, sliced
2 garlic cloves, finely chopped
250ml/8fl oz/1 cup double
  (heavy) cream
2 large egg yolks
salt and ground black pepper

1 Preheat the oven to 190°C/375°F/Gas 5. Cook the potatoes in salted boiling water for 3–4 minutes. Drain and set aside. Melt 25g/1oz/2 tbsp of the butter in a frying pan, add the leeks and fry, stirring occasionally, until softened. Remove from the heat, season, then stir in half the parsley and mixed herbs. Set aside.

2 Melt the remaining butter in a pan. Line a deep 23cm/9in loose-based cake tin (pan) with six to seven sheets of filo pastry, lightly brushing each layer with butter. Let the edges overhang the tin. Layer the potatoes, leek mixture and cheese in the tin, sprinkling some of the herbs and all of the garlic in between. Season.

3 Fold the overhanging pastry over the filling and cover with two sheets of filo, tucking in the sides. Brush with melted butter. Cover the pie loosely with foil. Bake for 35 minutes. (Keep the remaining filo covered with a damp dish towel.)

4 Beat together the cream, yolks and remaining herbs. Remove the foil from the pie, make a hole in the centre and gradually pour in the egg mixture. Reduce the oven to 180°C/350°F/Gas 4. Cut the remaining pastry into strips, arrange on top of the pie, brush with melted butter and bake for a further 25–30 minutes.

Nutritional information per portion: Energy 468kcal/1948kJ; Protein 10.7g; Carbohydrate 33g, of which sugars 3.5g; Fat 33.1g, of which saturates 20g; Cholesterol 137mg; Calcium 225mg; Fibre 3.2g; Sodium 218mg.

Spinach filo pie

This popular spinach and filo pastry pie is sometimes called spanakopita in its native Greece. There are several ways of making it, but feta is inevitably included.

SERVES 6

1kg/2¼ lb fresh spinach

4 spring onions (scallions), chopped

300g/11oz feta cheese, crumbled or
   coarsely grated

2 large eggs, beaten

30ml/2 tbsp chopped fresh parsley

15ml/1 tbsp chopped fresh dill

45ml/3 tbsp currants (optional)

about 8 sheets of filo pastry, each
   measuring 30 x 18cm/12 x 7in

150ml/¼ pint/²⁄₃ cup olive oil

ground black pepper

1 Break off any thick stalks from the spinach, then blanch the leaves in a very small amount of boiling water for 1–2 minutes until just wilted.

2 Drain and refresh under cold water. Drain again, squeeze the spinach dry and chop it roughly.

3 Place the spinach in a bowl with the spring onions and cheese. Pour in the eggs and stir in thoroughly. Mix in the herbs and currants, if using. Season with pepper.

4 Preheat the oven to 190°C/375°F/Gas 5. Brush a sheet of filo with oil and fit it into a 23cm/9in pie dish, allowing it to hang over the edges. Add three to four more sheets, placing them at different angles and brushing each with oil.

5 Spoon the filling into the filo pastry case, then top with all but one of the remaining filo sheets, brushing each sheet with oil as you go. Fold the overhanging filo pastry over the sheets on top to seal. Brush the reserved filo with oil and scrunch it over the top of the pie.

6 Brush the pie with oil. Sprinkle with a little water to stop the filo edges from curling, then place on a baking sheet. Bake for 40 minutes until golden and crisp. Allow the pie to cool for 15 minutes before serving.

Nutritional information per portion: Energy 396kcal/1640kJ; Protein 16.8g; Carbohydrate 13.8g, of which sugars 4g; Fat 30.7g, of which saturates 10.1g; Cholesterol 111mg; Calcium 528mg; Fibre 4.8g; Sodium 988mg.

Turkey and cranberry pie

The cranberries add a deliciously tart layer to this substantial meaty pie. Cranberry sauce can be used if fresh cranberries are not available. The pie freezes well.

SERVES 8

450g/1lb (bulk) pork sausage meat
450g/1lb lean minced (ground) pork
15ml/1 tbsp ground coriander
15ml/1 tbsp dried mixed herbs
finely grated rind of 2 large oranges
10ml/2 tsp grated fresh root ginger
10ml/2 tsp salt
450g/1lb turkey breast fillets
115g/4oz/1 cup fresh cranberries
1 egg, beaten
300ml/$\frac{1}{2}$ pint/1$\frac{1}{4}$ cups liquid aspic jelly
ground black pepper

FOR THE PASTRY

450g/1lb/4 cups plain (all-purpose) flour
5ml/1 tsp salt
150g/5oz/$\frac{2}{3}$ cup lard
150ml/$\frac{1}{4}$ pint/$\frac{2}{3}$ cup milk/water mixed

1 Place a baking sheet in an oven at 180°C/350°F/Gas 4 to preheat. In a bowl, mix together the sausage meat, pork, coriander, herbs, orange rind, ginger and salt. Season with black pepper to taste.

2 Make the pastry. Sift the flour into a bowl with the salt. Heat the lard in a small pan with the milk and water until just beginning to boil. Remove from the heat and allow to cool slightly. Quickly stir it into the flour to form a stiff dough. Knead until smooth. Cut off one-third for the lid, wrap in clear film (plastic wrap) and keep in a warm place. Roll out the rest while it is still warm, and use it to line the base and sides of a greased 20cm/8in loose-based, springform cake tin (pan).

3 Thinly slice the turkey breast. Flatten between two pieces of clear film (plastic wrap) with a rolling pin to 3mm/$\frac{1}{8}$in thick. Spoon half the pork mixture into the tin. Cover with half the turkey, then the cranberries, followed by the remaining turkey and the rest of the pork mixture. Roll out a lid with the remaining dough. Seal the edges with egg, and make a steam hole. Decorate the top, brush with egg and bake for 2 hours. Cover with foil if it gets too brown. Cool, then use a funnel to fill the pie with liquid aspic jelly. Leave to set, then turn out and serve.

Nutritional information per portion: Energy 670kcal/2801kJ; Protein 38.1g; Carbohydrate 50.8g, of which sugars 4.1g; Fat 36.2g, of which saturates 13.9g; Cholesterol 119mg; Calcium 155mg; Fibre 2.5g; Sodium 558mg.

Chicken and apricot filo pie

The filling for this unusual yet utterly delicious pie has a Middle Eastern flavour – chicken combined with apricots, bulgur wheat, nuts and spices.

SERVES 6

75g/3oz/¹⁄₂ cup bulgur wheat
75g/3oz/6 tbsp butter
1 onion, chopped
450g/1lb minced (ground) chicken
50g/2oz/¹⁄₄ cup ready-to-eat dried apricots, finely chopped
25g/1oz/¹⁄₄ cup chopped almonds
5ml/1 tsp ground cinnamon
2.5ml/¹⁄₂ tsp ground allspice
60ml/4 tbsp Greek (US strained plain) yogurt
15ml/1 tbsp chopped fresh chives
30ml/2 tbsp chopped fresh parsley
8 large sheets of filo pastry
salt and ground black pepper
chives, to garnish

1 Soak the bulgur wheat in 120ml/4fl oz/¹⁄₂ cup boiling water for about 10 minutes until the water is absorbed.

2 Heat 25g/1oz/2 tbsp of the butter in a frying pan, add the onion and chicken and gently fry until golden. Stir in the bulgur wheat and chopped apricots and almonds and cook for 2 minutes. Remove from the heat and stir in the cinnamon, allspice, yogurt, chives and parsley. Season with salt and pepper.

3 Preheat the oven to 200°C/400°F/Gas 6. Melt the remaining butter. Unroll the filo pastry and cut into 25cm/10in rounds. Keep the pastry covered with a damp dish towel to prevent it from drying out. Line a 23cm/9in loose-based flan tin (pan) with three filo rounds, brushing each with butter. Spoon in the chicken mixture and cover with three more rounds, brushing with melted butter.

4 Crumple the remaining two pastry rounds and place them on top of the pie, then brush over the remaining melted butter. Bake for about 30 minutes until the pastry is golden brown and crisp. Serve hot or cold, garnished with chives.

Nutritional information per portion: Energy 263kcal/1104kJ; Protein 21.9g; Carbohydrate 19.9g, of which sugars 3.8g; Fat 11.3g, of which saturates 5.2g; Cholesterol 70mg; Calcium 69mg; Fibre 1.6g; Sodium 106mg.

Spiced chicken and egg filo pie

This recipe is based on Bisteeya, one of the most elaborate and intriguing dishes in Moroccan cuisine. This version uses chicken instead of pigeon, and filo pastry instead of the traditional ouarka.

SERVES 4

30ml/2 tbsp sunflower oil

25g/1oz/2 tbsp butter

3 chicken quarters, with breasts attached

1¹/₂ Spanish onions, very finely chopped

generous pinch of ground ginger

generous pinch of saffron powder

10ml/2 tsp ground cinnamon,
    plus extra for dusting

40g/1¹/₂oz/¹/₃ cup flaked (sliced) almonds

1 large bunch fresh coriander (cilantro),
    finely chopped

1 large bunch fresh parsley, chopped

3 eggs, beaten

about 175g/6oz filo pastry,
    thawed if frozen

5–10ml/1–2 tsp icing (confectioners')
    sugar, plus extra for dusting (optional)

salt and ground black pepper

1 Heat the oil and butter in a pan, add the chicken pieces and cook, stirring, until browned. Add the onions, ginger, saffron, 2.5ml/¹/₂ tsp of the cinnamon and 300ml/¹/₂ pint/1¹/₄ cups water. Season, bring to the boil and then cover and simmer very gently for 45–55 minutes. When the chicken is cooked but still tender, transfer to a plate. Dry-fry the almonds until golden. Set aside. When the chicken is cool enough, remove the skin and bones. Cut into bitesize pieces.

2 Stir the coriander and parsley into the pan. Reduce the sauce until thickened. Add the beaten eggs. Stir over a gentle heat, until the eggs are lightly scrambled.

3 Preheat the oven to 180°C/350°F/Gas 4. Oil a shallow 25cm/10in round ovenproof dish. Place sheets of filo pastry in an even layer over the base and sides of the dish, letting the edges overhang. Lightly brush the pastry with oil. Make two more layers of filo, brushing with oil between layers.

4 Place the chicken in the pastry case, then spoon the egg and herb mixture on top. Level with a spoon. Place a layer of filo on top of the filling. Scatter with the almonds. Sprinkle with the remaining cinnamon and icing sugar, if using. Fold the edges of the filo over the almonds and then make four further layers of filo, brushing each with a little oil. Tuck the filo edges down the sides and brush the top with oil.

5 Bake the pie for 40–45 minutes until it is golden brown. Dust the top of the pie with icing sugar and cinnamon, creating a geometric design by using a paper template if you wish. Serve immediately.

Nutritional information per portion: Energy 497kcal/2081kJ; Protein 46.8g; Carbohydrate 28.4g, of which sugars 6.7g; Fat 22.7g, of which saturates 6g; Cholesterol 261mg; Calcium 139mg; Fibre 3.6g; Sodium 190mg.

Bacon and egg pie

Whole eggs are broken over smoked bacon and softened onions before being covered in pastry in a double-crust pie, in this celebration of the best of breakfast ingredients.

SERVES 4

30ml/2 tbsp sunflower oil

4 smoked bacon rashers (strips), cut into 4cm/1¹/₂in pieces

1 small onion, finely chopped

5 eggs

25ml/1¹/₂ tbsp chopped fresh parsley

salt and ground black pepper

a little milk, to glaze

FOR THE PASTRY

350g/12oz/3 cups plain (all-purpose) flour

pinch of salt

115g/4oz/¹/₂ cup butter, diced

50g/2oz/¹/₄ cup lard or white vegetable fat

75–90ml/5–6 tbsp chilled water

1 To make the pastry, sift the flour and salt into a large bowl and rub in the fat until the mixture resembles breadcrumbs. Sprinkle over most of the water. Mix to a pliable dough. Knead until smooth. Wrap in clear film (plastic wrap) and chill for 30 minutes.

2 Butter a deep 20cm/8in flan tin (pan). Roll out two-thirds of the pastry and use to line the flan tin. Cover and chill for 30 minutes.

3 Preheat the oven to 200°C/400°F/ Gas 6. Heat the oil in a pan, add the bacon and cook for a few minutes. Add the onion and cook until soft. Leave to cool on kitchen paper.

4 Cover the base of the case with the bacon mixture. Break the eggs on top, spreading them evenly apart. Tilt the tin so the egg whites flow together. Sprinkle with the parsley and season. Put a baking sheet in the oven to heat.

5 Roll out the remaining pastry, dampen the edges and place over the pie. Roll over the top with a rolling pin to seal the edges and remove excess pastry. Carefully cut curved lines from the pie's centre to within 2cm/³/₄in of the edge. Glaze with milk.

6 Bake for 10 minutes on the baking sheet, then reduce to 180°C/350°F/ Gas 4 and bake for 20 minutes more.

Nutritional information per portion: Energy 202kcal/843kJ; Protein 13.4g; Carbohydrate 9.7g, of which sugars 4.4g; Fat 12.5g, of which saturates 4.2g; Cholesterol 149mg; Calcium 125mg; Fibre 1.1g; Sodium 592mg.

Steak and kidney pie with mustard gravy

This is a tasty variation on a traditional favourite, perfect for a hearty family meal. The fragrant mustard, bay and parsley gravy complements the beef beautifully.

SERVES 4

450g/1lb puff pastry
40ml/2¹/₂ tbsp plain (all-purpose) flour
675g/1¹/₂lb rump (round) steak, cubed
175g/6oz lamb's kidneys
25g/1oz/2 tbsp butter
1 onion, chopped
15ml/1 tbsp English (hot) mustard
2 bay leaves
15ml/1 tbsp chopped fresh parsley
150ml/¹/₄ pint/²/₃ cup beef stock
1 egg, beaten

COOK'S TIP
When making a pie with a lid, a ceramic pie funnel can be used. It pokes up through the lid and acts as a chimney allowing steam to escape which might otherwise make the pastry soggy and prevent it from rising properly.

1 Roll out two-thirds of the pastry to a thickness of 3mm/¹/₈in. Use to line the base and sides of a 1.5 litre/ 2¹/₂ pint/6¹/₄ cup pie dish. Place a pie funnel in the centre. Put the flour in a bowl and season. Toss the steak in it. Remove the fat, skin and core from the kidneys, slice and toss with the steak.

2 Melt the butter in a pan. Add the onion and stir-fry over a low heat, until soft and translucent. Add the mustard, bay leaves, parsley and stock and stir well. Preheat the oven to 190°C/375°F/Gas 5. Place the steak and kidney in the pie dish and add the stock mixture.

3 Roll out the remaining puff pastry to a thickness of 3mm/¹/₈in to use for the pie lid. Brush the edges of the pastry case with beaten egg and cover with the lid. Press the edges firmly together to seal, then trim. Use the trimmings to decorate the top with pastry leaves.

4 Brush the pie with a little beaten egg and make a small hole in the centre of the pastry lid for the funnel. This will allow steam to escape as the pie cooks. Bake the pie in the preheated oven for about 1 hour until the pastry is risen, crispy and golden brown.

Nutritional information per portion: Energy 845kcal/3530kJ; Protein 53.7g; Carbohydrate 51g, of which sugars 2.8g; Fat 49.9g, of which saturates 10.1g; Cholesterol 249mg; Calcium 121mg; Fibre 1.2g; Sodium 565mg.

Chicken and mushroom pie

A classic pie that goes down well with diners of all ages. Porcini mushrooms are the perfect ingredient to intensify the flavour of the chicken and vegetable filling.

SERVES 6

15g/¹⁄₂ oz/¹⁄₄ cup dried porcini mushrooms
50g/2oz/¹⁄₄ cup butter
30ml/2 tbsp plain (all-purpose) flour
250ml/8fl oz/1 cup hot chicken stock
60ml/4 tbsp single (light) cream
1 onion, coarsely chopped
2 carrots, sliced
2 celery sticks, coarsely chopped
50g/2oz/³⁄₄ cup button (white)
    mushrooms, cut into quarters
450g/1lb cooked chicken meat, cubed

50g/2oz/¹⁄₂ cup fresh or frozen peas
salt and ground black pepper
beaten egg, to glaze

FOR THE PASTRY
225g/8oz/2 cups plain (all-purpose) flour
1.5ml/¹⁄₄ tsp salt
115g/4oz/¹⁄₂ cup cold butter, diced
65g/2¹⁄₂oz/¹⁄₃ cup white vegetable
    fat, diced
60–120ml/4–8 tbsp chilled water

1 To make the pastry, sift the flour and salt into a bowl. Cut or rub in the butter and white vegetable fat until the mixture resembles breadcrumbs. Sprinkle with 90ml/6 tbsp chilled water and mix until the dough holds together. If the dough is too crumbly, add a little more water, 15ml/1 tbsp at a time. Gather the dough into a ball and flatten it into a round. Wrap and chill for at least 30 minutes.

2 To make the filling, place the porcini mushrooms in a bowl. Add hot water to cover and leave to soak for 30 minutes. Drain in a muslin- (cheesecloth-) lined sieve (strainer), then dry well on kitchen paper. Preheat the oven to 190°C/375°F/Gas 5.

3 Melt half of the butter in a heavy pan. Whisk in the flour and cook until bubbling, whisking constantly. Add the hot stock and whisk over a medium heat until the mixture boils. Cook for 2–3 minutes, then whisk in the cream. Season to taste, and set aside.

4 Heat the remaining butter in a large frying pan and cook the onion and carrots over a low heat for 5 minutes. Add the celery and button mushrooms and cook for 5 minutes more. Stir in the cooked chicken, peas and drained porcini mushrooms. Add the chicken mixture to the cream sauce and stir. Adjust the seasoning if necessary. Spoon the mixture into a 2.5 litre/4 pint/2¹⁄₂ quart oval baking dish.

5 Roll out the pastry to about 3mm/¹⁄₈in. Cut out an oval 2.5cm/1in larger all around than the dish. Lay the pastry over the filling. Press around the edge to seal, then trim off the excess. Crimp the edges by pushing your forefinger into the pastry edge, and pinching the pastry with the other hand.

6 Press together the pastry trimmings and roll out again. Cut out mushroom shapes with a sharp knife and stick them on to the pastry lid with beaten egg. Glaze the lid with beaten egg. Cut several slits in the pastry to allow the steam to escape. Bake the pie for about 30 minutes, until the pastry has browned. Serve the pie hot.

COOK'S TIP
Using a combination of butter and white vegetable fat gives shortcrust pastry a lovely crumbly texture.

Nutritional information per portion: Energy 600kcal/2501kJ; Protein 23.7g; Carbohydrate 38.8g, of which sugars 3.7g; Fat 40g, of which saturates 21.8g; Cholesterol 132mg; Calcium 92mg; Fibre 2.7g; Sodium 226mg.

Parcels and shaped pastry cases

You'll find all manner of traditional and more unusual parcels and shaped pastry packages in this section. Pastry is amazingly versatile and can be wrapped around large or small joints of meat, rolled up for a strudel, slashed to make a jalousie, or cut and braided. In the following recipes, pastry is used not only to hold the filling, but also as a decoration for dishes, from the traditional Beef Wellington to the elegant Fillets of Sea Bream in Filo Pastry.

Mushroom, nut and prune jalousie

Jalousie, the French word for shutter, refers to this pie's slatted top. It has a rich nutty filling that will be enjoyed by vegetarians and meat-eaters alike.

SERVES 6

75g/3oz/¹/₃ cup green lentils, rinsed
5ml/1 tsp vegetable bouillon powder
15ml/1 tbsp sunflower oil
2 large leeks, sliced
2 garlic cloves, chopped
200g/7oz/3 cups field (portabello)
    mushrooms, finely chopped
10ml/2 tsp dried mixed herbs
75g/3oz/³/₄ cup chopped mixed nuts
15ml/1 tbsp pine nuts
75g/3oz/¹/₃ cup ready-to-eat
    pitted prunes
25g/1oz/¹/₂ cup fresh breadcrumbs
2 eggs, beaten
500g/1¹/₄lb puff pastry
salt and ground black pepper

1 Bring the lentils to the boil in a pan of water. Reduce the heat slightly and stir in the vegetable bouillon. Simmer for 20 minutes until tender. Set aside.

2 Heat the oil in a frying pan, add the leeks and garlic and fry for 5 minutes, until softened. Add the mushrooms and herbs and cook for 5 minutes. Transfer to a bowl. Stir in the nuts, pine nuts, prunes, breadcrumbs and lentils. Add two-thirds of the beaten egg and season. Preheat the oven to 220°C/425°F/Gas 7.

3 Roll out just under half the pastry to a 25 x 15cm/10 x 6in rectangle. Lay it on a dampened baking sheet. Roll out the rest to a 28 x 19cm/11 x 7¹/₂in rectangle, dust with flour, and fold in half lengthways. Make a series of cuts across the fold, 1cm/¹/₂in apart, leaving a 2.5cm/1in border.

4 Spoon the filling over the pastry base, leaving a 2.5cm/1in border. Dampen the edges with water. Open out the folded pastry and lay it over the filling. Seal the edges, trim the excess and crimp the edges. Brush with egg and bake for 25–30 minutes until golden.

Nutritional information per portion: Energy 480kcal/2004kJ; Protein 13.5g; Carbohydrate 42.3g, of which sugars 7.3g; Fat 30.5g, of which saturates 1.6g; Cholesterol 63mg; Calcium 99mg; Fibre 4.2g; Sodium 281mg.

Mushroom and quail's egg gougère

Gougère is a popular pastry from the Burgundy region of France. In this version it is filled with wild mushrooms and tiny, lightly boiled quail's eggs.

SERVES 4–6

25g/1oz/¼ cup cornflour (cornstarch)
150ml/¼ pint/²/₃ cup red wine/
 water mix
25g/1oz/2 tbsp butter
1 onion, chopped
2 celery sticks, sliced
350g/12oz/4–5 cups mixed mushrooms
150ml/¼ pint/²/₃ cup stock
dash of Worcestershire sauce
15ml/1 tbsp chopped fresh parsley
12 quail's eggs

FOR THE CHOUX PASTRY

75g/3oz/6 tbsp butter, diced
2.5ml/½ tsp salt
175ml/6fl oz/¾ cup water
100g/3¾oz/1 cup plain
 (all-purpose) flour
4 eggs
115g/4oz/1 cup grated Gruyère cheese

1 Preheat the oven to 220°C/425°F/Gas 7. To make the pastry, melt the butter with the salt and water. Bring to the boil. Remove from the heat, add the flour and beat with a wooden spoon until it forms a ball. Return to the heat. Cook, beating hard, for 1–2 minutes. Leave to cool slightly. Add two eggs, beating until glossy. Beat in the third egg, then as much of the fourth as needed, with half the cheese.

2 Put a round of baking parchment on a baking sheet. Place large spoonfuls of pastry close together in a 20cm/8in circle. Bake for 30 minutes, until risen and golden. Cut slits in the sides to release the steam and set aside to cool.

3 Mix the cornflour, wine and water. Fry the onion and celery in butter. Add the mushrooms, cook gently and add the wine mixture. Add the stock, and gradually the cornflour mixture. Cook until starting to thicken, then add the Worcestershire sauce and chopped fresh parsley. Cook until thick.

4 Boil the eggs for 1 minute. Cool and peel. Slice the gougère in half. Top with the filling and eggs. Replace the lid. Sprinkle with the remaining cheese, and return to the oven until the cheese melts.

Nutritional information per portion: Energy 603kcal/2513kJ; Protein 22.7g; Carbohydrate 35.1g, of which sugars 1.7g; Fat 40.5g, of which saturates 22.1g; Cholesterol 416mg; Calcium 321mg; Fibre 2.1g; Sodium 751mg.

Spicy potato strudel

Wrap up in crisp filo pastry a tasty mixture of vegetables cooked in a spicy, creamy sauce.
Serve with a good selection of chutneys or a yogurt and mint sauce.

SERVES 4

65g/2¹/₂oz/5 tbsp butter
1 onion, chopped
2 carrots, coarsely grated
1 courgette (zucchini), chopped
350g/12oz firm potatoes, chopped
10ml/2 tsp mild curry paste
2.5ml/¹/₂ tsp dried thyme
150ml/¹/₄ pint/²/₃ cup water
1 egg, beaten
30ml/2 tbsp single (light) cream
50g/2oz/¹/₂ cup grated Cheddar cheese
8 sheets of thawed filo pastry,
    thawed if frozen
salt and ground black pepper
sesame seeds, for sprinkling

1 Melt 25g/1oz/2 tbsp of the butter in a frying pan. Cook the onion, carrots, courgette and potatoes for 5 minutes, tossing to ensure they cook evenly. Stir in the curry paste. Cook for 1–2 minutes more until tender.

2 Add the thyme and water, and season. Bring to the boil. Reduce the heat and simmer for 10 minutes until tender, stirring often. Set aside to cool.

3 Put the vegetable mixture in a bowl and mix in the egg, cream and cheese. Chill until ready to fill the pastry.

4 Preheat the oven to 190°C/375°F/ Gas 5. Melt the remaining butter. Lay out four sheets of filo pastry, slightly overlapping, to form a large rectangle. Brush with butter and fit the other sheets on top. Brush with some more of the melted butter. Spoon the filling along one long side, then roll it up. Form it into a circle and place on a baking sheet. Brush with butter and sprinkle with sesame seeds.

5 Bake for 25 minutes, or until golden and crisp. Leave to stand for 5 minutes before cutting into slices and serving.

Nutritional information per portion: Energy 362kcal/1512kJ; Protein 9.8g; Carbohydrate 34.8g, of which sugars 6.5g; Fat 21.1g, of which saturates 12.7g; Cholesterol 98mg; Calcium 169mg; Fibre 3g; Sodium 227mg.

Mediterranean one-crust pie

This free-form pie encases a rich tomato, aubergine and kidney bean filling. If your pastry cracks, just patch it up – a rough appearance adds to the pie's rustic character.

SERVES 4

500g/1¼ lb aubergine (eggplant), cubed
1 red (bell) pepper
1 large onion, finely chopped
30ml/2 tbsp olive oil
1 courgette (zucchini), sliced
2 garlic cloves, crushed
15ml/1 tbsp chopped fresh oregano
200g/7oz can red kidney beans, drained
115g/4oz/1 cup pitted black olives
150ml/¼ pint/⅔ cup passata
    (bottled strained tomatoes)
1 egg, beaten, or a little milk
30ml/2 tbsp semolina

FOR THE PASTRY

75g/3oz/⅔ cup plain (all-purpose) flour
75g/3oz/⅔ cup wholemeal
    (whole-wheat) flour
75g/3oz/6 tbsp vegetable margarine
50g/2oz/⅔ cup grated Parmesan cheese
60–90ml/4–6 tbsp chilled water

1 Preheat the oven to 220°C/425°F/ Gas 7. To make the pastry, sift both the flours into a bowl, tipping in the bran. Rub in the margarine, then stir in the Parmesan. Mix in just enough chilled water to form a firm dough. Chill for 30 minutes. On a lightly floured surface, knead the dough into a smooth ball. Wrap in clear film (plastic wrap). Chill for 20 minutes.

2 Sprinkle the aubergine with salt in a colander and leave for 30 minutes. Rinse and pat dry. Roast the red pepper on a baking sheet in the oven for 20 minutes. Put the pepper in a plastic bag. When cool, remove, peel and seed. Dice the flesh. Set aside.

3 Fry the onion in the olive oil for 5 minutes, stirring, until soft. Add the aubergine and fry for 5 minutes more. Add the courgette, garlic and oregano. Cook for 5 minutes more, stirring. Add the kidney beans and olives, stir well, then add the passata. Season. Cook until heated through. Set aside.

4 Roll out the pastry to a rough 30cm/12in round. Place on a lightly oiled baking sheet. Brush with beaten egg or milk, sprinkle with semolina, leaving a 4cm/1½in border, then spoon over the filling. Fold up the pastry edges, leaving the middle open. Brush the pastry with the remaining egg and bake for 30–35 minutes.

Nutritional information per portion: Energy 554kcal/2318kJ; Protein 17.7g; Carbohydrate 56.6g, of which sugars 15.7g; Fat 30.2g, of which saturates 4.2g; Cholesterol 13mg; Calcium 295mg; Fibre 11.6g; Sodium 1353mg.

Ratatouille and Fontina strudel

Mix a colourful jumble of ratatouille vegetables with chunks of creamy Fontina cheese, then wrap in sheets of filo and bake for a delicious, summery party dish.

SERVES 6

1 small aubergine (eggplant), diced
45ml/3 tbsp extra virgin olive oil
1 onion, sliced
2 garlic cloves, crushed
1 red (bell) pepper, cored and sliced
1 yellow (bell) pepper, cored and sliced
2 courgettes (zucchini), cut into
    small chunks
generous pinch of dried mixed herbs
30ml/2 tbsp pine nuts
30ml/2 tbsp raisins
8 sheets of filo pastry, each measuring
    30 x 18cm/12 x 7in, thawed if frozen
50g/2oz/¼ cup butter, melted
130g/4½ oz/generous 1 cup diced
    Fontina cheese
salt and ground black pepper
dressed mixed salad, to serve

1 Layer the diced aubergine in a colander, sprinkling each layer with salt. Drain for 20 minutes, rinse well and pat dry. Heat the oil in a frying pan, add the onion, garlic, peppers and aubergine and gently fry over a low heat, stirring occasionally, for 10 minutes, or until soft and golden. Add the courgettes, herbs, and salt and pepper. Cook for 5 minutes until softened. Cool, then add the pine nuts and raisins.

2 Preheat the oven to 180°C/350°F/Gas 4. Brush two sheets of filo pastry with a little of the melted butter. Lay the filo sheets side by side, overlapping them slightly by about 5cm/2in, to make a large rectangle. Cover with the remaining filo, brushing each layer with melted butter. Spoon the vegetable mixture down one long side of the filo.

3 Sprinkle the cheese on top, then roll up and transfer to a non-stick baking sheet, curling the roll into a circle. Brush with the remaining butter. Bake for 30 minutes, cool for 10 minutes, then slice and serve with mixed salad.

Nutritional information per portion: Energy 327kcal/1359kJ; Protein 8.7g; Carbohydrate 22.8g, of which sugars 9.6g; Fat 22.4g, of which saturates 9.5g; Cholesterol 38mg; Calcium 106mg; Fibre 2.9g; Sodium 178mg.

Seafood gougère

In this recipe, the choux pastry is baked at the same time as its filling of lightly spiced haddock with mushrooms. This is an easy-to-prepare yet impressive supper dish.

SERVES 4

130g/4¹/₂oz/1 cup plus 30ml/2 tbsp
    plain (all-purpose) flour
1.5ml/¹/₄ tsp salt
130g/4¹/₂oz/9 tbsp butter
200ml/7fl oz/scant 1 cup water
3 eggs, beaten
150g/5oz Emmenthal or Gruyère
    cheese, grated
250g/9oz smoked haddock fillet
1 bay leaf
250ml/8fl oz/1 cup milk
1 small red onion, chopped
150g/5oz/2–2¹/₂ cups white (button)
    mushrooms, sliced
5ml/1 tsp mild curry paste (optional)
fresh lemon juice
30ml/2 tbsp chopped fresh parsley
salt and ground black pepper

1 Sift 100g/3³/₄oz/scant 1 cup of the flour on to a sheet of baking parchment and add the salt. Place 75g/3oz/6 tbsp of the butter in a pan, add the water, and heat gently. Once the butter has melted, bring to the boil. Tip in the flour mixture. Beat well. When the mixture comes away from the sides of the pan and forms a smooth paste, remove from the heat and leave to cool for 5 minutes.

2 Slowly work the beaten eggs into the dough, beating well, until it has the consistency of creamy mashed potato. You may not need all the egg. Stir in two-thirds of the cheese. Spoon the pastry around the edge of a lightly greased shallow ovenproof dish. Set aside. Preheat the oven to 180°C/350°F/Gas 4.

3 Put the haddock in a baking dish with the bay leaf. Pour in the milk, cover and bake for 15 minutes until just cooked. Set aside the fish. Discard the bay leaf but retain the milk. Melt the remaining butter in a frying pan. Add the onion and mushrooms and sauté for 5 minutes. Add the curry paste and remaining flour. Gradually add the hot milk. Heat, stirring, until smooth. Simmer for 2–3 minutes. Add the lemon juice and parsley, and season. Increase the heat to 200°C/400°F/Gas 6. Skin and flake the fish. Spoon into the centre of the uncooked pastry, with the mushrooms. Sprinkle with the remaining cheese. Bake for 35–40 minutes.

Nutritional information per portion: Energy 597kcal/2485kJ; Protein 30.7g; Carbohydrate 26.8g, of which sugars 1.6g; Fat 41.1g, of which saturates 24.2g; Cholesterol 261mg; Calcium 391mg; Fibre 1.6g; Sodium 1101mg.

Scallops and wild mushrooms in a shell

From the depths of the sea and the forest floor come two flavours that marry perfectly in a smooth creamy sauce. Crisp pastry completes the dish.

SERVES 4

350g/12oz puff pastry
1 egg, beaten
75g/3oz/6 tbsp butter
12 scallops, trimmed and thickly sliced
2 shallots, chopped
1/2 celery stick, cut into strips
1/2 carrot, cut into strips

225g/8oz/3 cups assorted wild
    mushrooms, trimmed and sliced
60ml/4 tbsp dry vermouth
150ml/1/4 pint/2/3 cup crème fraîche
4 egg yolks
15ml/1 tbsp lemon juice
celery salt and cayenne pepper, to taste

1 Roll out the puff pastry on a floured surface, then cut out four 13cm/5in shell shapes, using a paper template if you need to. Mark a shell pattern on each with a knife, and brush with a little beaten egg. Place on a baking sheet and chill for 1 hour. Preheat the oven to 200°C/400°F/Gas 6.

2 Melt one third of the butter in a pan. Season the scallops and cook in the pan for 30 seconds over a high heat. Set aside.

3 Score an inner shell 2.5cm/1in from the outer edge of each pastry shape. Bake the shapes for 20–25 minutes until golden. Set aside on a wire rack.

4 Fry the shallots, celery and carrot gently in the remaining butter. Add the mushrooms and cook until the juices run.

5 Pour in the vermouth and then increase the heat to evaporate the pan juices. Add the crème fraîche and cooked scallops and bring to a simmer (do not boil).

6 Remove the pan from the heat and blend in the egg yolks. Return the pan to a gentle heat and cook for a moment or two until the sauce has thickened to the consistency of thin cream, then remove the pan from the heat. Season with celery salt and cayenne pepper and add the lemon juice.

7 Gently split the pastry shapes open and place the bases on four plates. Spoon in the filling and arrange the lids on top. Serve with potatoes and salad, if you like.

Nutritional information per portion: Energy 698kcal/2896kJ; Protein 10.1g; Carbohydrate 35.3g, of which sugars 3.5g; Fat 57.7g, of which saturates 21.6g; Cholesterol 284mg; Calcium 110mg; Fibre 0.9g; Sodium 410mg.

Tuna and egg galette

This stunningly colourful pie is surprisingly easy to make using ready-rolled puff pastry. If you prefer to make your own pastry, you will need 500g/1¼lb.

SERVES 4

2 sheets of ready-rolled puff pastry

1 egg, beaten

60ml/4 tbsp olive oil

175g/6oz tuna steak

2 onions, sliced

1 red (bell) pepper, chopped

2 garlic cloves, crushed

45ml/3 tbsp capers, drained

5ml/1 tsp grated lemon rind

30ml/2 tbsp lemon juice

5 eggs

30ml/2 tbsp flat leaf parsley, to garnish

1 Preheat the oven to 190°C/375°F/Gas 5. Lay a sheet of puff pastry on a floured baking sheet and cut to a 28 x 18cm/11 x 7in rectangle. Glaze the whole sheet with beaten egg.

2 Cut the second sheet of puff pastry to the same shape. Cut out the centre and reserve for another recipe, leaving a 2.5cm/1in border. Lift the pastry border on to the first sheet. Brush the border with beaten egg and prick the base with a fork. Bake in the hot oven for about 15 minutes until golden and well risen.

3 Heat 30ml/2 tbsp of the oil in a frying pan and fry the tuna steak for about 3 minutes on each side until golden but still pale pink in the middle. Transfer to a plate and flake into small pieces.

4 Add the remaining oil to the pan and fry the onions, red pepper and garlic for 6–8 minutes until softened, stirring occasionally. Remove from the heat and stir in the tuna, capers and lemon rind and juice. Season well.

5 Spoon the filling into the pastry case and level the surface with the back of a spoon. Break the eggs into the filling, cover the tart with lightly oiled foil and return to the oven for about 10 minutes, or until the eggs have just cooked through. Garnish with chopped parsley and serve at once.

Nutritional information per portion: Energy 544kcal/2263kJ; Protein 21.7g; Carbohydrate 27.7g, of which sugars 4.6g; Fat 39.5g, of which saturates 10.1g; Cholesterol 260mg; Calcium 102mg; Fibre 1.9g; Sodium 320mg.

Fillets of sea bream in filo pastry

Any firm fish fillets can be used for this dish. Each little parcel is a meal in itself and can be prepared several hours in advance, which makes this ideal for entertaining.

SERVES 4

8 small waxy salad potatoes

200g/7oz sorrel, stalks removed

30ml/2 tbsp olive oil

4 sea bream fillets, about 175g/6oz each
  (scaled but not skinned)

16 sheets of filo pastry, thawed if frozen

50g/2oz/¼ cup butter, melted

120ml/4fl oz/½ cup fish stock

250ml/8fl oz/1 cup double (heavy) cream

finely diced red (bell) pepper, to garnish

1 Preheat the oven to 200°C/400°F/Gas 6. Cook the salad potatoes in lightly salted boiling water for 15–20 minutes, until just tender. Drain and set aside to cool. Shred half the sorrel by piling up six or eight leaves at a time, rolling them up like a fat cigar and slicing them with a sharp knife.

2 Thinly slice the potatoes lengthways. Brush a baking tray with a little oil. Lay a sheet of filo pastry on the tray, brush it with oil, then lay a second sheet crossways over the first. Repeat with two more sheets.

3 Arrange a quarter of the sliced potatoes in the centre of the pastry, season well and add a quarter of the shredded sorrel. Lay a bream fillet on top, skin side up. Season well.

4 Loosely fold the filo pastry up and over to make a neat parcel. Make three more parcels in the same way. Place on the baking tray and brush them with half the butter. Bake for 20 minutes until the filo is puffed up and golden brown.

5 Meanwhile, make the sorrel sauce. Heat the remaining butter in a small pan, add the reserved sorrel and cook until it wilts. Stir in the fish stock and cream. Heat almost to boiling point, stirring constantly. Season and keep hot. Serve the fish parcels garnished with red pepper and offer the sauce separately, in its own bowl.

VARIATION
Use small spinach leaves or baby chard in place of sorrel, if you like.

Nutritional information per portion: Energy 651kcal/2710kJ; Protein 35.8g; Carbohydrate 23.2g, of which sugars 3.3g; Fat 46.8g, of which saturates 23.2g; Cholesterol 159mg; Calcium 222mg; Fibre 2g; Sodium 359mg.

Chicken and couscous parcels

Based on the Turkish börek or boreg, these savoury rich pastry parcels are served at room temperature with a yogurt sauce, spiked with cayenne and cooled with mint.

SERVES 4

50g/2oz/¹/₃ cup couscous
45ml/3 tbsp olive oil
1 onion, chopped
115g/4oz/1¹/₂ cups mushrooms
1 garlic clove, crushed
115g/4oz cooked chicken, diced
30ml/2 tbsp walnuts, chopped
30ml/2 tbsp raisins
60ml/4 tbsp chopped fresh parsley
5ml/1 tsp chopped fresh thyme
2 eggs, hard-boiled and peeled

FOR THE PASTRY
400g/14oz/3¹/₂ cups self-raising
    (self-rising) flour

1 egg, plus extra for glazing
150ml/¹/₄ pint/²/₃ cup natural
    (plain) yogurt
150ml/¹/₄ pint/²/₃ cup olive oil
grated rind of ¹/₂ lemon

FOR THE YOGURT SAUCE
200ml/7fl oz/scant 1 cup natural
    (plain) yogurt
45ml/3 tbsp chopped fresh mint
2.5ml/¹/₂ tsp caster
    (superfine) sugar
1.5ml/¹/₄ tsp cayenne pepper
1.5ml/¹/₄ tsp celery salt
a little milk or water (optional)

1 Preheat the oven to 190°C/375°F/Gas 5. Place the couscous in a bowl and just cover with boiling water. Soak for 10 minutes, or until all the liquid has been absorbed.

2 Heat the oil in a frying pan, add the onion and cook over a medium heat until soft but without letting it colour. Add the mushrooms and crushed garlic and cook until the juices begin to run. Increase the heat to evaporate the juices.

3 Transfer the onion and mushroom mixture to a large mixing bowl. Add the diced chicken, chopped walnuts, raisins, chopped parsley and thyme and couscous and stir well. Roughly chop the eggs and stir them into the mixture with seasoning to taste.

4 To make the pastry, sift the flour and 5ml/1 tsp salt into a bowl. Make a well in the centre, add the egg, yogurt, olive oil and lemon rind, and mix together with a round-bladed knife.

5 On a lightly floured surface, roll out the pastry to a 30cm/12in round. Pile the filling into the centre of the pastry round and bring the edges over to enclose the filling.

6 Place the parcel seam side down on a baking sheet and gently flatten. Glaze with beaten egg and bake for 25 minutes.

7 Meanwhile, make the sauce. Mix together all the ingredients, adding milk or water if the mixture is too thick. Spoon a little sauce over each serving.

VARIATIONS
Alternative fillings for these parcels include mixed cheese and herbs; mushrooms with ground cumin and coriander; or a spicy potato and vegetable mixture.

Nutritional information per portion: Energy 885kcal/3707kJ; Protein 28.3g; Carbohydrate 97.2g, of which sugars 14.5g; Fat 45.5g, of which saturates 7.1g; Cholesterol 164mg; Calcium 369mg; Fibre 4.5g; Sodium 156mg.

Lamb pie with pear and mint sauce

Cooking lamb with fruit is an idea derived from traditional Persian cuisine. The ginger and mint add a delightful bite to the mild flavours in this dish.

SERVES 6

400g/14oz can pears in juice
50g/2oz/¼ cup butter
1 small onion, chopped
grated rind of 1 lemon
75g/3oz/1 cup coarse wholemeal
   (whole-wheat) breadcrumbs

1.5ml/¼ tsp ground ginger
1 small egg, beaten
900g/2lb boned and rolled loin of lamb
8 large sheets of filo pastry, thawed if frozen
10ml/2 tsp finely chopped fresh mint,
   plus a few mint sprigs to garnish

1 Preheat the oven to 180°C/350°F/Gas 4. Drain the pears, reserving the juice. Set half the pears aside and chop the rest. Melt 15g/½oz/1 tbsp of the butter in a pan and add the onion. Cook until soft. Put in a bowl and add the lemon rind, breadcrumbs, chopped pears and ginger. Bind with the egg and season well.

2 Open out the lamb, fat side down, and season. Place the pear stuffing along the middle and roll the meat around it. Secure with skewers while you tie it up with string (twine). Heat a roasting pan in the oven and brown the lamb slowly all over. This will take 20–30 minutes. Remove from the oven, leave to cool and then chill until needed.

3 Increase the temperature to 200°C/400°F/Gas 6. Melt the remaining butter. Brush two pastry sheets with butter and overlap, making a square. Continue layering the rest of the sheets, brushing with butter.

4 Place the roll of lamb diagonally across one corner of the pastry. Fold the corner over the lamb, fold in the sides, and brush the pastry well with melted butter. Roll up the lamb in the pastry, tucking in the edges as you go. Place the filo-wrapped lamb, seam side down, on a buttered baking sheet. Brush all over with the remaining butter. Bake for about 30 minutes until the pastry is crisp and golden.

5 To make the sauce, process the reserved pears along with their juice and the mint in a food processor or blender. Spoon into a bowl and serve with the lamb, garnished with a few mint sprigs.

Nutritional information per portion: Energy 482kcal/2022kJ; Protein 33.5g; Carbohydrate 34.8g, of which sugars 6.4g; Fat 24.2g, of which saturates 12.2g; Cholesterol 132mg; Calcium 69mg; Fibre 2g; Sodium 277mg.

Beef Wellington

This dish, a fillet of beef baked in puff pastry, is a variation of the classic French boeuf en croûte. The English name was applied in 1815 in honour of the Duke of Wellington.

SERVES 6

1.6kg/3¼lb fillet (tenderloin) of beef
45ml/3 tbsp sunflower oil
115g/4oz/1½ cups button (white)
    mushrooms, chopped
2 garlic cloves, crushed

175g/6oz smooth liver pâté
30ml/2 tbsp chopped fresh parsley
400g/14oz puff pastry
1 egg, beaten
salt and ground black pepper

1 Preheat the oven to 220°C/425°F/Gas 7. Tie the beef with string (twine). Heat 30ml/2 tbsp of the oil in a frying pan, and brown the beef on all sides for 10 minutes. Put in a roasting pan and roast for 20 minutes. Remove and set aside to cool. Leave the oven on.

2 Heat the remaining oil in a frying pan and cook the mushrooms and garlic for about 5 minutes until soft. Beat the mushroom mixture into the pâté with the chopped parsley, and season well. Set aside to cool.

3 Roll out the puff pastry into a sheet large enough to enclose the beef, plus a strip to spare. Trim off the spare pastry. Spread the pâté mixture down the middle of the pastry. Untie the beef and lay it on top of the pâté mixture.

4 Brush the edges of the pastry with beaten egg and fold the pastry over the meat to enclose it in a neat parcel. Seal the edges well. Place the meat parcel on a baking sheet, seam side down.

5 Cut decorative leaf shapes from the reserved pastry. Brush the parcel with beaten egg, decorate with the pastry leaves and brush with egg. Chill for about 10 minutes.

6 Bake the beef for 50–60 minutes, covering it loosely with foil after about 30 minutes to prevent the pastry from over-browning. Transfer to a serving platter and leave to stand for about 10 minutes. Serve in thick slices, and garnish each portion with parsley.

Nutritional information per portion: Energy 872kcal/3632kJ; Protein 69.5g; Carbohydrate 25g, of which sugars 1g; Fat 56.1g, of which saturates 13.5g; Cholesterol 236mg; Calcium 62mg; Fibre 0.2g; Sodium 620mg.

Sweet shortcrust pastries

This is a tantalizing collection of small sweet pastries to suit any occasion. Traditional Lemon Curd Tarts with their tangy filling, and more substantial Baked Apple Dumplings, are perennial favourites, along with daintier tartlets — some made from flavoured pastries, including chocolate and coffee. This chapter also contains unusual pastries from around the world, such as Gazelles' Horns from Morocco with their orange-scented almond paste filling, and fragrant Greek Fruit and Nut Pastries.

Summer fruit brûlée tartlets

This quantity of pastry is enough for eight tartlets, so freeze half for another day. The brûlée topping is best added no more than two hours before the tarts are served.

MAKES 4

4 egg yolks
50g/2oz/¼ cup caster (superfine) sugar
15ml/1 tbsp cornflour (cornstarch)
a few drops of vanilla extract
300ml/½ pint/¼ cup creamy milk
225g/8oz/2 cups mixed summer fruits
50g/2oz/½ cup icing (confectioners') sugar

FOR THE PASTRY

250g/9oz/2¼ cups plain
   (all-purpose) flour
pinch of salt
25g/1oz/¼ cup ground almonds
15ml/1 tbsp icing (confectioners') sugar
150g/5oz/²/₃ cup chilled butter, diced
1 egg yolk
about 45ml/3 tbsp chilled water

1 Make the pastry. Mix the flour, salt, ground almonds and icing sugar in a bowl. Rub in the butter. Add the egg yolk and enough chilled water to form a soft dough. Knead gently, then cut it in half. Wrap half in clear film (plastic wrap) and freeze for use later. Cut the rest into quarters and roll out. Stamp out rounds big enough to line four tartlet tins (muffin pans). Use your fingertips to mould it to the tin, letting the excess hang over the edges. Chill for 30 minutes.

2 Preheat the oven to 200°C/400°F/Gas 6. Line the pastry cases with baking parchment and baking beans. Bake blind for 10 minutes. Remove the paper and beans. Return to the oven for 5 minutes until golden. Cool, then trim carefully.

3 To make the custard, beat the egg yolks, caster sugar, cornflour and vanilla extract in a bowl. Warm the milk in a pan and whisk into the egg yolk mixture. Return to the cleaned pan. Heat until thickened, stirring. Do not boil. Remove from the heat and press a circle of baking parchment on the surface. Let it cool.

4 Sprinkle the fruits into the cases, spoon over the custard and chill for 2 hours. Sift over the icing sugar and place under a hot grill (broiler) to caramelize.

Nutritional information per portion: Energy 743kcal/3099kJ; Protein 13.6g; Carbohydrate 75.2g, of which sugars 20.7g; Fat 45g, of which saturates 23.8g; Cholesterol 342mg; Calcium 250mg; Fibre 4g; Sodium 282mg.

Red grape and cheese tartlets

Fruit and cheese make a natural combination in this simple recipe. Look out for small, pale, mauve-coloured or red grapes. These are often seedless, and sweeter than large black varieties.

MAKES 6

225g/8oz/1 cup curd (farmer's) cheese
150ml/¼ pint/⅔ cup double
   (heavy) cream
2.5ml/½ tsp vanilla extract
30ml/2 tbsp icing (confectioners') sugar
200g/7oz/2 cups red grapes, halved,
   seeded if necessary
60ml/4 tbsp apricot conserve
15ml/1 tbsp water

FOR THE PASTRY

200g/7oz/1¾ cups plain
   (all-purpose) flour
15ml/1 tbsp caster (superfine) sugar
150g/5oz/⅔ cup butter
2 egg yolks
15ml/1 tbsp chilled water

1 To make the pastry, sift the flour and sugar into a mixing bowl. Rub in the butter until the mixture resembles breadcrumbs. Add the egg yolks and water and mix to a dough. Knead lightly until smooth. Wrap and chill for 30 minutes.

2 Preheat the oven to 200°C/400°F/Gas 6. Roll out the pastry and use to line six deep 10cm/4in fluted tartlet tins (muffin pans). Prick the bases and line with foil and baking beans. Bake for 10 minutes, remove the foil and beans, then bake for a further 5 minutes until golden. Remove from the tins and cool.

3 Meanwhile, beat the curd cheese, double cream, vanilla extract and icing sugar in a small bowl. Divide the mixture among the pastry cases. Smooth the surface and arrange the halved grapes attractively on top.

4 Strain the apricot conserve into a pan. Add the water and heat, stirring constantly, until smooth and glossy. Spoon the glaze over the grapes. Leave to cool, then chill before serving.

Nutritional information per portion: Energy 559kcal/2330kJ; Protein 10.4g; Carbohydrate 45.1g, of which sugars 19.7g; Fat 39.3g, of which saturates 23.9g; Cholesterol 164mg; Calcium 123mg; Fibre 1.3g; Sodium 331mg.

Tia Maria truffle tartlets

Sophisticated and seriously indulgent, these mini coffee pastry cases are filled with a chocolate liqueur truffle centre and topped with fresh ripe berries.

MAKES 6

300ml/½ pint/1¼ cups double
   (heavy) cream
225g/8oz/¾ cup seedless blackberry jam
150g/5oz plain (semisweet) chocolate
45ml/3 tbsp Tia Maria liqueur
450g/1lb/4 cups mixed berries

FOR THE PASTRY

225g/8oz/2 cups plain (all-purpose) flour
15ml/1 tbsp caster (superfine) sugar
150g/5oz/⅔ cup butter, diced
1 egg yolk
30ml/2 tbsp strong brewed coffee, chilled

1 Preheat the oven to 200°C/400°F/Gas 6, placing a large baking sheet in the oven to heat. To make the pastry, sift the flour and sugar into a large bowl. Rub or cut in the butter until the mixture resembles fine breadcrumbs.

2 Blend the egg yolk with the coffee, add to the bowl and mix to a stiff dough. Knead on a floured surface for a few seconds until smooth. Wrap in clear film (plastic wrap) and chill for 20 minutes.

3 Roll out the pastry and use to line six 10cm/4in fluted tartlet tins (muffin pans). Prick the bases with a fork and line with foil and baking beans. Place on the hot baking sheet and bake for 10 minutes. Remove the foil and beans and bake for a further 8–10 minutes. Allow to cool in the tins.

4 To make the filling, slowly bring the cream and 175g/6oz/generous ½ cup of the jam to the boil, stirring constantly.

5 Remove the pan from the heat, add the chocolate and 30ml/2 tbsp of the liqueur. Stir until melted. Leave to cool, then spoon the mixture into the tartlet cases and smooth the tops. Place on a baking tray and chill for 40 minutes.

6 Heat the remaining jam and liqueur and stir until smooth. Arrange the fruit on the tarts, then brush the jam glaze over. Chill until ready to serve.

Nutritional information per portion: Energy 844kcal/3519kJ; Protein 7.1g; Carbohydrate 79g, of which sugars 50.2g; Fat 55.9g, of which saturates 34.3g; Cholesterol 157mg; Calcium 112mg; Fibre 2.6g; Sodium 182mg.

Lemon curd tarts

These tasty little tarts are a popular tea-time treat in the north of England. They have a curd cheese and currant filling on a tangy layer of lemon curd.

MAKES 24

225g/8oz/1 cup curd (farmer's) cheese
2 eggs, beaten
75g/3oz/6 tbsp caster (superfine) sugar
5ml/1 tsp finely grated lemon rind
50g/2oz/¼ cup currants
60ml/4 tbsp lemon curd
thick cream, to serve

FOR THE PASTRY

275g/10oz/2½ cups plain
   (all-purpose) flour
pinch of salt
75g/3oz/6 tbsp butter, diced
50g/2oz/¼ cup lard or white
   vegetable fat
60ml/4 tbsp chilled water

1 Make the pastry. Sift the flour and salt into a bowl. Rub in the fat until it resembles breadcrumbs. Sprinkle the water over and mix to a dough. Knead on a lightly floured surface for a few seconds until smooth. Chill.

2 Preheat the oven to 180°C/350°F/ Gas 4. Roll out the pastry thinly, stamp out 24 rounds using a 7.5cm/3in plain pastry (cookie) cutter and use to line mini tartlet tins (muffin pans) or cupcake tins (pans). Chill until needed.

3 Cream the curd cheese with the eggs, sugar and lemon rind in a mixing bowl, then stir in the currants. Place 2.5ml/½ tsp of the lemon curd into the base of each tartlet case.

4 Spoon the filling into each case, then flatten the tops and bake for 35–40 minutes until just turning golden. Serve the tarts either warm or cold, topped with thick cream.

Nutritional information per portion: Energy 125kcal/526kJ; Protein 3.1g; Carbohydrate 15.8g, of which sugars 6.5g; Fat 6.1g, of which saturates 3.1g; Cholesterol 27mg; Calcium 34mg; Fibre 0.4g; Sodium 68mg.

Pecan tassies

Cream cheese pastry has a rich flavour that goes well with the pecan filling in these tiny tartlets, which take their name from a Scottish word meaning 'a small cup'.

MAKES 24

2 eggs
175g/6oz/³/₄ cup firmly packed soft dark brown sugar
5ml/1 tsp vanilla extract
large pinch of salt
25g/1oz/2 tbsp butter, melted
115g/4oz/1 cup pecan nuts

FOR THE PASTRY
115g/4oz/¹/₂ cup butter
400g/14oz/1³/₄ cups cream cheese
115g/4oz/1 cup plain (all-purpose) flour

1 Place a baking sheet in the oven and preheat to 180°C/350°F/Gas 4. Grease two 12-cup mini tartlet tins (muffin pans) or cupcake tins (pans). Cut up the butter and cream cheese and place in a mixing bowl. Sift over the flour and mix to a smooth dough.

2 Roll out the dough thinly on a lightly floured surface. Using a 6cm/2¹/₂in fluted pastry (cookie) cutter, stamp out 24 pastry rounds. Line the mini tartlet cups with the rounds and chill.

3 To make the filling, whisk the eggs in a bowl. Whisk in the brown sugar, a few tablespoons at a time, then add the vanilla, salt and butter. Set aside. Reserve 24 perfect pecan halves for decoration and chop the rest.

4 Place a spoonful of chopped nuts in each mini tartlet cup and cover with the filling. Set a pecan half on top of each. Bake on the hot baking sheet for about 20 minutes, until puffed and set. Transfer to a rack to cool. Serve at room temperature.

Nutritional information per portion: Energy 139kcal/576kJ; Protein 1.6g; Carbohydrate 9g, of which sugars 5.3g; Fat 10.9g, of which saturates 4.9g; Cholesterol 33mg; Calcium 20mg; Fibre 0.4g; Sodium 56mg.

Baked apple dumplings

Not many people will be able to resist this tasty treat. The sharpness of the fruit contrasts perfectly with the maple syrup drizzled over this delightful pastry parcel.

MAKES 8

8 firm cooking apples, peeled
1 egg white
130g/4¹/₂oz/²/₃ cup caster
    (superfine) sugar
45ml/3 tbsp double (heavy) cream,
    plus extra whipped cream, to serve
2.5ml/¹/₂ tsp vanilla extract
250ml/8fl oz/1 cup maple syrup

FOR THE PASTRY

475g/1lb 2oz/4¹/₂ cups plain
    (all-purpose) flour
2.5ml/¹/₂ tsp salt
350g/12oz/1¹/₂ cups butter or white
    vegetable fat, diced
175–250ml/6–8fl oz/³/₄–1 cup
    chilled water

1 Make the pastry. Sift the flour and salt into a bowl. Rub in the butter or fat. Sprinkle over 175ml/6fl oz/³/₄ cup water and mix until it holds together. Gather into a ball, wrap in clear film (plastic wrap) and chill for 20 minutes.

2 Preheat the oven to 220°C/425°F/ Gas 7. From the stem end, core each apple without cutting the base. Roll out the pastry. Cut squares almost big enough to enclose an apple; brush with egg white and set an apple in the centre of each. Cut pastry rounds to cover the tops. Combine the sugar, cream and vanilla extract in a bowl.

3 Spoon filling into each apple, place a pastry circle on top, then bring up the sides of the pastry square to enclose it, fitting the larger piece of pastry snuggly around the apple. Moisten the joins where they overlap. Make leaves and stalks with the trimmings to decorate.

4 Set 2cm/³/₄in apart in a greased baking dish and bake for 30 minutes. Lower the temperature to 180°C/ 350°F/Gas 4. Bake for 20 minutes until golden. Mix the juices in the dish with the maple syrup and drizzle over the dumplings. Serve hot with cream.

Nutritional information per portion: Energy 713kcal/2988kJ; Protein 6.6g; Carbohydrate 94.7g, of which sugars 49.5g; Fat 36.8g, of which saturates 22.9g; Cholesterol 93mg; Calcium 108mg; Fibre 3g; Sodium 361mg.

Greek fruit and nut pastries

Aromatic sweet pastry crescents, known as moshopoungia in Greece, are packed with candied citrus peel and walnuts, which have been soaked in a coffee syrup.

MAKES 16

60ml/4 tbsp clear honey
60ml/4 tbsp strong brewed coffee
75g/3oz/¹/₂ cup mixed candied citrus peel, finely chopped
175g/6oz/1¹/₂ cups walnuts, chopped
1.5ml/¹/₄ tsp freshly grated nutmeg
milk, to glaze
caster (superfine) sugar, for sprinkling

FOR THE PASTRY

450g/1lb/4 cups plain (all-purpose) flour
2.5ml/¹/₂ tsp ground cinnamon
2.5ml/¹/₂ tsp baking powder
pinch of salt
150g/5oz/²/₃ cup butter
30ml/2 tbsp caster (superfine) sugar
1 egg
120ml/4fl oz/¹/₂ cup chilled milk

1 Preheat the oven to 180°C/350°F/ Gas 4. To make the pastry, sift the flour, cinnamon, baking powder and salt into a bowl. Rub in the butter until it resembles breadcrumbs. Stir in the sugar. Make a well. Beat the egg and milk together and pour into the well. Mix to a soft dough. Divide into two and wrap each piece in clear film (plastic wrap). Chill for 30 minutes.

2 Meanwhile, mix the honey and coffee in a bowl. Add the candied peel, walnuts and nutmeg. Stir well, cover and leave for 20 minutes.

3 Roll out one piece of dough to 3mm/ ¹/₈in thick. Stamp out rounds with a 10cm/4in pastry (cookie) cutter.

4 Place a heaped teaspoon of filling on one side of each round. Brush the edges with milk, then fold over and press together to seal. Repeat with the second piece of pastry until all the filling has been used.

5 Place the pastries on greased baking sheets, brush with milk and sprinkle with caster sugar. Make a steam hole in each and bake for 35 minutes.

Nutritional information per portion: Energy 278kcal/1162kJ; Protein 5g; Carbohydrate 30.2g, of which sugars 8.7g; Fat 16.1g, of which saturates 5.7g; Cholesterol 32mg; Calcium 69mg; Fibre 1.5g; Sodium 80mg.

Whisky-laced mince pies

Mincemeat gets the luxury treatment with the addition of glacé pineapple, cherries and whisky to make a marvellous filling for these traditional festive pies. Serving them with a dollop of whisky butter is pure indulgence, and makes a perfect yuletide treat.

MAKES 12–15

225g/8oz/1 cup mincemeat
50g/2oz/¼ cup glacé (candied) pineapple
50g/2oz/¼ cup glacé (candied) cherries
30ml/2 tbsp whisky
1 egg, beaten or a little milk
icing (confectioners') sugar, for dusting

FOR THE PASTRY
1 egg yolk
5ml/1 tsp grated orange rind

15ml/1 tbsp caster (superfine) sugar
225g/8oz/2 cups plain (all-purpose) flour
150g/5oz/⅔ cup butter, diced

FOR THE WHISKY BUTTER
75g/3oz/6 tbsp butter, softened
175g/6oz/1½ cups icing
   (confectioners') sugar, sifted
30ml/2 tbsp whisky
5ml/1 tsp grated orange rind

1 To make the pastry, mix the egg yolk with the orange rind, caster sugar and 10ml/2 tsp chilled water in a bowl. Set aside. Sift the flour into a seperate mixing bowl. Rub in the butter. Stir in the egg mixture and mix to a dough. Wrap in clear film (plastic wrap) and chill for 30 minutes.

2 Mix the mincemeat, pineapple and cherries. Spoon over the whisky and leave to soak. Roll out three-quarters of the pastry. Stamp out fluted rounds to line 12–15 cupcake tins (pans). Roll out the remaining pastry and stamp out star shapes.

3 Preheat the oven to 200°C/400°F/Gas 6. Spoon a little filling into each pastry case and top with a star. Brush with a little beaten egg or milk and bake for 20–25 minutes until golden. Leave to cool.

4 Meanwhile, make the whisky butter. Place the butter, icing sugar, whisky and grated orange rind in a small bowl and beat with a wooden spoon until light and fluffy.

5 To serve, lift off each pastry star, pipe a swirl of whisky butter on top of the filling, then replace the star. Dust the mince pies with a little icing sugar.

Nutritional information per portion: Energy 195kcal/818kJ; Protein 1.8g; Carbohydrate 26.3g, of which sugars 14.8g; Fat 9.5g, of which saturates 5.3g; Cholesterol 35mg; Calcium 36mg; Fibre 0.8g; Sodium 75mg.

Baked sweet ravioli

These delicious sweet ravioli are made with a rich pastry flavoured with lemon and filled with a mixture of ricotta cheese, candied fruits and chocolate.

SERVES 4

175g/6oz/³/4 cup ricotta cheese
50g/2oz/¹/4 cup caster
    (superfine) sugar
4ml/³/4 tsp vanilla extract
small egg, beaten, plus 1 egg yolk
15ml/1 tbsp mixed candied fruits
25g/1oz dark (bittersweet) chocolate,
    finely chopped
icing (confectioners') sugar and grated
    chocolate, to serve

FOR THE PASTRY

225g/8oz/2 cups plain
    (all-purpose) flour
65g/2¹/2oz/¹/3 cup caster
    (superfine) sugar
90g/3¹/2oz/scant ¹/2 cup butter, diced
1 egg
5ml/1 tsp finely grated lemon rind

1 To make the pastry, place the flour and sugar in a food processor and, with the motor running at full speed, slowly add the butter until fully worked in. With the motor running, add the egg and lemon rind, to form a dough that just holds together. Lay it on one sheet on clear film (plastic wrap) and cover with another, then flatten into a round. Chill. Press the ricotta through a sieve (strainer) into a bowl. Stir in the sugar, vanilla extract, egg yolk, candied fruits and chocolate.

2 Allow the pastry to return to room temperature and then divide in half. Roll each half between sheets of clear film to make a 15 x 56cm/6 x 22in rectangle. Preheat the oven to 180°C/350°F/Gas 4. Arrange heaped teaspoonfuls of filling in two rows along one of the rectangles, leaving a 2.5cm/1in margin around each. Brush between the mounds with egg, place the second rectangle on top, and press down between each mound of filling to seal.

3 Use a 6cm/2¹/2in plain pastry (cookie) cutter to cut around each mound. Pinch the edges with your fingertips to seal. Bake on a greased baking sheet for 15 minutes. Serve warm, sprinkled with icing sugar and grated chocolate.

Nutritional information per portion: Energy 628kcal/2636kJ; Protein 13.1g; Carbohydrate 81.4g, of which sugars 38.5g; Fat 30.1g, of which saturates 17.7g; Cholesterol 162mg; Calcium 119mg; Fibre 2.1g; Sodium 186mg.

Gazelles' horns

These horn-shaped pastries, filled with almond paste, are commonly served at wedding ceremonies in their native Morocco, where they are a firm favourite.

MAKES ABOUT 16

200g/7oz/scant 2 cups ground almonds
115g/4oz/1 cup icing (confectioners')
    sugar, plus extra for dusting
30ml/2 tbsp orange flower water
25g/1oz/2 tbsp butter, melted
2 egg yolks, beaten
2.5ml/¹/₂ tsp ground cinnamon

FOR THE PASTRY

200g/7oz/1³/₄ cups plain
    (all-purpose) flour
pinch of salt
25g/1oz/2 tbsp butter, melted
about 30ml/2 tbsp orange flower water
1 egg yolk, beaten
60–90ml/4–6 tbsp chilled water

1 Mix the ground almonds, icing sugar, orange flower water, melted butter, egg yolks and cinnamon in a mixing bowl to make a smooth paste.

2 To make the pastry, sift the flour and salt into a bowl. Add the melted butter, orange flower water and three-quarters of the egg yolk. Stir in enough chilled water to make a soft dough. Quickly and lightly, knead the pastry until smooth and elastic, then roll it out thinly. Cut it into long strips about 7.5cm/3in wide.

3 Preheat the oven to 180°C/350°F/Gas 4. Roll small pieces of the almond paste into thin sausages 7.5cm/3in long with tapering ends. Line these along one side of the pastry strips, about 3cm/1¹/₄in apart. Dampen the edges, then fold the other half of the strip over the filling and press the edges together.

4 Using a pastry wheel, cut around each sausage to make a crescent. Pinch the edges together to seal. Prick with a fork. Brush with egg yolk. Bake on a buttered baking sheet for 12–16 minutes. Allow to cool, then dust with icing sugar.

Nutritional information per portion: Energy 182kcal/762kJ; Protein 4.4g; Carbohydrate 18.1g, of which sugars 8.2g; Fat 10.7g, of which saturates 2.5g; Cholesterol 44mg; Calcium 56mg; Fibre 1.3g; Sodium 23mg.

Greek chocolate mousse tartlets

If you are a chocolate fan, you will adore these tarts, with their dark rich chocolate pastry, creamy filling and yet more chocolate drizzled over the top.

MAKES 6

200g/7oz white chocolate, broken up
120ml/4fl oz/½ cup milk
10ml/2 tsp powdered gelatine
30ml/2 tbsp caster (superfine) sugar
5ml/1 tsp vanilla extract
2 eggs, separated
250g/9oz/1 cup Greek (US strained
   plain) yogurt
melted dark (bittersweet) chocolate

FOR THE PASTRY

115g/4oz/1 cup plain (all-purpose) flour
25g/1oz/¼ cup icing (confectioners') sugar
25g/1oz/¼ cup unsweetened
   cocoa powder
75g/3oz/6 tbsp butter
2 eggs
2.5ml/½ tsp vanilla extract

1 To make the pastry, sift the flour, sugar and cocoa powder into a mixing bowl. Rub in the butter. Combine the eggs and vanilla in a small bowl. Add to the dry ingredients and mix to a soft dough. Knead until smooth. Wrap in clear film (plastic wrap) and chill for 20 minutes.

2 Roll out the pastry and use to line six deep 10cm/4in loose-based tartlet tins (muffin pans). Cover and chill for 20 minutes. Preheat the oven to 190°C/375°F/Gas 5.

3 Prick the base of each pastry case all over with a fork. Line with baking parchment, fill with baking beans and bake blind for 10 minutes. Remove the paper and beans, return the cases to the oven and bake for a further 15 minutes, or until the pastry is firm. Cool completely in the tins.

4 To make the filling, melt the white chocolate in a bowl set over a pan of hot water. Pour the milk into a pan, sprinkle over the gelatine and heat gently, stirring until the gelatine dissolves. Remove from the heat and stir in the chocolate. Whisk together the sugar, vanilla extract and egg yolks in a bowl, then beat in the chocolate mixture. Beat in the yogurt until evenly mixed. Chill until starting to set.

5 Whisk the egg whites in a grease-free bowl until stiff, then gently fold into the mixture. Divide among the tartlet cases and leave to set. Drizzle the melted dark chocolate over the tartlets to decorate.

Nutritional information per portion: Energy 490kcal/2048kJ; Protein 12.9g; Carbohydrate 46.2g, of which sugars 31.2g; Fat 30g, of which saturates 16.6g; Cholesterol 155mg; Calcium 235mg; Fibre 1.1g; Sodium 238mg.

Sweet puff and filo pastries

Crisp puff pastry and light-as-a-feather filo make some of the most memorable pastries. They rise to airy heights and often need just the simplest of fillings, such as whipped cream and fresh fruit, to create a tempting treat for afternoon tea or a dessert that will have everyone eager for second helpings. Try the delicate flavours of Almond Cream Puffs, Peach and Redcurrant Tartlets or sweet and sticky Almond and Date Filo Parcels. These pastries may be small, but they are difficult to resist.

Mini mille-feuille

This pâtisserie classic is a delectable combination of tender puff pastry with luscious pastry cream. As it is difficult to cut, making individual servings is a brilliant solution.

SERVES 4

450g/1lb rough puff or puff pastry
6 egg yolks
65g/2¹/₂oz/¹/₃ cup caster
(superfine) sugar
45ml/3 tbsp plain (all-purpose) flour
350ml/12fl oz/1¹/₂ cups milk
30ml/2 tbsp Kirsch or cherry liqueur
450g/1lb/2²/₃ cups raspberries
icing (confectioners') sugar, for dusting

1 Sprinkle two buttered baking sheets with a little very cold water. Roll out the pastry to 3mm/¹/₈in thick. Cut out 12 rounds with a 10cm/4in plain pastry (cookie) cutter. Place on the baking sheets, prick a few times with a fork, and chill for 30 minutes. Preheat the oven to 200°C/400°F/Gas 6. Bake for 15–20 minutes until golden, then transfer to wire racks to cool.

2 Whisk the egg yolks and sugar for 2 minutes until light and creamy, then whisk in the flour until just blended. Bring the milk to the boil, then whisk into the egg mixture. Return to the pan, bring to the boil and boil for 2 minutes, whisking constantly. Remove from the heat. Whisk in the liqueur. Pour into a bowl, press a piece of clear film (plastic wrap) on to the surface and set aside.

3 To assemble, carefully split the pastry rounds in half. Spread each with a little pastry cream. Arrange a layer of raspberries over the cream and top with a second pastry round. Spread with a little more cream and a few more raspberries. Top with a third pastry round and dust with icing sugar.

Nutritional information per portion: Energy 702kcal/2943kJ; Protein 16.5g; Carbohydrate 79.1g, of which sugars 30.4g; Fat 37.8g, of which saturates 3.4g; Cholesterol 308mg; Calcium 258mg; Fibre 3.2g; Sodium 406mg.

Almond cream puffs

These sweet little pies consist of crisp, flaky layers of pastry surrounding a delicious, creamy filling. They are best served warm, so reheat any that become cold before eating.

MAKES 10

275g/10oz puff pastry
2 egg yolks
15ml/1 tbsp plain (all-purpose) flour
30ml/2 tbsp ground almonds
30ml/2 tbsp caster (superfine) sugar
a few drops of vanilla or almond extract
150ml/¼ pint/⅔ cup double (heavy) cream, whipped
milk, to glaze
icing (confectioners') sugar, for dusting

1 Roll out the pastry thinly on a lightly floured surface, and cut out ten 7.5cm/3in plain rounds and ten 6.5cm/2½in fluted rounds. Keep the smaller rounds for the tops, and use the larger ones to line a patty tin (muffin pan) or cupcake tin (pan). Chill for about 10 minutes. Preheat the oven to 200°C/400°F/Gas 6.

2 Whisk the egg yolks with the flour, almonds, sugar and vanilla extract. Fold in the cream and spoon into the pastry cases. Brush the rims with milk, add the tops and seal the edges. Glaze with milk.

3 Bake for 20–25 minutes until golden. Cool slightly, then dust with icing sugar before serving.

VARIATION
Another tasty option is to use desiccated (dry unsweetened shredded) coconut instead of ground almonds.

Nutritional information per portion: Energy 225kcal/933kJ; Protein 3.2g; Carbohydrate 14.9g, of which sugars 3.9g; Fat 17.6g, of which saturates 5.5g; Cholesterol 61mg; Calcium 39mg; Fibre 0.3g; Sodium 91mg.

Poached pear tartlets with chocolate sauce

In this delicious recipe puff pastry is shaped and topped with spicy poached pears. The chocolate sauce complements the pastries beautifully, creating a simply scrumptious dessert.

SERVES 6

3 firm pears, peeled
450ml/³⁄₄ pint/scant 2 cups water
strip of thinly pared orange rind
1 vanilla pod (bean)
1 bay leaf
50g/2oz/¹⁄₄ cup granulated
   (white) sugar
350g/12oz puff pastry

40g/1¹⁄₂oz/¹⁄₃ cup unsweetened
   cocoa powder
75ml/5 tbsp double (heavy) cream
15g/¹⁄₂oz/1 tbsp butter, softened
15ml/1 tbsp soft light brown sugar
25g/1oz/¹⁄₄ cup walnuts, chopped
1 egg, beaten
15g/¹⁄₂oz/1 tbsp caster (superfine) sugar

1 Halve the pears. Scoop out just the cores with a melon baller or small spoon. Put the water in a pan with the orange rind, vanilla pod, bay leaf and sugar. Bring to the boil, stirring. Add the pears and more water to cover. Cook gently, covered, for 15 minutes until tender. Set the pears aside and reserve the syrup.

2 Roll out the pastry and cut out six pear shapes, slightly larger than the pear halves. Place the shapes on greased baking sheets and chill for 30 minutes.

3 Remove the orange rind, vanilla pod and bay leaf from the reserved syrup, then return the syrup to the heat and boil rapidly for 10 minutes. Blend the cocoa powder with 60ml/4 tbsp cold water in a separate pan.

4 Stir a few spoonfuls of the syrup into the cocoa paste. Whisk the paste into the syrup in the pan. Cook until reduced to about 150ml/¹⁄₄ pint/²⁄₃ cup. Remove from the heat and add the cream. Stir well.

5 Preheat the oven to 200°C/400°F/Gas 6. In a bowl, mix together the butter, sugar and walnuts. Gently pat the pears dry with kitchen paper, then spoon a little filling into each cavity.

6 Lightly brush the pastry pear shapes with a little egg. Put a pear half, filled side down, in the centre of each pastry shape. Lightly sprinkle the pastries with a little caster sugar and bake for 12 minutes, or until the pastry has puffed up around the pear and is golden brown. Drizzle over some of the warm chocolate sauce and serve immediately.

Nutritional information per portion: Energy 443kcal/1847kJ; Protein 6.7g; Carbohydrate 44.2g, of which sugars 22.5g; Fat 28.4g, of which saturates 6.8g; Cholesterol 54mg; Calcium 73mg; Fibre 2.6g; Sodium 277mg.

Mango and tamarillo pastries

These fruit-topped pastry slices are the perfect companion for a cup of afternoon tea. Ready-rolled puff pastry is perfect if you are short of time.

MAKES 8

225g/8oz puff pastry
1 egg yolk, lightly beaten
115g/4oz white marzipan
40ml/2¹/₂ tbsp ginger or
    apricot conserve
1 mango, peeled and thinly sliced
2 tamarillos, halved and sliced
caster (superfine) sugar, for sprinkling

1 Preheat the oven to 200°C/400°F/Gas 6. Roll out the pastry thinly and trim it to a 30 x 25cm/12 x 10in rectangle. Cut this into eight rectangles and place on baking sheets.

2 Using the point of a small sharp knife, score the surface of each piece of pastry in a diamond pattern, then brush lightly with the egg yolk to glaze. Cut the marzipan into eight thin slices and lay one slice on each pastry rectangle. Top each with a teaspoonful of the ginger or apricot conserve and spread evenly.

3 Top the pastries with alternate slices of mango and tamarillo. Sprinkle with a little caster sugar, then bake for about 20 minutes until the pastry is puffed up and golden. Transfer the pastries to a wire rack to cool, then place on dessert plates. Sprinkle with more caster sugar before serving.

Nutritional information per portion: Energy 202kcal/847kJ; Protein 3.2g; Carbohydrate 28.4g, of which sugars 18.3g; Fat 9.5g, of which saturates 0.4g; Cholesterol 25mg; Calcium 43mg; Fibre 1.2g; Sodium 95mg.

Nectarine puff pastry tarts

These simple, fresh fruit pastries are easy to put together, but the puff pastry gives them an elegant look. You could use peaches, apples or pears instead of nectarines.

SERVES 6

15g/¹/₂oz/1 tbsp butter
225g/8oz rough puff or puff pastry
450g/1lb nectarines
30ml/2 tbsp caster (superfine) sugar
freshly grated nutmeg
crème fraîche or lightly whipped cream,
   to serve (optional)

1 Lightly butter a large baking sheet and sprinkle lightly with water. Roll out the puff pastry to a large rectangle, measuring about 40 x 25cm/15 x 10in, and then cut it into six smaller rectangles. Transfer to the baking sheet.

2 Scallop the edges of each piece of pastry with the back of a small knife. Then, using the tip, score a border 1cm/¹/₂in from the edge of each rectangle. Chill the pastry shapes for 30 minutes. Preheat the oven to 200°C/400°F/Gas 6.

3 Halve the nectarines, removing the stones (pits). Cut the fruit into thin slices. Arrange the slices in the centre of the pastry rectangles, leaving the border uncovered. Sprinkle the fruit with caster sugar and freshly grated nutmeg.

4 Bake for 12–15 minutes until the edges of the pastry cases are puffed up and the fruit is tender. Transfer the tarts to a wire rack to cool slightly, then remove and serve warm, with a little crème fraîche or whipped cream, if you like.

Nutritional information per portion: Energy 208kcal/873kJ; Protein 3.2g; Carbohydrate 25.9g, of which sugars 12.5g; Fat 11.3g, of which saturates 1.3g; Cholesterol 5mg; Calcium 30mg; Fibre 0.9g; Sodium 133mg.

Plum and marzipan pastries

Ready-rolled puff pastry has been used here for speed and convenience. However, if you make your own puff pastry, the squares should measure 15cm/6in.

MAKES 6

375g/13oz ready-rolled puff pastry
3 red plums
90ml/6 tbsp plum jam
115g/4oz/¹⁄₂ cup white marzipan,
   coarsely grated
1 egg, beaten

50g/2oz/¹⁄₂ cup flaked
   (sliced) almonds

FOR THE GLAZE
30ml/2 tbsp plum jam
15ml/1 tbsp water

1 Preheat the oven to 220°C/425°F/Gas 7. Unroll the pastry, cut it into six equal squares and then place on one or two dampened baking sheets.

2 Halve and stone (pit) the red plums. Place 15ml/1 tbsp jam into the centre of each puff pastry square, leaving a border all round. Divide the marzipan among them. Place half a plum, hollow side down, on top of each marzipan mound.

3 Brush the edges of the pastry with beaten egg. Bring up the corners of the pastry and lightly press the edges together, then open out the corners at the top. Glaze the pastries with some more beaten egg, then press a sixth of the almonds on each.

4 Bake the pastries for 20–25 minutes, or until lightly golden. Meanwhile, make the glaze. Heat the jam and water in a pan, stirring until smooth.

5 Press the jam and water mixture through a sieve (strainer) into a bowl. Lightly brush it over the pastries while they are still warm. Leave the pastries to cool on a wire rack before serving at room temperature.

Nutritional information per portion: Energy 416kcal/1746kJ; Protein 6.6g; Carbohydrate 51.8g, of which sugars 29.2g; Fat 22.4g, of which saturates 0.6g; Cholesterol 0mg; Calcium 73mg; Fibre 1.2g; Sodium 205mg.

Peach and redcurrant tartlets

Tart redcurrants and sweet peaches make a winning combination in these simple tartlets.
Small bunches of redcurrants make easy ornaments, dusted with a little icing sugar.

MAKES 4

25g/1oz/2 tbsp butter, melted

16 sheets of filo pastry, each measuring
    15cm/6in square, thawed if frozen

150ml/¼ pint/⅔ cup double
    (heavy) cream

130g/4½oz peach and mango fromage
    frais or yogurt

vanilla extract

15ml/1 tbsp icing (confectioners') sugar,
    sifted, plus extra for dusting

2 peaches, halved and stoned (pitted)

50g/2oz/½ cup redcurrants, plus
    redcurrant sprigs, to decorate

1 Preheat the oven to 190°C/375°F/Gas 5. Use a little of the butter to lightly grease four individual tartlet tins (muffin pans). Brush the pastry squares with a little more butter, stack them in fours, then place in the tartlet tins to make four pastry cases.

2 Bake for about 15 minutes until golden. Cool the filo cases on a wire rack before removing them from the tins.

3 To make the filling, whip the cream to soft peaks, then lightly fold in the fromage frais or yogurt with a few drops of the vanilla extract and icing sugar. Divide among the tartlet cases.

4 Slice the peaches and arrange the slices on top of the filling, with a few redcurrants. Decorate with the redcurrant sprigs and dust with icing sugar.

COOK'S TIP

To strip redcurrants from their stalks, pull the strips through the tines of a fork so that they drop into a bowl.

Nutritional information per portion: Energy 431kcal/1801kJ; Protein 6.4g; Carbohydrate 41.9g, of which sugars 13.2g; Fat 27.6g, of which saturates 17g; Cholesterol 71mg; Calcium 112mg; Fibre 2.2g; Sodium 60mg.

Walnut and vanilla ice palmiers

These wonderful walnut pastries are delicious when served freshly baked but, for convenience, you can make them ahead and reheat them in a medium oven.

MAKES 6

75g/3oz/³⁄₄ cup walnut pieces
350g/12oz puff pastry
1 egg, beaten
45ml/3 tbsp caster (superfine) sugar
about 200ml/7fl oz/scant 1 cup vanilla
   ice cream

1 Preheat the oven to 200°C/400°F/ Gas 6. Lightly grease a large baking sheet with butter. Chop the walnuts finely. On a lightly floured surface roll the pastry to a thin rectangle measuring 30 x 20cm/12 x 8in.

2 Trim the edges of the pastry. Brush with the egg. Sprinkle over all but 45ml/3 tbsp of the walnuts and all but 30ml/2 tbsp of the sugar.

3 Press the walnuts gently into the pastry with a rolling pin, then roll up the pastry from one short edge to the centre. Roll up the other side until the two rolls meet.

4 Brush the points where the rolls meet in the middle with a little beaten egg. Using a sharp knife, carefully cut the pastry into 1cm/¹⁄₂in slices.

5 Lay the slices on their sides and flatten them with a rolling pin. Transfer to the baking sheet. Brush the slices with more beaten egg and sprinkle with the reserved walnuts and sugar.

6 Bake for 15 minutes, or until pale golden. Serve the palmiers warm, in pairs, sandwiched together with ice cream.

Nutritional information per portion: Energy 398kcal/1661kJ; Protein 6.4g; Carbohydrate 38g, of which sugars 16.3g; Fat 25.7g, of which saturates 2.8g; Cholesterol 10mg; Calcium 93mg; Fibre 0.4g; Sodium 205mg.

Apricot filo purses

These little filo parcels conceal a delectable apricot and mincemeat filling. They provide the perfect excuse for using up any mincemeat and marzipan.

MAKES 8

350g/12oz filo pastry, thawed if frozen
50g/2oz/¼ cup butter, melted
8 apricots, halved and stoned (pitted)
60ml/4 tbsp mincemeat
12 ratafia biscuits (almond
   macaroons), crushed
30ml/2 tbsp grated marzipan
icing (confectioners') sugar, for dusting
whipped cream, flavoured with brandy,
   to serve (optional)

1 Preheat the oven to 200°C/400°F/ Gas 6. Cut the sheets of pastry into 32 squares, each about 18cm/7in. Brush four of the squares with a little melted butter and stack them, giving each layer a quarter turn to create a star shape. Repeat with the remaining filo squares to make eight stars.

2 Place an apricot half, hollow side up, in the centre of each pastry star. Mix the mincemeat, ratafias and marzipan together and spoon a little into the hollow in each apricot half.

3 Top with another apricot half, then bring the corners of each pastry star together and gently squeeze to make a gathered purse.

4 Place the purses on a baking sheet and brush each with a little melted butter. Bake for about 20 minutes, or until the pastry is golden and crisp.

5 Lightly dust the purses with icing sugar. Serve them immediately, with whipped cream, flavoured with a little brandy, if you like.

Nutritional information per portion: Energy 62kcal/263kJ; Protein 0.9g; Carbohydrate 11.3g, of which sugars 7.1g; Fat 1.8g, of which saturates 0.2g; Cholesterol 0mg; Calcium 17mg; Fibre 0.8g; Sodium 24mg.

Almond and date filo parcels

It is worth buying a pot of good honey, such as orange blossom or heather, for dipping these delicious pastries into – it makes all the difference.

MAKES ABOUT 30

15ml/1 tbsp sunflower oil

225g/8oz/2 cups blanched almonds

115g/4oz/²/₃ cup pitted dates

25g/1oz/2 tbsp butter, softened

5ml/1 tsp ground cinnamon

1.5ml/¼ tsp almond extract

40g/1¹/₂oz/¹/₃ cup icing (confectioners') sugar

30ml/2 tbsp orange flower water

10 sheets of filo pastry, thawed if frozen

50g/2oz/¼ cup butter, melted

120ml/4fl oz/¹/₂ cup clear honey

dates, to serve (optional)

1 Heat the oil in a pan, add the almonds and fry until golden, stirring. Drain on kitchen paper, cool, then grind in a clean coffee or spice mill. Pound the dates by hand or process in a blender or a food processor.

2 Combine the almonds, dates, softened butter, cinnamon, almond extract and icing sugar in a mixing bowl, blender or food processor. Add a little orange flower water to taste. Mix or process to a smooth paste. If it feels stiff, work in a little extra flower water, but only 5ml/1 tsp at a time, until smooth.

3 Preheat the oven to 180°C/350°F/Gas 4. Brush a sheet of filo pastry with melted butter. Cut into three equal strips. Cover remaining sheets with a damp dish towel.

4 Place a walnut-sized piece of the almond and date paste at the end of each strip. Fold one corner of the pastry over the filling to make a triangle and then continue folding to make a neat triangular package. Brush with butter. Repeat to make about 30 pastries.

5 Place the pastries on a buttered baking sheet and bake for 30 minutes until golden. Cook them in batches, if possible, as once cooked they must be dipped immediately in honey.

6 While the filo parcels are cooking, pour the clear honey and a little orange flower water into a pan and heat very gently. As soon as the pastries are cooked, lower them one by one into the honey mixture and turn them so that they are coated. Transfer to a plate and cool, then serve.

Nutritional information per portion: Energy 101kcal/420kJ; Protein 2g; Carbohydrate 8.8g, of which sugars 6g; Fat 6.7g, of which saturates 1.7g; Cholesterol 5mg; Calcium 25mg; Fibre 0.7g; Sodium 17mg.

Elegant
fruit tarts

Of all pastries, shortcrust is probably the most popular. Many of the pastries in this chapter are made exclusively with butter, which gives them the best flavour; others contain a small amount of white vegetable fat to make the pastry even more crumbly. Shortcrust has a particular affinity with fruit, a fact that is celebrated in sweet treats such as Alsace Plum Tart, Rustic Apple Tart and utterly irresistible Fresh Orange Tart with its creamy citrus custard filling.

Orange sweetheart tart

Stunning to look at and delectable to eat, this tart has a crisp shortcrust pastry case, spread with apricot jam and filled with frangipane, then topped with tangy orange slices.

SERVES 8

200g/7oz/scant 1 cup sugar
250ml/8fl oz/1 cup fresh orange juice
2 large navel oranges
75g/3oz/³⁄4 cup blanched almonds
50g/2oz/¹⁄4 cup butter
1 egg
15ml/1 tbsp plain (all-purpose) flour
45ml/3 tbsp apricot jam

FOR THE PASTRY

175g/6oz/1¹⁄2 cups plain
    (all-purpose) flour
2.5ml/¹⁄2 tsp salt
75g/3oz/6 tbsp butter, diced
45ml/3 tbsp chilled water

1 To make the pastry, sift the flour and salt into a mixing bowl. Rub in the butter until it resembles breadcrumbs. Sprinkle over the water and mix to a dough. Knead until smooth. Wrap in clear film (plastic wrap) and chill for 30 minutes.

2 Roll out the pastry to a thickness of 5mm/¹⁄4in on a floured surface. Use to line a 20cm/8in heart-shaped flan tin (pan). Trim the edges. Chill until needed.

3 Put 150g/5oz/³⁄4 cup of the sugar into a pan with the orange juice. Bring to the boil and boil steadily for about 10 minutes, or until the liquid is thick and syrupy.

4 Cut the oranges into 5mm/¹⁄4in slices, leaving the peel on. Add to the syrup. Simmer gently for 10 minutes, or until glazed. Transfer to a wire rack to dry. Reserve the syrup. When cool, cut in half. Preheat the oven to 200°C/400°F/Gas 6, with a baking sheet placed in it.

5 Grind the almonds finely in a food processor, blender or nut grinder. With an electric mixer, cream the butter and remaining sugar until light and fluffy. Beat in the egg and 30ml/2 tbsp of the orange syrup. Add the ground almonds and mix well, then add the flour.

6 Melt the jam over a low heat, then brush it evenly over the inside of the pastry case. Pour in the almond mixture. Bake for 20 minutes, or until set. Leave to cool in the tin. Starting at the top of the heart shape and working down to the point, arrange overlapping orange slices on top of the tart. Boil the remaining syrup until thick. Brush on top to glaze.

Nutritional information per portion: Energy 405kcal/1699kJ; Protein 6.4g; Carbohydrate 53.7g, of which sugars 36.8g; Fat 19.8g, of which saturates 9g; Cholesterol 81mg; Calcium 98mg; Fibre 2g; Sodium 123mg.

Rustic apple tart

This easy apple tart looks as though it has come straight from the kitchen of a French farmhouse. Cooking the apples before putting them on the pastry prevents a soggy crust.

SERVES 6

900g/2lb cooking apples, peeled, quartered and cored
15ml/1 tbsp lemon juice
50g/2oz/¼ cup caster (superfine) sugar
40g/1½oz/3 tbsp butter
crème fraîche or lightly whipped cream, to serve

FOR THE PASTRY

225g/8oz/2 cups plain (all-purpose) flour
pinch of salt
15ml/1 tbsp caster (superfine) sugar
150g/5oz/⅔ cup butter, diced
1 egg yolk
30ml/2 tbsp chilled water

1 To make the pastry, sift the flour, salt and sugar into a bowl. Rub in the butter until it resembles fine breadcrumbs. Combine the egg and water, sprinkle over the dry ingredients and mix to a dough. Knead for a few seconds until smooth. Wrap in clear film (plastic wrap) and chill for 30 minutes.

2 Slice the apple quarters and place in a bowl. Sprinkle with the lemon juice and sugar, and toss to combine. Melt the butter in a frying pan over a medium heat and add the apples. Cook, stirring freqently, for about 12 minutes until just turning golden. Set aside. Preheat the oven to 190°C/375°F/Gas 5.

3 On a lightly floured surface, roll out the pastry to a 30cm/12in round and trim the edge if uneven. Carefully transfer to a baking sheet. Heap the apple slices on the pastry, leaving a 5cm/2in border all round the edge of the pastry.

4 Gather the pastry border around the apple slices, enclosing those closest to the rim and leaving the centre open. Bake the tart for 35–40 minutes until the pastry is crisp and golden brown. Serve warm, with crème fraîche or whipped cream.

Nutritional information per portion: Energy 372kcal/1560kJ; Protein 5.1g; Carbohydrate 49.1g, of which sugars 23.7g; Fat 18.7g, of which saturates 11.2g; Cholesterol 76mg; Calcium 86mg; Fibre 3.9g; Sodium 142mg.

Alsace plum tart

Fruit and custard tarts are typical of the Alsace region of France. Some have a yeast dough base instead of pastry. Use other seasonal fruits or a mixture if you like.

SERVES 6–8

450g/1lb ripe plums, halved and
    stoned (pitted)
30ml/2 tbsp Kirsch or plum brandy
30ml/2 tbsp seedless raspberry jam
2 eggs
50g/2oz/¼ cup caster (superfine) sugar
175ml/6fl oz/¾ cup double (heavy) cream
grated rind of ½ lemon
1.5ml/¼ tsp vanilla extract

FOR THE PASTRY

200g/7oz/1¾ cups plain
    (all-purpose) flour
pinch of salt
25g/1oz/¼ cup icing
    (confectioners') sugar
100g/3½ oz/scant ½ cup butter, diced
2 egg yolks
15ml/1 tbsp chilled water

1 To make the pastry, sift the flour, salt and sugar into a bowl. Rub in the butter until it resembles breadcrumbs. Mix the egg yolks and water together, sprinkle over the dry ingredients and mix to a soft dough.

2 Lightly knead for a few seconds until smooth. Wrap in clear film (plastic wrap) and chill for 30 minutes. Preheat the oven to 200°C/400°F/Gas 6. Mix the plums with the Kirsch or plum brandy in a bowl and set aside for 30 minutes.

3 Roll out the pastry thinly and use to line a 23cm/9in flan tin (pan). Cover and chill for 30 minutes. Prick the base all over with a fork. Line with foil and baking beans. Bake for 15 minutes until slightly dry and set. Remove the foil and beans. Brush the base with a thin layer of jam, bake for a further 5 minutes, then cool on a wire rack. Lower the oven to 180°C/350°F/Gas 4.

4 Beat the eggs and sugar until combined, then beat in the cream, lemon rind, vanilla extract and any plum juice. Arrange the plums, cut side down, in the pastry case. Pour over the custard mixture. Bake for 30 minutes and serve warm.

Nutritional information per portion: Energy 396kcal/1652kJ; Protein 5.5g; Carbohydrate 37.2g, of which sugars 18.2g; Fat 25.2g, of which saturates 14.7g; Cholesterol 155mg; Calcium 74mg; Fibre 1.7g; Sodium 104mg.

Belgian plum tart

This stunning open tart is made with a yeast dough and topped with fragrant cinnamon-scented plums. It is also delicious made with apricots, cherries, apples or pears.

SERVES 6–8

675g/1½lb fresh ripe plums, quartered
60ml/4 tbsp soft light brown sugar
15ml/1 tbsp ground cinnamon
15ml/1 tbsp sweet dessert wine
5ml/1 tsp cornflour (cornstarch)

FOR THE PASTRY
250g/9oz/2¼ cups plain (all-purpose) flour, plus extra for dusting

50g/2oz/¼ cup sugar
15ml/1 tbsp easy-blend (rapid-rise) dried yeast
2.5ml/½ tsp salt
1 egg, beaten
100ml/3½fl oz/scant ½ cup milk
50–75g/2–3oz/4–6 tbsp unsalted butter, softened

1 To make the pastry, sift the flour into a bowl. Stir in the sugar, yeast and salt. Make a well in the centre and pour in the beaten egg and half the milk. Stir, gradually incorporating the dry ingredients until the mixture starts to hold together. Add the extra milk, if needed. Finally add the softened butter and mix with your fingertips to a soft dough.

2 On a floured surface, knead the dough lightly, form it into a ball and place in a large, lightly oiled bowl. Cover with clear film (plastic wrap) and leave to rise in a warm place for about 30 minutes or until doubled in bulk.

3 Meanwhile, prepare the filling. Put the plums in a bowl. Sprinkle with 45ml/3 tbsp of the brown sugar and two-thirds of the cinnamon. Add the wine, stir well and leave to stand while the dough is rising, stirring occasionally. Preheat the oven to 220°C/425°F/Gas 7 and place a baking sheet inside to heat. Grease a 23cm/9in loose-bottomed tart or flan tin (pan) and dust it lightly with flour.

4 Knock back (punch down) the dough. Roll it out and line the pan. Trim and crimp the edges and prick the base. Sprinkle with the remaining brown sugar and cinnamon. Leave to stand for 15 minutes.

5 Sift the cornflour over the plums, then layer them in the pastry case. Place the tin on the baking sheet in the oven. Bake for 30–45 minutes, until the pastry is golden brown. Leave to cool on a wire rack for about 15 minutes. Remove from the tin, slice and serve warm.

Nutritional information per portion: Energy 304kcal/1285kJ; Protein 5.9g; Carbohydrate 57.5g, of which sugars 23.6g; Fat 6.7g, of which saturates 3.7g; Cholesterol 38mg; Calcium 100mg; Fibre 2.7g; Sodium 56mg.

Pear and almond cream tart

This glorious tart makes a truly indulgent dessert. Vary it according to the season – it is equally successful made with nectarines, peaches, apricots or apples.

SERVES 6

3 firm pears
a little lemon juice
15ml/1 tbsp peach brandy
60ml/4 tbsp peach preserve, strained

FOR THE PASTRY

200g/7oz/1¾ cups plain (all-purpose) flour
pinch of salt
25g/1oz/¼ cup icing (confectioners') sugar
100g/3½oz/scant ½ cup butter, diced
2 egg yolks
15ml/1 tbsp chilled water

FOR THE ALMOND CREAM FILLING

100g/3½oz/generous ¾ cup
**   blanched almonds**
50g/2oz/¼ cup caster (superfine) sugar
65g/2½oz/5 tbsp butter
1 egg, plus 1 egg white
a few drops of almond extract

1 To make the pastry, sift the flour with the salt and sugar. Rub in the butter. Mix the egg yolks and water, sprinkle over the dry ingredients and mix to a dough. Knead until smooth. Wrap in clear film (plastic wrap). Chill for 30 minutes.

2 Roll out the pastry and use to line a 23cm/9in flan tin (pan), then chill for 30 minutes. Meanwhile, make the filling. Pulse the almonds and caster sugar in a food processor until finely ground but not pasty. Add the butter and process until creamy. Mix in the egg, egg white and almond extract.

3 Preheat the oven to 190°C/375°F/Gas 5 with a baking sheet in it. Peel and halve the pears, remove the cores and rub them lightly with lemon juice. Lay them cut side down and slice thinly crossways, keeping the slices together.

4 Pour the almond cream filling into the case. Slide a palette knife under one pear half and fan out the slices. Transfer to the tart, arranging the fruit like spokes of a wheel. Remove a few slices from each half first, to fill in any gaps in the centre. Bake on the hot baking sheet for 50–55 minutes until set. Cool. Heat the brandy and preserve in a pan and brush over the top to glaze.

Nutritional information per portion: Energy 544kcal/2271kJ; Protein 8.4g; Carbohydrate 51.5g, of which sugars 24.4g; Fat 34.7g, of which saturates 11.7g; Cholesterol 63mg; Calcium 106mg; Fibre 3.9g; Sodium 330mg.

Apricot frangipane tart with Kirsch

Take a light pastry case, fill it with moist almond sponge and top it with slices of fresh apricot and crushed macaroons, and the result is simply sensational.

SERVES 6

12 apricots, stoned (pitted), some halved, some thickly sliced
75g/3oz ratafia biscuits (almond macaroons), crushed
natural (plain) yogurt or single (light) cream, to serve

FOR THE PASTRY
225g/8oz/2 cups plain (all-purpose) flour
115g/4oz/$^{1}/_{2}$ cup butter, diced
10ml/2 tsp finely grated lime rind
60–90ml/4–6 tbsp chilled water

FOR THE FILLING
25g/1oz/2 tbsp butter, softened
30ml/2 tbsp soft light brown sugar
15ml/1 tbsp plain (all-purpose) flour
50g/2oz/$^{1}/_{2}$ cup ground almonds
1 egg, beaten
45ml/3 tbsp Kirsch

1 To make the pastry, sift the flour into a mixing bowl, then rub or cut in the butter until the mixture resembles fine breadcrumbs. Stir in the grated lime rind and add enough chilled water to make a soft dough. Wrap in clear film (plastic wrap) and chill for 30 minutes.

2 Meanwhile, make the filling. Cream the butter with the sugar in a large bowl, then stir in the flour, ground almonds, egg and Kirsch.

3 Preheat the oven to 200°C/400°F/Gas 6. Roll out the pastry on a floured surface to a 40 x 16cm/16 x 6$^{1}/_{2}$in rectangle and use to line a 35 x 12cm/ 14 x 4$^{1}/_{2}$in flan tin (pan).

4 Spread the filling in the base of the flan case and arrange the apricots on top. Scatter over the crushed ratafia biscuits.

5 Bake for about 40 minutes, or until the pastry is golden. Serve warm or cold, with yogurt or cream.

Nutritional information per portion: Energy 483kcal/2024kJ; Protein 7.9g; Carbohydrate 53.2g, of which sugars 19g; Fat 27g, of which saturates 13.6g; Cholesterol 81mg; Calcium 113mg; Fibre 3.3g; Sodium 199mg.

Summer berry tart

A simple crisp pastry case is all that is needed to set off this classic filling of vanilla-flavoured custard topped with a luscious mixture of summer berry fruits.

SERVES 6–8

3 egg yolks
50g/2oz/1/4 cup caster (superfine) sugar
30ml/2 tbsp cornflour (cornstarch)
30ml/2 tbsp plain (all-purpose) flour
5ml/1 tsp vanilla extract
300ml/1/2 pint/11/4 cups milk
150ml/1/4 pint/2/3 cup double
   (heavy) cream
800g/13/4lb/41/2–5 cups
   summer berries

60ml/4 tbsp redcurrant jelly
30ml/2 tbsp raspberry liqueur

FOR THE PASTRY
185g/61/2oz/12/3 cups plain
   (all-purpose) flour
pinch of salt
115g/4oz/1/2 cup butter, diced
1 egg yolk
30ml/2 tbsp chilled water

1 To make the pastry, sift the flour and salt into a bowl. Rub in the butter until the mixture resembles breadcrumbs. Mix the egg yolk with the chilled water and sprinkle over the dry ingredients. Mix to a firm dough, then knead until smooth. Wrap in clear film (plastic wrap) and chill for 30 minutes.

2 Roll out the pastry and use to line a 25cm/10in fluted flan tin (pan). Wrap in clear film and chill. Put a baking sheet in the oven and preheat to 200°C/400°F/Gas 6. Prick the base, line with foil and baking beans and bake for 15 minutes. Remove the foil and beans. Bake for 10 minutes, then cool.

3 Beat the egg yolks, sugar, cornflour, flour and vanilla extract together. Bring the milk to the boil in a pan. Slowly pour on to the egg mixture, whisking all the time.

4 Pour the custard into the cleaned pan and cook over a low heat, stirring constantly, until thickened. Return to a clean bowl, cover the surface with a piece of clear film and set aside to cool. Whip the cream until thick, then fold into the custard. Spoon the custard into the pastry case and spread it evenly.

5 Arrange the fruit on top. Gently heat the redcurrant jelly and liqueur together until melted. Allow to cool, then brush over the fruit. Serve the tart within 3 hours.

Nutritional information per portion: Energy 394kcal/1644kJ; Protein 6.5g; Carbohydrate 36.4g, of which sugars 12.5g; Fat 25.7g, of which saturates 15g; Cholesterol 159mg; Calcium 125mg; Fibre 1.9g; Sodium 121mg.

Exotic fruit tranche

This simple fruit flan provides a colourful visual feast for diners, and is a wonderful way to make the most of a small selection of brightly coloured exotic fruit.

SERVES 8

150ml/¼ pint/⅓ cup double (heavy) cream, plus extra to serve
250g/9oz/generous 1 cup mascarpone
25g/1oz/¼ cup icing (confectioners') sugar, sifted
grated rind of 1 orange
450g/1lb/3 cups mixed seasonal fruits
90ml/6 tbsp apricot conserve, strained
15ml/1 tbsp white or coconut rum

FOR THE PASTRY
175g/6oz/1½ cups plain (all-purpose) flour
50g/2oz/¼ cup butter, diced
25g/1oz/2 tbsp white vegetable fat
50g/2oz/¼ cup caster (superfine) sugar
2 egg yolks
about 15ml/1 tbsp chilled water
115g/4oz/scant ½ cup apricot conserve

1 Make the pastry. Sift the flour into a bowl and rub in the fat. Stir in the caster sugar. Add the egg yolks and enough water to make a soft dough.

2 Roll out the pastry between two sheets of clear film (plastic wrap) and use to line a 35 x 12cm/14 x 4½in fluted tranche tin (pan). Allow the excess pastry to hang over the edge of the tin and chill for 30 minutes.

3 Preheat the oven to 200°C/400°F/ Gas 6. Prick the base of the pastry and line with parchment and baking beans.

4 Bake for 10–12 minutes. Lift out the paper and beans and return the pastry to the oven for 5 minutes. Trim off the excess pastry. Brush the inside of the case with the warmed apricot conserve to form a seal. Leave to cool on a wire rack.

5 Whip the cream to soft peaks. Stir it into the mascarpone with the icing sugar and orange rind. Spread evenly in the cooled pastry case and top with the prepared fruits. Warm the apricot conserve with the rum in a pan, and drizzle or brush over the fruit to glaze.

Nutritional information per portion: Energy 429kcal/1801kJ; Protein 6.4g; Carbohydrate 53.3g, of which sugars 36.9g; Fat 22.2g, of which saturates 12.7g; Cholesterol 99mg; Calcium 105mg; Fibre 2.1g; Sodium 136mg.

Prune tart with custard filling

Brandy-soaked prunes and a classic custard filling combine to simple but delicious effect in this recipe. This dessert is wonderful, served either warm or cold.

SERVES 6–8

225g/8oz/1 cup stoned (pitted) prunes
50ml/2fl oz/¼ cup brandy
300ml/½ pint/1¼ cups milk
a few drops of vanilla extract
4 egg yolks
45ml/3 tbsp caster (superfine) sugar
30ml/2 tbsp cornflour (cornstarch)
25g/1oz/¼ cup flaked (sliced) almonds
icing (confectioners') sugar, for dusting
thick cream, to serve

FOR THE PASTRY

175g/6oz/1½ cups plain
    (all-purpose) flour
pinch of salt
50g/2oz/¼ cup caster (superfine) sugar
90g/3½oz/scant ½ cup butter, diced
1 egg

1 Place the prunes in a small bowl with the brandy to soak. Preheat the oven to 200°C/400°F/Gas 6. To make the pastry, put the flour, salt, sugar and butter in a food processor. Set aside 5ml/1 tsp of the egg white and add the remaining egg to the processor. Process to a pliable dough. Shape into a ball and leave to rest for 10 minutes.

2 Roll out the pastry and use to line a lightly floured 28 x 18cm/11 x 7in loose-based tin (pan). Chill for 30 minutes. Line with foil and baking beans. Bake for 15 minutes, remove the foil and beans and bake for 10–15 minutes more. Brush the pastry base with the reserved egg white while it is still hot. Set aside to cool.

3 Bring the milk and vanilla to the boil in a pan. In a small bowl, whisk the egg yolks and sugar until thick, pale and fluffy, then whisk in the cornflour. Strain in the milk and whisk until there are no lumps.

4 Return the mixture to the cleaned pan. Bring it back to the boil, whisking to remove any lumps. Cook for about 2 minutes until thick and smooth. Set aside. Press baking parchment on to the surface so a skin does not form.

5 Add any prune liquid to the custard, then spread it over the pastry. Arrange the prunes and sprinkle the almonds on top. Dust with icing sugar. Bake for 10 minutes. Serve warm with cream.

Nutritional information per portion: Energy 362kcal/1518kJ; Protein 7.1g; Carbohydrate 42.1g, of which sugars 23.6g; Fat 18.1g, of which saturates 9.1g; Cholesterol 157mg; Calcium 117mg; Fibre 2.5g; Sodium 122mg.

Date and almond tart

Fresh dates make an unusual but delicious filling for a tart, especially when teamed with a sponge filling flavoured with ground almonds and orange flower water.

SERVES 6

90g/3¹/₂oz/scant ¹/₂ cup butter
90g/3¹/₂oz/scant ¹/₂ cup caster
   (superfine) sugar
1 egg, beaten
90g/3¹/₂oz/scant 1 cup ground almonds
30ml/2 tbsp plain (all-purpose) flour
30ml/2 tbsp orange flower water
12–13 fresh dates, halved and
   stoned (pitted)
60ml/4 tbsp apricot jam

FOR THE PASTRY
175g/6oz/1¹/₂ cups plain
   (all-purpose) flour
75g/3oz/6 tbsp butter, diced
1 egg
15ml/1 tbsp chilled water

1 Preheat the oven to 200°C/400°F/Gas 6 with a baking sheet in it. To make the pastry, sift the flour into a bowl, then rub in the butter. Add the egg and water, then work to a dough. Wrap in clear film (plastic wrap) and chill for 20 minutes.

2 Roll out the pastry and use to line a 20cm/8in flan tin (pan). Prick the base with a fork, then chill until needed. Cream the butter and sugar in a bowl with a wooden spoon until light, then beat in the egg. Stir in the ground almonds, flour and 15ml/1 tbsp of the orange flower water. Mix thoroughly.

3 Spread the almond filling evenly over the base of the pastry case. Arrange the dates, cut side down, on the mixture. Bake the tart on the hot baking sheet for 10–15 minutes, then lower the oven to 180°C/350°F/Gas 4. Bake for 15 minutes more, or until pale golden and set. Transfer to a wire rack to cool.

4 Gently heat the apricot jam in a pan, then press through a sieve (strainer) into a bowl. Stir in the remaining orange flower water. Brush over the tart and serve.

Nutritional information per portion: Energy 478kcal/2003kJ; Protein 6.2g; Carbohydrate 61.1g, of which sugars 33.7g; Fat 25g, of which saturates 14.9g; Cholesterol 122mg; Calcium 82mg; Fibre 1.7g; Sodium 199mg.

One-crust rhubarb pie

This method can be used for all sorts of fruit and is really foolproof. It doesn't matter how rough the pie looks when it goes into the oven; it comes out looking fantastic!

SERVES 6

1 egg yolk, beaten
25g/1oz/3 tbsp semolina
450g/1lb rhubarb
75g/3oz/6 tbsp caster (superfine) sugar
1–2 pieces stem (crystallized) ginger in
 syrup, drained and finely chopped
25g/1oz/¼ cup chopped hazelnuts
30ml/2 tbsp golden sugar

FOR THE PASTRY

225g/8oz/2 cups plain (all-purpose) flour
pinch of salt
115g/4oz/½ cup butter, diced
45–60ml/3–4 tbsp chilled water

1 To make the pastry, sift the flour and salt into a bowl. Rub in the butter. Sprinkle over 45ml/3 tbsp of the water and mix together to a soft dough, adding more water if needed. Wrap in clear film (plastic wrap) and chill for 30 minutes.

2 Preheat the oven to 200°C/400°F/Gas 6. Roll out the pastry to a 35cm/14in round. Lay it over the rolling pin and transfer it to a large baking sheet. Brush a little egg yolk over the pastry round. Sprinkle the semolina evenly over the centre of the pastry, leaving a wide margin all round.

3 Cut the rhubarb into 2.5cm/1in pieces and mix in a bowl with the sugar and ginger. Pile the rhubarb into the middle of the pastry round. Draw the pastry up roughly around the filling so that it encloses it, but does not cover it completely.

4 Glaze the pastry rim with any remaining egg yolk. Sprinkle with the hazelnuts and golden sugar. Bake for 30–35 minutes, or until the pastry is golden brown.

Nutritional information per portion: Energy 389kcal/1633kJ; Protein 5.6g; Carbohydrate 49.7g, of which sugars 19.6g; Fat 20.1g, of which saturates 5.6g; Cholesterol 42mg; Calcium 139mg; Fibre 2.5g; Sodium 239mg.

Fresh orange tart

Finely grated orange rind gives this rich shortcrust pastry its wonderful colour and flavour.
A creamy custard filling and fresh oranges turn it into a sophisticated dessert.

SERVES 9

2 eggs, plus 2 egg yolks
150g/5oz/²/₃ cup caster
   (superfine) sugar
150ml/¹/₄ pint/²/₃ cup single
   (light) cream
finely grated rind and juice of 1 orange
6–8 oranges
fresh mint sprigs, to decorate

FOR THE PASTRY
175g/6oz/1¹/₂ cups plain
   (all-purpose) flour
90g/3¹/₂oz/scant ¹/₂ cup butter, diced
15ml/1 tbsp caster (superfine) sugar
finely grated rind of 1 orange
1 egg yolk
about 10ml/2 tsp orange juice

1 To make the pastry, sift the flour and rub or cut in the butter. Stir in the sugar and orange rind. Beat the egg yolk with the orange juice, then add to the dry ingredients and mix to a firm dough.

2 Lightly and quickly knead the dough until smooth. Roll out and use to line a 20cm/8in square fluted tin (pan). Wrap and chill for 30 minutes.

3 Put a baking sheet in the oven and preheat to 200°C/400°F/Gas 6. Prick the pastry case all over with a fork and line with foil and baking beans. Place on the hot baking sheet and bake blind for 12 minutes. Remove the foil and beans and bake the pastry for a further 5 minutes.

4 Whisk the eggs, yolks and sugar in a bowl until foamy. Whisk in the cream, followed by the orange rind and juice. Pour into the pastry case and bake for 30–35 minutes until firm. Remove from the oven and leave to cool on a wire rack still in the tin.

5 Peel the oranges, removing all the white pith and separate the segments by cutting between the membranes. Arrange the segments in rows on top of the tart. Chill until ready to serve, then carefully remove the tart from the tin and decorate with sprigs of fresh mint.

Nutritional information per portion: Energy 500kcal/2093kJ; Protein 8.6g; Carbohydrate 59.4g, of which sugars 37.4g; Fat 27g, of which saturates 7.7g; Cholesterol 50mg; Calcium 129mg; Fibre 3.1g; Sodium 137mg.

Rich and indulgent desserts

Although sweet pies and pastries filled with

fruit are delicious, for pure indulgence, velvety

smooth coffee custard tart is unbeatable.

Also included in this mouthwatering selection

are decadent rich desserts, such as the

luxurious Dark Chocolate and Hazelnut Tart,

the creamy Baked Cheesecake with Kissel,

and familiar classics, such as Yorkshire Curd

Tart, American Pumpkin Pie and the French

delight, Lemon Tart.

American pumpkin pie

This spicy sweet pie is traditionally served at Thanksgiving, or at Hallowe'en to use the pulp from the hollowed-out pumpkin lanterns.

SERVES 8

900g/2lb piece of pumpkin
2 large eggs
75g/3oz/scant ¹/₂ cup soft light
   brown sugar
60ml/4 tbsp golden (light corn) syrup
250ml/8fl oz/1 cup double (heavy) cream
15ml/1 tbsp mixed spice
2.5ml/¹/₂ tsp salt
icing (confectioners') sugar, for dusting

FOR THE PASTRY

200g/7oz/1³/₄ cups plain
   (all-purpose) flour
2.5ml/¹/₂ tsp salt
90g/3¹/₂oz/scant ¹/₂ cup butter, diced
1 egg yolk
15ml/1 tbsp chilled water

1 To make the pastry, sift the flour and salt into a bowl. Rub in the butter, then mix in the egg yolk and enough chilled water to make a soft dough. Roll into a ball, wrap it in clear film (plastic wrap) and chill for 30 minutes.

2 Peel and seed the pumpkin. Cut the flesh into cubes. Place in a pan and cover with water. Bring to the boil and simmer for 15–20 minutes until tender. Mash well until smooth, then spoon into a sieve (strainer) and set over a bowl to drain. Preheat the oven to 200°C/400°F/Gas 6.

3 Roll out the pastry. Line a 23cm/ 9in loose-based flan tin (pan). Prick the base all over. Line with foil and baking beans. Chill for 15 minutes. Bake for 10 minutes, remove the foil and beans, then bake for a further 5 minutes.

4 Lower the oven temperature to 190°C/375°F/Gas 5. Tip the pumpkin into a bowl and beat in the eggs, sugar, syrup, cream, mixed spice and salt to make a smooth filling. Pour into the pastry case. Bake for 40 minutes until set. Dust generously with icing sugar. Serve at room temperature.

Nutritional information per portion: Energy 416kcal/1736kJ; Protein 5.3g; Carbohydrate 38.2g, of which sugars 18.6g; Fat 28g, of which saturates 16.9g; Cholesterol 114mg; Calcium 98mg; Fibre 1.9g; Sodium 360mg.

Cider pie

Few can resist this delectable pie, with its rich cider filling. Decorate with pretty pastry apples, dotted around the edge of the pie.

SERVES 6

600ml/1 pint/2¹⁄₂ cups (hard) cider
15g/¹⁄₂ oz/1 tbsp butter
250ml/8fl oz/1 cup maple syrup
60ml/4 tbsp water
2 eggs, at room temperature, separated
    and yolks beaten
5ml/1 tsp grated nutmeg
icing (confectioners') sugar, for dusting

FOR THE PASTRY

175g/6oz/1¹⁄₂ cups plain
    (all-purpose) flour
1.5ml/¹⁄₄ tsp salt
10ml/2 tsp sugar
115g/4oz/¹⁄₂ cup cold butter, diced
about 60ml/4 tbsp chilled water

1 To make the pastry, sift the flour, salt and sugar into a bowl. Rub in the butter. Sprinkle the chilled water over, and combine with a fork until it holds together. Flatten into a round, wrap in clear film (plastic wrap) and chill for 30 minutes.

2 Pour the cider into a pan and boil until only 175ml/6fl oz/³⁄₄ of a cup remains. Set aside. Roll out the pastry between two large sheets of baking parchment to 3mm/¹⁄₈in thick. Use to line a 23cm/9in pie dish. Trim the edge, leaving a 1cm/¹⁄₂in overhang.

3 Fold the overhang under to form a rim. Press the rim down with a fork and scallop the edge. Chill for at least 20 minutes. Preheat the oven to 180°C/350°F/Gas 4. Put the butter, maple syrup, water and cider in a pan and simmer gently for 5–6 minutes. Cool slightly, then whisk in the yolks.

4 Whisk the egg whites to stiff peaks. Gently fold in the cider mixture. Pour the filling into the case evenly and sprinkle with the grated nutmeg. Bake for 30–35 minutes, until set and golden. Dust with icing sugar and serve.

Nutritional information per portion: Energy 452kcal/1897kJ; Protein 5.1g; Carbohydrate 60.1g, of which sugars 37.8g; Fat 20g, of which saturates 11.9g; Cholesterol 110mg; Calcium 70mg; Fibre 0.9g; Sodium 275mg.

Butternut squash and maple pie

This American-style pie has a rich shortcrust pastry case and a creamy filling, sweetened with maple syrup and flavoured with fresh ginger and a dash of brandy.

SERVES 10

1 small butternut squash, halved
   and peeled with the seeds removed
60ml/4 tbsp water
2.5cm/1in piece of fresh grated
   root ginger
120ml/4fl oz/½ cup double
   (heavy) cream
90ml/6 tbsp maple syrup
45ml/3 tbsp light muscovado (brown) sugar
3 eggs, lightly beaten
30ml/2 tbsp brandy
1.5ml/¼ tsp grated nutmeg
beaten egg, to glaze
cream, to serve

FOR THE PASTRY

175g/6oz/1½ cups plain
   (all-purpose) flour
pinch of salt
115g/4oz/½ cup butter, diced
10ml/2 tsp caster (superfine) sugar
1 egg, lightly beaten

1 To make the pastry, sift the flour and salt into a bowl. Rub in the butter. Add the sugar and egg. Mix to a dough. Wrap in clear film (plastic wrap). Chill for 30 minutes.

2 Cut the butternut squash into cubes. Cover with water in a pan, then cover and cook gently for 15 minutes. Stir in the ginger and cook, uncovered, for 5 minutes until the liquid has evaporated. Cool, then purée in a food processor until smooth.

3 Roll out the pastry and use to line a 23cm/ 9in flan tin (pan). Use the leftover pastry trimmings to make maple leaf shapes. Brush the rim of the case with a little beaten egg.

4 Decorate the rim with the leaves. Cover with clear film and chill for 30 minutes. Put a baking sheet in the oven. Preheat to 200°C/400°F/Gas 6.

5 Prick the base. Line with foil and fill with baking beans. Bake on the baking sheet for 12 minutes. Remove the foil and beans; bake for 5 minutes more.

6 Brush the base with beaten egg and return to the oven for 3 minutes. Lower the temperature to 180°C/ 350°F/Gas 4. Mix 200g/7oz/scant 1 cup of the butternut purée with the cream, syrup, sugar, eggs, brandy and grated nutmeg. Pour into the pastry case. Bake for 30 minutes until lightly set. Serve slightly cooled, with cream.

Nutritional information per portion: Energy 266kcal/1109kJ; Protein 4g; Carbohydrate 26.2g, of which sugars 13.7g; Fat 16.1g, of which saturates 4.6g; Cholesterol 74mg; Calcium 56mg; Fibre 1.4g; Sodium 92mg.

Walnut pie

Sweetened with coffee-flavoured maple syrup, this pie has a rich and sticky texture. The walnuts can be replaced by pecan nuts for an authentic American pie.

SERVES 8

30ml/2 tbsp ground coffee
175ml/6fl oz/³⁄₄ cup maple syrup
25g/1oz/2 tbsp butter, softened
175g/6oz/³⁄₄ cup soft light brown sugar
3 eggs, beaten
5ml/1 tsp vanilla extract
115g/4oz/1 cup walnut halves
crème fraîche or vanilla ice cream,
    to serve

FOR THE PASTRY

150g/5oz/1¹⁄₄ cups plain
    (all-purpose) flour
pinch of salt
25g/1oz/¹⁄₄ cup icing
    (confectioners') sugar
75g/3oz/6 tbsp butter, diced
2 egg yolks

1 Preheat the oven to 200°C/400°F/ Gas 6. To make the pastry, sift the flour, salt and icing sugar into a bowl. Rub in the butter. Add the egg yolks and mix well to form a soft dough.

2 Knead the pastry until smooth. Wrap in clear film (plastic wrap) and chill for 30 minutes. Roll out the pastry and use to line a 20cm/8in fluted flan tin (pan). Line with baking parchment and baking beans and bake for 10 minutes. Remove the paper and beans and bake for 5 minutes until brown. Set aside.

3 Lower the oven temperature to 180°C/350°F/Gas 4. Heat the coffee and maple syrup in a pan until almost boiling. Set aside to cool slightly. Mix the butter and sugar in a bowl, then beat in the eggs. Strain the reserved maple syrup mixture into the bowl, add the vanilla extract and stir.

4 Arrange the walnuts in the pastry case. Carefully pour in the filling. Bake for 30–35 minutes, until lightly browned and firm. Cool for a few minutes before serving warm with crème fraîche or vanilla ice cream.

Nutritional information per portion: Energy 462kcal/1938kJ; Protein 7.2g; Carbohydrate 58.5g, of which sugars 44.1g; Fat 23.8g, of which saturates 8.3g; Cholesterol 148mg; Calcium 75mg; Fibre 1.1g; Sodium 166mg.

Chocolate, pear and pecan pie

In this recipe the timeless classic pecan pie gets a delicious and tempting new twist with the delicious addition of rich dark chocolate and succulent, juicy pears.

SERVES 8–10

3 small pears, peeled
165g/5½ oz/scant ¾ cup caster (superfine) sugar
150ml/¼ pint/⅔ cup water
pared rind of 1 lemon
50g/2oz plain (semisweet) chocolate, broken into pieces
50g/2oz/¼ cup butter, diced
225g/8oz/scant ¾ cup golden (light corn) syrup
3 eggs, beaten
5ml/1 tsp vanilla extract
150g/5oz/1¼ cups pecan nuts, chopped

FOR THE PASTRY

175g/6oz/½ cup plain (all-purpose) flour
115g/4oz/½ cup butter, diced
25g/1oz/2 tbsp caster (superfine) sugar
1 egg yolk
10–15ml/2–3 tsp chilled water

1 To make the pastry, sift the flour into a mixing bowl and rub in the butter. Stir in the sugar. Mix the egg yolk with 10ml/2 tsp of the water, add to the bowl and mix to a dough. Knead until smooth. Wrap in clear film (plastic wrap). Chill for 30 minutes. Preheat the oven to 200°C/400°F/Gas 6. Roll out the pastry and use to line a deep 23cm/9in fluted flan tin (pan). Chill for 20 minutes, then line with foil and baking beans. Bake for 10 minutes. Remove the foil and beans and bake for 5 minutes more. Set aside to cool.

2 Halve and core the pears. Place 50g/2oz/¼ cup of the sugar in a pan with the water and lemon rind. Bring to the boil. Add the pears. Cover, lower the heat and simmer for 10 minutes. Set the pears aside to cool and discard the liquid.

3 Melt the chocolate in a bowl over a pan of simmering water. Beat in the butter and set aside. In a separate pan, heat the remaining sugar and syrup until most of the sugar has dissolved. Bring to the boil and simmer for 2 minutes. Whisk the eggs into the chocolate, then whisk in the syrup mixture. Stir in the vanilla and pecan nuts. Lay the pears flat side down and make cuts, lengthways, down each pear (do not cut right through). Arrange in the case. Pour the pecan mixture over. Bake for 25–30 minutes until set. Allow to cool before serving.

Nutritional information per portion: Energy 499kcal/2090kJ; Protein 5.8g; Carbohydrate 59.9g, of which sugars 46.3g; Fat 28g, of which saturates 11g; Cholesterol 113mg; Calcium 68mg; Fibre 2.4g; Sodium 186mg.

Almond and pine nut tart

This traditional Italian tart, similar to the homely Bakewell tart from Derbyshire in the north of England, is an appealing dessert with its melt-in-the mouth pastry and flavourful filling.

SERVES 8

115g/4oz/¹/₂ cup butter, softened
115g/4oz/¹/₂ cup caster
    (superfine) sugar
1 egg, plus 2 egg yolks
150g/5oz/1¹/₄ cups ground almonds
115g/4oz/1¹/₃ cups pine nuts
60ml/4 tbsp seedless raspberry jam
icing (confectioners') sugar, for dusting
whipped cream, to serve

FOR THE PASTRY
175g/6oz/1¹/₂ cups plain
    (all-purpose) flour
65g/2¹/₂ oz/¹/₃ cup caster
    (superfine) sugar
1.5ml/¹/₄ tsp baking powder
pinch of salt
115g/4oz/¹/₂ cup chilled butter, diced

1 To make the pastry, sift the flour, sugar, baking powder and salt on to a clean, dry cold surface or marble pastry board. Make a well in the centre and put in the diced butter and egg yolk. Gradually work the flour mixture into the butter and egg yolk, using just your fingertips, until you have a soft, pliable dough.

2 This dough is too sticky to roll, so press it with your fingers into a 23cm/9in loose-based fluted flan tin (pan). Chill for 30 minutes.

3 Cream the butter and sugar with an electric mixer, then beat in the egg and egg yolks a little at a time with a wooden spoon, alternating them with the almonds. Beat in the nuts. Preheat the oven to 160°C/325°F/Gas 3.

4 Spread the jam over the base. Spoon in the filling. Bake for 30–35 minutes, until a skewer inserted in the centre of the tart comes out clean.

5 Transfer the tart to a wire rack and leave to cool. Carefully remove the side of the tin, leaving the tart on the tin base. Dust with icing sugar and serve with whipped cream.

Nutritional information per portion: Energy 643kcal/2675kJ; Protein 10.2g; Carbohydrate 47.7g, of which sugars 30.5g; Fat 47g, of which saturates 17.3g; Cholesterol 161mg; Calcium 108mg; Fibre 2.3g; Sodium 193mg.

Dark chocolate and hazelnut tart

This crisp, hazelnut-flavoured pastry tastes wonderful with its luxurious chocolate filling, creating an indulgently rich dessert which will tempt just about everyone.

SERVES 10

300ml/¹/₂ pint/1¹/₄ cups double
   (heavy) cream
150ml/¹/₄ pint/²/₃ cup creamy milk
150g/5oz dark (bittersweet) chocolate
4 eggs
50g/2oz/¹/₄ cup caster (superfine) sugar
5ml/1 tsp vanilla extract
15ml/1 tbsp plain (all-purpose) flour
115g/4oz/1 cup toasted hazelnuts
10ml/2 tsp icing (confectioners') sugar

FOR THE PASTRY

150g/5oz/1¹/₄ cups plain
   (all-purpose) flour
pinch of salt
45ml/3 tbsp caster (superfine) sugar
50g/2oz/¹/₂ cup toasted
   ground hazelnuts
90g/3¹/₂oz/scant ¹/₂ cup butter, diced
1 egg, lightly beaten

1 To make the pastry, sift the flour, salt and sugar in a bowl. Mix in the hazelnuts. Rub in the butter. Make a well in the centre, add the beaten egg and mix to a dough. Knead until smooth. Wrap in clear film (plastic wrap). Chill for 30 minutes.

2 Roll out the pastry and use to line a 23cm/9in loose-based heart-shaped flan tin (pan). Trim the edges. Cover and chill for a further 30 minutes.

3 Re-roll the pastry trimmings into a long strip, about 30cm/12in long. Cut this into six strips, each 5mm/¹/₄ in wide. Make two plaits (braids) with three strips in each. Curve into a heart shape and press ends gently to join together. Carefully place on a baking sheet lined with baking parchment and chill.

4 Put a heavy baking sheet in the oven and preheat to 200°C/400°F/Gas 6. Prick the pastry case base. Line with foil and baking beans. Bake blind for 10 minutes. Remove the foil and beans and bake for a further 5 minutes. Bake the plait on the shelf below for 10 minutes.

5 Bring the cream and milk to the boil in a pan. Add the chocolate and stir until melted. Whisk the eggs, caster sugar, vanilla and flour together. Pour the hot chocolate cream over the egg mixture, whisking all the time. Stir in the hazelnuts. Pour the mixture into the pastry case and bake for 25 minutes. Allow to cool. Transfer from the tin to a serving plate. Place the plait on top, then dust with icing sugar.

Nutritional information per portion: Energy 544kcal/2261kJ; Protein 8.8g; Carbohydrate 35.6g, of which sugars 22.5g; Fat 41.8g, of which saturates 19.2g; Cholesterol 158mg; Calcium 105mg; Fibre 2g; Sodium 106mg.

Honey and pine nut tart

Wonderful tarts of all descriptions are to be found throughout France, and this recipe recalls the flavours of the south, with its sunny Mediterranean influences.

SERVES 6

115g/4oz/1/2 cup butter, diced
115g/4oz/1/2 cup caster (superfine) sugar
3 eggs, beaten
175g/6oz/2/3 cup sunflower honey
grated rind and juice of 1 lemon
225g/8oz/2 2/3 cups pine nuts
pinch of salt
icing (confectioners') sugar, for dusting
crème fraîche or vanilla ice cream,
    to serve (optional)

FOR THE PASTRY

225g/8oz/2 cups plain (all-purpose) flour
115g/4oz/1/2 cup butter, diced
30ml/2 tbsp icing (confectioners') sugar
1 egg
15ml/1 tbsp chilled water

1 Preheat the oven to 180°C/350°F/Gas 4. To make the pastry, sift the flour into a large mixing bowl. Rub in the butter. Stir in the icing sugar. Add the egg and water and mix to form a soft dough. Knead lightly until smooth.

2 Roll out the pastry and use to line a 23cm/9in flan tin (pan). Prick the base with a fork, then chill for 10 minutes. Line with baking parchment and fill with baking beans. Bake for 10 minutes. Remove the paper and beans. Set aside.

3 Cream the butter and caster sugar until the mixture is light and fluffy. Beat in the eggs one at a time. In a small pan, gently melt the honey, then add it to the butter mixture with the lemon rind and juice. Mix well. Stir in the pine nuts and salt, blending well, then pour the filling evenly into the pastry case.

4 Bake for 45 minutes until the filling is lightly browned and set. Leave to cool slightly in the tin, then remove and dust with icing sugar. Serve warm, or at room temperature, with crème fraîche or vanilla ice cream, if you like.

Nutritional information per portion: Energy 899kcal/3750kJ; Protein 13.4g; Carbohydrate 78.4g, of which sugars 49.8g; Fat 61.4g, of which saturates 22.8g; Cholesterol 209mg; Calcium 97mg; Fibre 1.9g; Sodium 285mg.

Lemon tart

This classic French tart is one of the most delicious desserts there is. A rich lemon curd is contained in a crisp pastry case. Crème fraîche is an optional – but nice – extra.

SERVES 6

6 eggs, beaten
350g/12oz/1½ cups caster
  (superfine) sugar
115g/4oz/½ cup butter
grated rind and juice of 4 lemons
icing (confectioners') sugar, for dusting

FOR THE PASTRY
225g/8oz/2 cups plain
  (all-purpose) flour
115g/4oz/½ cup butter, diced
30ml/2 tbsp icing
  (confectioners') sugar
1 egg
5ml/1 tsp vanilla extract
15ml/1 tbsp chilled water

1 Preheat the oven to 200°C/400°F/Gas 6. To make the pastry, sift the flour into a mixing bowl and rub in the butter. Stir in the icing sugar. Add the egg, vanilla extract and most of the chilled water, then work to a soft dough. Add a few more drops of water if necessary. Knead quickly and lightly until smooth.

2 Roll out the pastry on a floured surface and use to line a 23cm/9in flan tin (pan). Prick the base all over with a fork. Line with baking parchment and fill with baking beans. Bake the pastry case for 10 minutes. Remove the paper and beans and set the pastry case aside while you make the filling.

3 Put the eggs, sugar and butter into a pan, and stir over a low heat until all the sugar has dissolved. Add the lemon rind and juice, and continue cooking, stirring constantly, until it has thickened slightly. Pour the mixture into the pastry case.

4 Bake for 20 minutes, until the filling is just set. Transfer the tart to a wire rack to cool. Dust the surface generously with icing sugar just before serving.

Nutritional information per portion: Energy 268kcal/1121kJ; Protein 5.6g; Carbohydrate 27g, of which sugars 10.9g; Fat 16.1g, of which saturates 5.8g; Cholesterol 148mg; Calcium 57mg; Fibre 0.7g; Sodium 173mg.

Yorkshire curd tart

The distinguishing characteristic of Yorkshire curd tarts is allspice, or 'clove pepper' as it was known locally. This tart tastes superb and is not too sweet.

SERVES 8

90g/3½oz/scant ½ cup soft light
   brown sugar
large pinch of ground allspice
3 eggs, beaten
grated rind and juice of 1 lemon
40g/1½oz/3 tbsp butter, melted
450g/1lb/2 cups curd (farmer's) cheese
75g/3oz/scant ½ cup raisins
cream, to serve (optional)

FOR THE PASTRY
225g/8oz/2 cups plain (all-purpose) flour
115g/4oz/½ cup butter, diced
1 egg yolk
15–30ml/1–2 tbsp chilled water

1 To make the pastry, place the flour in a mixing bowl. Rub in the butter. Stir in the egg yolk and add just enough water to bind the mixture together to form a dough.

2 Put the dough on a floured surface, knead lightly and briefly, then form into a ball. Roll out the pastry thinly and use to line a 20cm/8in fluted loose-based flan tin (pan). Cover with clear film (plastic wrap) and chill for 15 minutes.

3 Preheat the oven to 190°C/375°F/ Gas 5. Mix the sugar with the ground allspice in a bowl, then stir in the eggs, lemon rind and juice, butter, curd cheese and raisins. Mix well.

4 Pour the filling into the pastry case, then bake for 40 minutes, or until the pastry is cooked and the filling is lightly set and golden brown. Cut the tart into wedges while it is still slightly warm, and serve with cream, if you like.

Nutritional information per portion: Energy 480kcal/2005kJ; Protein 16.2g; Carbohydrate 48.2g, of which sugars 23.7g; Fat 27g, of which saturates 15.8g; Cholesterol 173mg; Calcium 153mg; Fibre 1.2g; Sodium 451mg.

Coffee custard tart

For sheer decadence, try this crisp walnut pastry case, flavoured with vanilla and filled with a smooth creamy coffee custard. It is baked until lightly set and topped with cream.

SERVES 6–8

1 vanilla pod (bean)
30ml/2 tbsp ground coffee
300ml/¹/₂ pint/1¹/₄ cups single
   (light) cream
150ml/¹/₄ pint/²/₃ cup milk
2 eggs, plus 2 egg yolks
50g/2oz/¹/₄ cup caster (superfine) sugar
icing (confectioners') sugar, for dusting
whipped cream, to serve

FOR THE PASTRY

175g/6oz/1¹/₂ cups plain
   (all-purpose) flour
30ml/2 tbsp icing (confectioners') sugar
115g/4oz/¹/₂ cup butter, diced
75g/3oz/³/₄ cup walnuts, chopped
1 egg yolk
5ml/1 tsp vanilla extract
10ml/2 tsp chilled water

1 To make the pastry, sift the flour and sugar together. Rub in the butter. Stir in the walnuts. Mix together the egg yolk, vanilla and water in a bowl. Add to the dry ingredients and mix to a smooth dough. Wrap in clear film (plastic wrap). Chill for 20 minutes. Preheat the oven to 200°C/400°F/ Gas 6 with a heavy baking sheet in it.

2 Roll out the pastry and use to line a 20cm/8in flan tin (pan). Trim the edges and then chill for 20 minutes. Prick the base with a fork, fill with foil and baking beans and bake for 10 minutes on the baking sheet.

3 Remove the foil and beans. Bake for 10 minutes more. Reduce the oven temperature to 150°C/300°F/Gas 2.

4 Meanwhile, split the vanilla pod and scrape out the seeds. Put both in a pan with the coffee, cream and milk. Heat until almost boiling, remove from the heat, cover and infuse for 10 minutes. Whisk the eggs, egg yolks and caster sugar together in a bowl. Bring the cream mixture to the boil and pour on the egg mixture, stirring. Strain into the pastry case. Bake for 40–45 minutes. Cool. Dust with icing sugar and top with whipped cream.

Nutritional information per portion: Energy 408kcal/1698kJ; Protein 8.1g; Carbohydrate 29.6g, of which sugars 12.8g; Fat 29.5g, of which saturates 13.8g; Cholesterol 176mg; Calcium 119mg; Fibre 1g; Sodium 129mg.

Baked cheesecake with kissel

As with all classic cheesecakes, this simple German version is baked in a rich shortcrust pastry case, flavoured here with lemon. Kissel is a traditional red berry compôte.

SERVES 8–10

675g/1¹/₂lb/3 cups low-fat soft cheese
4 eggs, separated
150g/5oz/²/₃ cup caster (superfine) sugar
45ml/3 tbsp cornflour (cornstarch)
150ml/¹/₄ pint/²/₃ cup sour cream
finely grated rind and juice of ¹/₂ lemon
5ml/1 tsp vanilla extract
fresh mint sprigs, to decorate

FOR THE PASTRY

225g/8oz/2 cups plain (all-purpose) flour
115g/4oz/¹/₂ cup butter, diced
15ml/1 tbsp caster (superfine) sugar
finely grated rind of ¹/₂ lemon
1 egg, beaten

FOR THE KISSEL

450g/1lb/4–4¹/₂ cups prepared red berry fruit
50g/2oz/¹/₄ cup caster (superfine) sugar
120ml/4fl oz/¹/₂ cup water
15ml/1 tbsp arrowroot

1 To make the pastry, sift the flour into a mixing bowl. Rub in the butter. Stir in the sugar and lemon rind. Add the beaten egg. Mix to a dough, wrap in clear film (plastic wrap) and chill for 30 minutes. Roll out the pastry and use to line a 25cm/10in loose-based fluted flan tin (pan). Chill for 1 hour.

2 Drain the soft cheese in a sieve (strainer) over a bowl for 1 hour. Preheat the oven to 200°C/400°F/Gas 6. Prick the pastry case base, fill with crumpled foil and bake for 5 minutes. Remove the foil. Bake for 5 minutes, then remove.

3 Lower the oven to 180°C/350°F/Gas 4. Mix the soft cheese in a bowl with the egg yolks and caster sugar. Blend the cornflour in a cup with a little sour cream. Add to the cheese mixture with the remaining sour cream, lemon rind and juice and vanilla extract. Mix thoroughly. Whisk the egg whites until stiff. Fold into the cheese mixture, one-third at a time. Pour the filling into the case. Bake for 1–1¹/₄ hours. Let the cheesecake cool down in the oven, then chill for 2 hours.

4 To make the kissel, gently cook the fruit, caster sugar and water in a pan, until the sugar dissolves and the juices run. Remove the fruit with a slotted spoon and set aside, retaining the juices. Mix the arrowroot with a little cold water. Stir into the retained juices. Bring to the boil, stirring. Return the fruit to the pan, mix, then cool. Drizzle over the chilled cheesecake. Decorate with mint and berries.

Nutritional information per portion: Energy 431kcal/1807kJ; Protein 16.6g; Carbohydrate 49.2g, of which sugars 27.9g; Fat 21.1g, of which saturates 12.2g; Cholesterol 145mg; Calcium 163mg; Fibre 1.8g; Sodium 412mg.

Classic
sweet pies

There are some sweet pies that are so popular that recipes for them can be found in many countries. Classics such as Deep-dish Apple Pie and Blueberry Pie come into this category, along with Linzertorte, Shoofly Pie and Treacle Tart. Over the centuries, cooks creating these pies have lovingly decorated them. Some are topped with pastry shapes that hint at what lies beneath, while others have lattice or crumble crusts or conceal their fillings under swirls of meringue.

Deep-dish apple pie

This all-time classic favourite is made with rich shortcrust pastry. Inside, sugar, spices and flour create a deliciously thick and syrupy sauce with the apple juices.

SERVES 6

115g/4oz/¹/₂ cup caster (superfine) sugar
45ml/3 tbsp plain (all-purpose) flour
2.5ml/¹/₂ tsp ground cinnamon
finely grated rind of 1 orange
900g/2lb tart cooking apples
1 egg white, lightly beaten
30ml/2 tbsp golden sugar
whipped cream, to serve

FOR THE PASTRY

350g/12oz/3 cups plain (all-purpose) flour
pinch of salt
175g/6oz/³/₄ cup butter, diced
about 75ml/5 tbsp chilled water

1 To make the pastry, sift the flour and salt into a bowl and rub in the butter. Sprinkle over the water and mix to a firm, soft dough. Knead lightly until smooth. Wrap in clear film (plastic wrap) and chill for 30 minutes.

2 Combine the caster sugar, flour, cinnamon and orange rind in a bowl. Peel, core and thinly slice the apples. Add to the sugar mixture, then toss gently.

3 Put a baking sheet in the oven and preheat to 200°C/400°F/Gas 6. Roll out just over half the pastry and use to line a 23cm/9in pie dish that is 4cm/1¹/₂in deep. Allow to overhang the edges slightly. Spoon in the filling, doming it in the centre.

4 Roll out the remaining pastry to form the lid. Lightly brush the edges with a little water, then place the lid over the apple filling. Trim the pastry with a sharp knife. Gently press the edges together to seal, then knock up the edge. Re-roll the pastry trimmings and cut out apple and leaf shapes. Brush the top of the pie with egg white. Arrange the pastry apples and leaves on top.

5 Brush again with egg white, then sprinkle with golden sugar. Make two small slits in the top of the pie to allow steam to escape.

6 Bake for 30 minutes, then lower the oven temperature to 180°C/350°F/Gas 4 and bake for a further 15 minutes until the pastry is golden and the apples are soft – check by inserting a small sharp knife or skewer through one of the slits in the top of the pie. Serve hot, with some whipped cream.

Nutritional information per portion: Energy 591kcal/2488kJ; Protein 7.4g; Carbohydrate 89.9g, of which sugars 39.8g; Fat 25g, of which saturates 15.3g; Cholesterol 62mg; Calcium 117mg; Fibre 4.4g; Sodium 193mg.

Peach leaf pie

Juicy, lightly spiced peach slices are covered with a decorative crust made entirely from individual pastry leaves to make this spectacular pie.

SERVES 8

1.2kg/2½ lb ripe peaches
juice of 1 lemon
115g/4oz/½ cup sugar
45ml/3 tbsp cornflour (cornstarch)
1.5ml/¼ tsp grated nutmeg
2.5ml/½ tsp ground cinnamon
25g/1oz/2 tbsp butter, diced
1 egg, beaten with 45ml/1 tbsp water,
    to glaze

FOR THE PASTRY

225g/8oz/2 cups plain (all-purpose) flour
4ml/¾ tsp salt
115g/4oz/½ cup cold butter, diced
40g/1½ oz/3 tbsp white vegetable
    fat, diced
75–90ml/5–6 tbsp chilled water

1 To make the pastry, sift the flour and salt into a bowl. Rub in the butter and fat. Sprinkle over just enough of the water to bind the dry ingredients, and use a fork to bring it together to form a soft dough. Gather into two balls, one slightly larger than the other. Wrap each in clear film (plastic wrap). Chill for 30 minutes. Put a baking sheet in the oven and preheat to 220°C/425°F/Gas 7.

2 Drop a few peaches at a time into a pan of boiling water, leave for 20 seconds, then transfer to a bowl of cold water. When cool, peel and slice, then mix with the lemon juice, sugar, cornflour and spices. Set aside.

3 Roll out the larger piece of pastry to 3mm/⅛in thick. Line a 23cm/9in pie plate and chill. Roll out the other piece and cut out enough 7.5cm/3in long leaf shapes to cover the pie. Mark on veins with a knife. Brush the base with egg glaze. Add the peaches, piling to a dome in the centre. Dot with butter.

4 Make a ring of leaves around the outside, attaching them with a dab of egg glaze. Place another ring of leaves above. Continue, until the pie is covered. Brush with egg glaze. Bake on the hot baking sheet for 10 minutes. Lower the oven to 180°C/350°F/Gas 4 and continue to bake for 35–40 minutes until golden.

Nutritional information per portion: Energy 390kcal/1638kJ; Protein 4.4g; Carbohydrate 53.8g, of which sugars 27.2g; Fat 19g, of which saturates 10.7g; Cholesterol 52mg; Calcium 62mg; Fibre 3.2g; Sodium 152mg.

Shoofly pie

An unsweetened pastry case made with a simple combination of butter and cream cheese complements the wonderful dark sweet filling of this pie from the American Deep South.

SERVES 8

115g/4oz/1 cup plain (all-purpose) flour
115g/4oz/1/2 cup firmly packed soft dark brown sugar
1.5ml/1/4 tsp each salt, ground ginger, cinnamon, mace and nutmeg
75g/3oz/6 tbsp cold butter, diced
2 eggs
185g/6 1/2 oz/1/2 cup black treacle (molasses)
120ml/4fl oz/1/2 cup boiling water
1.5ml/1/2 tsp bicarbonate of soda (baking soda)

FOR THE PASTRY
115g/4oz/1/2 cup cream cheese
115g/4oz/1/2 cup butter, diced
115g/4oz/1 cup plain (all-purpose) flour

1 To make the pastry, put the cream cheese and butter in a mixing bowl. Sift over the flour, and rub in to bind the dough. Wrap in clear film (plastic wrap). Chill for at least 30 minutes.

2 Preheat the oven to 190°C/375°F/ Gas 5. Mix the flour, brown sugar, salt, spices and butter in a bowl. Rub in with your fingertips until it resembles coarse breadcrumbs, then set aside.

3 Roll out the dough to a thickness of 3mm/1/8in and use to line a 23cm/ 9in pie plate. Trim and flute the edges.

4 Spoon one-third of the filling mixture into the pastry case. Whisk the eggs with the treacle in a large bowl. Put a baking sheet in the oven.

5 Pour the boiling water into a bowl and stir in the bicarbonate of soda; it will foam. Add immediately to the egg mixture and whisk. Pour into the pastry case and sprinkle the remaining filling mixture over evenly.

6 Place on the hot baking sheet and bake for 35 minutes, or until browned. Cool, then serve at room temperature.

Nutritional information per portion: Energy 472kcal/1975kJ; Protein 5.2g; Carbohydrate 53g, of which sugars 31g; Fat 28.1g, of which saturates 17.1g; Cholesterol 112mg; Calcium 201mg; Fibre 0.9g; Sodium 248mg.

Blueberry pie

American blueberries or European bilberries can be used for this pie. You may need to add a little more sugar if you are lucky enough to find native bilberries.

SERVES 6

800g/1¾lb/7 cups blueberries
75g/3oz/6 tbsp caster (superfine) sugar,
   plus extra for sprinkling
45ml/3 tbsp cornflour (cornstarch)
grated rind and juice of ½ orange
grated rind of ½ lemon
2.5ml/½ tsp ground cinnamon
15g/½oz/1 tbsp butter, diced
1 egg, beaten
whipped cream, to serve

FOR THE PASTRY

275g/10oz/2½ cups plain
   (all-purpose) flour
pinch of salt
75g/3oz/6 tbsp butter, diced
50g/2oz/¼ cup white vegetable fat
60–75ml/4–5 tbsp chilled water

1 To make the pastry, sift the flour and salt into a bowl and rub in the fat. Sprinkle over most of the water and mix to a soft dough. Add more water if necessary. Knead lightly. Wrap in clear film (plastic wrap) and chill. Preheat the oven to 200°C/400°F/Gas 6. Roll out half the pastry and use to line a 23cm/9in pie dish, allowing the excess pastry to overhang the edge.

2 In a bowl, mix the blueberries, caster sugar, cornflour, orange rind and juice, lemon rind and cinnamon. Spoon into the pastry case and dot with butter.

3 Roll out the remaining pastry to make a lid for the pie. Trim off the excess, leaving a rim all round. Cut the rim at 2.5cm/1in intervals, then fold each pastry section over on itself to form a triangle. Re-roll the trimmings and cut out pastry decorations. Attach them to the pastry lid with a little beaten egg.

4 Glaze the pastry with the beaten egg and sprinkle with caster sugar. Bake for 30 minutes, or until golden. Serve warm or cold with whipped cream.

Nutritional information per portion: Energy 458kcal/1915kJ; Protein 4.7g; Carbohydrate 60g, of which sugars 20.4g; Fat 23.8g, of which saturates 1.3g; Cholesterol 5mg; Calcium 95mg; Fibre 5.6g; Sodium 143mg.

Key lime pie

This pie is one of America's classic favourites. As the name suggests, it originated in the Florida Keys, but it is now a hugely popular pie all over the world.

SERVES 10

4 eggs, separated

400g/14oz can skimmed, sweetened condensed milk

grated rind and juice of 3 limes

a few drops of green food colouring

30ml/2 tbsp caster (superfine) sugar

300ml/¹/₂ pint/1¹/₄ cups double (heavy) cream

2–3 limes, thinly sliced

thinly pared lime rind and fresh mint sprigs

FOR THE PASTRY

225g/8oz/2 cups plain (all-purpose) flour

115g/4oz/¹/₂ cup chilled butter, diced

30ml/2 tbsp caster (superfine) sugar

pinch of salt

2 egg yolks

30ml/2 tbsp chilled water

1 To make the pastry, sift the flour into a bowl and rub in the butter. Add the sugar, salt, egg yolks and enough water to bind. Knead to a soft dough, then roll out thinly and use to line a deep 21cm/8¹/₂in fluted flan tin (pan). Allow the excess to overhang the edge. Prick the base all over, wrap in clear film (plastic wrap) and chill for 30 minutes. Preheat the oven to 200°C/400°F/Gas 6.

2 Trim off the excess pastry from around the edge of the pastry case, then line with baking parchment and fill with baking beans. Bake for 10 minutes, remove the beans and parchment and bake for 10 minutes more to lightly brown.

3 Beat the egg yolks until light and creamy, then beat in the condensed milk, lime rind and juice. Add the food colouring, and beat until the mixture is thick. Whisk the egg whites in a grease-free bowl until stiff peaks form. Whisk in the sugar, then fold into the lime mixture. Reduce the oven to 160°C/325°F/Gas 3.

4 Pour the filling into the case. Bake for 20 minutes. Cool, then chill. Whip the cream and spoon around the edge. Add lime twists and rind, and mint sprigs.

Nutritional information per portion: Energy 510kcal/2126kJ; Protein 9.2g; Carbohydrate 46.6g, of which sugars 29.4g; Fat 33.2g, of which saturates 19.5g; Cholesterol 196mg; Calcium 182mg; Fibre 0.7g; Sodium 163mg.

Mississippi mud pie

This is the ultimate in chocolate desserts – a deep pastry case, filled with chocolate custard and topped with a fluffy rum mousse and a smothering of whipped cream.

SERVES 6–8

3 eggs, separated
20ml/4 tsp cornflour (cornstarch)
75g/3oz/6 tbsp caster (superfine) sugar
400ml/14fl oz/1¾ cups milk
150g/5oz plain (semisweet) chocolate, broken up
5ml/1 tsp vanilla extract
15ml/1 tbsp powdered gelatine
45ml/3 tbsp water

30ml/2 tbsp dark rum
175g/6fl oz/¾ cup double (heavy) cream
a few chocolate curls, to decorate

FOR THE PASTRY
250g/9oz/2¼ cups plain (all-purpose) flour
150g/5oz/⅔ cup butter, diced
2 egg yolks
15–30ml/1–2 tbsp chilled water

1 To make the pastry, sift the flour into a bowl and rub in the butter. Stir in the egg yolks with just enough chilled water to make a soft dough. Roll out on a lightly floured surface and use to line a deep 23cm/9in flan tin (pan). Chill for 30 minutes. Preheat the oven to 190°C/375°F/Gas 5. Prick the pastry all over with a fork, line with foil and baking beans, then bake blind for 10 minutes.

2 Remove the foil and beans, return the pie to the oven and bake for a further 10 minutes until the pastry is crisp and golden. Cool in the tin.

3 To make the custard filling, mix the egg yolks, cornflour and 30ml/2 tbsp of the sugar in a bowl. Heat the milk in a pan until almost boiling, then beat into the egg mixture. Return to the cleaned pan. Stir over a low heat until thickened and smooth. Pour half into a bowl. Melt the chocolate, then add to the custard in the bowl. Add the vanilla extract and mix well. Spread in the case, cover closely with baking parchment to prevent a skin from forming, cool, then chill until set.

4 Sprinkle the gelatine over the water in a bowl, leave until spongy, then place over a pan of simmering water to dissolve. Stir into the remaining custard, along with the rum. Whisk the egg whites until stiff peaks form, whisk in the rest of the sugar, then quickly fold into the custard before it sets. Spoon the mixture over the chocolate custard to cover completely. Chill until set, then remove the pie from the tin to serve. Spread whipped cream over the top and decorate with chocolate curls.

Nutritional information per portion: Energy 571kcal/2385kJ; Protein 9.4g; Carbohydrate 53.5g, of which sugars 22.7g; Fat 36.2g, of which saturates 21.2g; Cholesterol 196mg; Calcium 160mg; Fibre 1.3g; Sodium 180mg.

Lemon meringue pie

Crisp shortcrust is filled with a mouthwatering lemon cream filling and heaped with soft golden-topped meringue. This classic dessert never fails to please.

SERVES 6

3 large eggs, separated
150g/5oz/ ²⁄₃ cup caster (superfine) sugar
grated rind and juice of 1 lemon
25g/1oz/¹⁄₂ cup fresh white breadcrumbs
250ml/8fl oz/1 cup milk

FOR THE PASTRY
115g/4oz/1 cup plain (all-purpose) flour
pinch of salt
50g/2oz/¹⁄₄ cup butter, diced
50g/2oz/¹⁄₄ cup lard or white vegetable
   fat, diced
15ml/1 tbsp caster (superfine) sugar
15ml/1 tbsp chilled water

1 To make the pastry, sift the flour and salt into a bowl. Rub in the fats. Stir in the caster sugar and enough chilled water to make a soft dough. Roll out on a lightly floured surface and use to line a 21cm/8¹⁄₂in pie plate. Chill until needed.

2 Meanwhile, place the egg yolks and 30ml/2 tbsp of the caster sugar in a bowl. Add the lemon rind, juice, breadcrumbs and milk. Mix and leave to soak for 1 hour. Preheat the oven to 200°C/400°F/Gas 6. Beat the filling until smooth and pour into the case.

3 Bake for 20 minutes, or until the filling has just set. Cool on a wire rack for 30 minutes, or until a slight skin has formed on the surface.

4 Lower the oven to 180°C/350°F/Gas 4. Whisk the egg whites until stiff peaks form. Gradually whisk in the remaining caster sugar to form a glossy meringue. Spoon on top of the lemon filling, spreading right to the edge of the pastry, using the back of a spoon. Swirl the meringue slightly. Bake for 20–25 minutes until crisp and golden. Cool slightly, then serve.

Nutritional information per portion: Energy 357kcal/1497kJ; Protein 6.8g; Carbohydrate 42.8g, of which sugars 25.1g; Fat 18.9g, of which saturates 9g; Cholesterol 129mg; Calcium 108mg; Fibre 0.7g; Sodium 137mg.

Rhubarb meringue pie

The sharp tang of rhubarb with its sweet meringue topping will really tantalize the taste buds. This pie is delicious hot or cold with cream or vanilla ice cream.

SERVES 6

675g/1¹/₂lb rhubarb, chopped
250g/9oz/generous 1 cup caster
    (superfine) sugar
grated rind and juice of 3 oranges
3 eggs, separated
75ml/5 tbsp cornflour (cornstarch)
whipped cream, to serve

FOR THE PASTRY
200g/7oz/1³/₄ cups plain
    (all-purpose) flour
25g/1oz/¹/₄ cup ground walnuts
115g/4oz/¹/₂ cup butter, diced
30ml/2 tbsp sugar
1 egg yolk, beaten with 15ml/1 tbsp water

1 To make the pastry, sift the flour into a bowl and add the walnuts. Rub in the butter. Stir in the sugar and egg yolks to make a firm dough. Knead lightly, wrap in clear film (plastic wrap). Chill for 30 minutes.

2 Preheat the oven to 190°C/375°F/Gas 5. Roll out the pastry and use to line a 23cm/9in fluted flan tin (pan). Prick the base. Line with foil and baking beans. Bake for 15 minutes. Put the rhubarb in a pan with 75g/3oz/6 tbsp of sugar. Add the orange rind. Cook over a low heat until tender.

3 Remove the foil and beans from the pastry case, brush all over with egg yolk, and bake for 15 minutes more. Mix the cornflour and orange juice in a bowl. Remove the rhubarb from the heat, then add the cornflour mixture and return to the heat. Bring to the boil and stir constantly for 1–2 minutes. Cool, then beat in the remaining egg yolk. Pour into the pastry case.

4 Whisk the egg whites to form soft peaks. Gradually whisk in the remaining sugar. Swirl over the filling, then bake for 25 minutes. Serve with whipped cream.

Nutritional information per portion: Energy 567kcal/2388kJ; Protein 8.4g; Carbohydrate 89.5g, of which sugars 52.6g; Fat 22g, of which saturates 11.1g; Cholesterol 136mg; Calcium 202mg; Fibre 2.8g; Sodium 168mg.

Plum crumble pie

Polenta adds a wonderful golden hue and crunchiness to the crumble topping for this pie, which makes a perfect contrast to the ripe, juicy plum filling.

SERVES 6–8

10ml/2 tsp caster (superfine) sugar
15ml/1 tbsp polenta
450g/1lb dark plums
25g/1oz/¼ cup rolled oats
15ml/1 tbsp demerara (raw) sugar
custard or cream, to serve

FOR THE PASTRY

115g/4oz/1 cup plain
   (all-purpose) flour

115g/4oz/1 cup wholemeal
   (whole-wheat) flour
150g/5oz/⅔ cup caster (superfine) sugar
115g/4oz/1 cup polenta
5ml/1 tsp baking powder
pinch of salt
150g/5oz/10 tbsp butter, diced
1 egg, beaten
15ml/1 tbsp olive oil
about 60ml/4 tbsp chilled water

1 To make the pastry, mix the dry ingredients in a large bowl. Rub in the butter until the mixture resembles fine breadcrumbs. Stir in the egg, olive oil and chilled water to form a dough. Grease a 23cm/9in springform cake tin (pan). Press two-thirds of the dough evenly over the base and sides of the tin. Wrap the remaining dough in clear film (plastic wrap) and chill.

2 Preheat the oven to 180°C/350°F/Gas 4. Sprinkle the sugar and polenta into the pastry case. Cut the plums in half and remove the stones, then place the plums, cut side down, on top of the polenta base.

3 Unwrap the piece of chilled dough, crumble it between your fingers into a mixing bowl, then add the oats. Mix lightly. Sprinkle the mixture evenly over the plums, then sprinkle the demerara sugar on top.

4 Bake the pie for 50 minutes. Leave for 15 minutes, then remove from the tin. Leave to cool for a while on a wire rack. Serve in slices with custard or cream.

VARIATION

Almonds and plums make a good combination. Add 60ml/4 tbsp flaked (sliced) almonds to the oat topping.

Nutritional information per portion: Energy 426kcal/1787kJ; Protein 6.4g; Carbohydrate 60.5g, of which sugars 26.5g; Fat 18.9g, of which saturates 10.2g; Cholesterol 64mg; Calcium 53mg; Fibre 3.2g; Sodium 127mg.

Boston banoffee pie

Simply press this wonderfully biscuity pastry into the tin, rather than rolling it out. Add the fudge-toffee filling and sliced banana topping and it'll prove irresistible.

SERVES 6

115g/4oz/¹/₂ cup butter, diced
200g/7oz can skimmed, sweetened
    condensed milk
115g/4oz/¹/₂ cup soft brown sugar
30ml/2 tbsp golden (light corn) syrup
2 small bananas, sliced
a little lemon juice
whipped cream, to decorate
5ml/1 tsp grated plain (semisweet)
    chocolate, to decorate

FOR THE PASTRY
150g/5oz/1¹/₄ cups plain
    (all-purpose) flour
115g/4oz/¹/₂ cup butter, diced
50g/2oz/¹/₄ cup caster
    (superfine) sugar

1 Preheat the oven to 160°C/325°F/ Gas 3. In a food processor, process the flour and diced butter until crumbed. Stir in the caster sugar and mix to form a soft, pliable dough. Press the dough into a 20cm/8in loose-based flan tin (pan) and bake for 30 minutes.

2 To make the filling, place the butter in a pan with the condensed milk, brown sugar and syrup. Heat gently, stirring, until the butter has melted and the sugar has dissolved.

3 Bring to a gentle boil and cook for 7–10 minutes, stirring constantly, until the mixture thickens and turns a light caramel colour. Pour the hot caramel filling into the pastry case and leave until completely cold.

4 Sprinkle the banana slices with lemon juice and arrange in overlapping circles on top of the filling, leaving a gap in the centre. Pipe a generous swirl of whipped cream in the centre and sprinkle with grated chocolate.

Nutritional information per portion: Energy 608kcal/2547kJ; Protein 6.4g; Carbohydrate 78.5g, of which sugars 58.9g; Fat 32g, of which saturates 20.1g; Cholesterol 82mg; Calcium 169mg; Fibre 1.1g; Sodium 299mg.

Treacle tart

Traditional shortcrust pastry is perfect for this old-fashioned favourite, with its sticky lemon and golden syrup filling and twisted lattice topping.

SERVES 4–6

260g/9¹/₂oz/generous ³/₄ cup golden
   (light corn) syrup
75g/3oz/1¹/₂ cups fresh
   white breadcrumbs
grated rind of 1 lemon
30ml/2 tbsp lemon juice
custard, to serve

FOR THE PASTRY

150g/5oz/1¹/₄ cups plain
   (all-purpose) flour
2.5ml/¹/₂ tsp salt
130g/4¹/₂oz/9 tbsp chilled
   butter, diced
45–60/3–4 tbsp chilled water

1 To make the pastry, combine the flour and salt in a bowl. Rub in the butter. With a fork, stir in just enough water to bind the dough. Gather into a smooth ball and knead lightly until smooth. Wrap in clear film (plastic wrap). Chill for at least 20 minutes.

2 On a lightly floured surface, roll out the pastry to 3mm/¹/₈in thick. Transfer to a 20cm/8in fluted flan tin (pan) and trim off the overhang. Chill the pastry case for 20 minutes. Reserve the trimmings. Put a baking sheet in the oven and preheat to 200°C/400°F/Gas 6. Warm the syrup in a pan until it melts.

3 Remove the syrup from the heat. Stir in the breadcrumbs and lemon rind. Leave to stand for 10 minutes, then add more breadcrumbs if too moist and thin. Stir in the lemon juice, and spread evenly in the pastry case.

4 Roll out the pastry trimmings and cut into 10–12 thin strips. Twist the strips into spirals. Lay half of them on the filling. Arrange the remaining strips at right angles to form a lattice. Press the ends on to the rim. Bake the tart on the hot baking sheet for 10 minutes. Lower the oven to 190°C/375°F/Gas 5. Bake for 15 minutes, until golden. Serve warm with custard.

Nutritional information per portion: Energy 420kcal/1764kJ; Protein 4.1g; Carbohydrate 63.5g, of which sugars 35.1g; Fat 18.4g, of which saturates 11.3g; Cholesterol 46mg; Calcium 62mg; Fibre 1.1g; Sodium 344mg.

Italian chocolate ricotta tart

Creamy ricotta cheese packed with mixed peel and dark chocolate chips is baked in a chocolate and sherry pastry case for a luxuriously rich tart with maximum flavour.

SERVES 6

2 egg yolks
115g/4oz/¹/₂ cup caster (superfine) sugar
500g/1¹/₄lb/2¹/₂ cups ricotta cheese
finely grated rind of 1 lemon
90ml/6 tbsp dark (bittersweet)
   chocolate chips
75ml/5 tbsp chopped mixed peel
45ml/3 tbsp chopped angelica

FOR THE PASTRY

225g/8oz/2 cups plain (all-purpose) flour
30ml/2 tbsp unsweetened cocoa powder
60ml/4 tbsp caster (superfine) sugar
115g/4oz/¹/₂ cup butter, diced
60ml/4 tbsp dry sherry

1 Preheat the oven to 200°C/400°F/Gas 6. To make the pastry, sift the flour and cocoa into a bowl, then stir in the sugar. Rub in the butter until the mixture resembles fine breadcrumbs, then work in the dry sherry, using your fingertips, until the mixture binds to a firm, smooth dough.

2 Roll out three-quarters of the pastry on a lightly floured surface and use to line a 24cm/9¹/₂in loose-based flan tin (pan). Chill for 20 minutes.

3 Beat the egg yolks and sugar in a bowl, then add the ricotta cheese. Beat the mixture with a wooden spoon to combine thoroughly. Stir in the lemon rind, chocolate chips, mixed peel and angelica. Scrape the ricotta mixture into the pastry case and level the surface.

4 Roll out the remaining pastry thinly and cut into narrow strips, then arrange these in a lattice over the filling. Bake for 15 minutes, then lower the oven temperature to 180°C/350°F/Gas 4 and bake for 30–35 minutes more until golden brown. Leave to cool in the tin.

COOK'S TIP
This chocolate tart is best served at room temperature so, if made in advance, chill it when cool, then, when needed, bring to room temperature before serving.

Nutritional information per portion: Energy 701kcal/2938kJ; Protein 14.2g; Carbohydrate 83.4g, of which sugars 54.1g; Fat 35.6g, of which saturates 21.3g; Cholesterol 144mg; Calcium 115mg; Fibre 3g; Sodium 223mg.

Linzertorte

Use a good quality jam or conserve to fill the cinnamon and almond pastry case in this traditional Austrian speciality, and dust it with icing sugar before serving.

SERVES 8–10

225g/8oz/³⁄₄ cup raspberry jam
1 egg yolk
icing (confectioners') sugar,
  for dusting
custard, to serve

FOR THE PASTRY
200g/7oz/scant 1 cup butter
200g/7oz/scant 1 cup caster
  (superfine) sugar
3 eggs, plus 1 egg yolk
2.5ml/¹⁄₂ tsp ground cinnamon
grated rind of ¹⁄₂ lemon
115g/4oz/2 cups fine sweet biscuit
  (cookie) crumbs
150g/5oz/1¹⁄₄ cups ground almonds
225g/8oz/2 cups plain (all-purpose)
  flour, sifted

1 Preheat the oven to 190°C/375°F/Gas 5. To make the pastry, cream the butter and sugar together until light. Slowly add the eggs and one of the egg yolks, beating all the time, then add the cinnamon and rind. Stir the crumbs and ground almonds into the mixture. Mix well, then add the sifted flour. Knead to form a dough, then wrap in clear film (plastic wrap). Chill for about 30 minutes.

2 Roll out two-thirds of the pastry on a lightly floured surface and use to line a deep 25cm/10in loose-based flan tin (pan). Press the pastry into the sides and trim the edge. Spread the raspberry jam generously and evenly over the base of the pastry case. Roll out the remaining pastry into a long rectangle. Cut the rectangle into even strips with a sharp knife and arrange in a lattice pattern over the jam filling.

3 Lightly beat the remaining egg yolk in a small bowl, then brush it evenly over the pastry rim and lattice. Bake the flan for 45 minutes, until golden brown. Leave to cool in the tin before turning out on to a wire rack. Just before serving, sift a little icing sugar over the top. Serve with custard, if you like.

Nutritional information per portion: Energy 537kcal/2247kJ; Protein 8.5g; Carbohydrate 63g, of which sugars 39.1g; Fat 29.7g, of which saturates 12.8g; Cholesterol 125mg; Calcium 106mg; Fibre 2.1g; Sodium 223mg.

Crunchy apple and almond flan

Do not be tempted to put any sugar with the apples, as this makes them produce too much liquid. All the sweetness is in the pastry and the crunchy topping.

SERVES 8

115g/4oz/1 cup plain (all-purpose) flour
1.5ml/¼ tsp mixed spice
50g/2oz/¼ cup butter, diced
50g/2oz/¼ cup demerara (raw) sugar
50g/2oz/½ cup flaked (sliced) almonds
675g/1½lb cooking apples, peeled, cored
    and thinly sliced
25g/1oz/3 tbsp raisins
sifted icing (confectioners') sugar,
    for dusting

FOR THE PASTRY

175g/6oz/1½ cups plain (all-purpose) flour
75g/3oz/6 tbsp butter, diced
25g/1oz/¼ cup ground almonds
25g/1oz/2 tbsp caster (superfine) sugar
1 egg yolk
15ml/1 tbsp cold water
1.5ml/¼ tsp almond extract

1 To make the pastry, place the flour in a mixing bowl and rub in the butter. Stir in the ground almonds and sugar. Whisk together the egg yolk, water and almond extract and mix into the dry ingredients to form a dough. Knead until smooth, wrap in clear film (plastic wrap) and leave in a cool place for 20 minutes.

2 Meanwhile, make the topping. Sift the flour and mixed spice into a bowl and rub in the butter with your fingertips. Stir in the demerara sugar and flaked almonds. Roll out the pastry. Line a 23cm/9in loose-based flan tin (pan), pressing the pastry neatly into the edges and making a lip around the top edge. Trim off the excess. Chill for 15 minutes.

3 Place a baking sheet in the oven and preheat to 190°C/375°F/Gas 5. Arrange the apple slices in the pastry case in overlapping concentric circles, doming the centre. Sprinkle over the raisins. Cover the apples with the crunchy topping, pressing it on lightly. Bake the flan on the hot baking sheet for 25–30 minutes. Cool in the tin for 10 minutes. Serve warm or cold, dusted with icing sugar.

Nutritional information per portion: Energy 358kcal/1499kJ; Protein 6.2g; Carbohydrate 42.5g, of which sugars 14.6g; Fat 19.3g, of which saturates 8.8g; Cholesterol 59mg; Calcium 86mg; Fibre 3.2g; Sodium 102mg.

Puff, choux and filo pastry desserts

Puff and similar pastries are repeatedly rolled and folded to trap the air within the buttery layers, expanding on baking to produce wonderfully light results. Elegant and airy, choux is perfect for sweet fillings, while bought filo could not be easier to use. Simply brush with melted butter and stack, then cut, fold or scrunch to the desired shape. From Tarte Tatin and Bakewell Tart to Apple Strudel and Coffee Cream Profiteroles, whatever the pastry, the result is bound to be superb.

Peach and brandy pie

Slices of juicy, ripe peach, gently cooked in butter and sugar, are encased in crisp puff pastry to make this fragrant fruit pie – simple but delicious.

SERVES 8

6 large, firm, ripe peaches	**FOR THE GLAZE**
40g/1¹/₂oz/3 tbsp butter	1 egg
45ml/3 tbsp brandy	5ml/1 tsp water
75g/3oz/6 tbsp caster (superfine) sugar	15ml/1 tbsp granulated (white) sugar
450g/1lb puff pastry	
vanilla ice cream, to serve	

1 Immerse the peaches in boiling water for 30 seconds. Lift out with a slotted spoon, dip in cold water, then peel. Halve, stone (pit) and slice the peaches.

2 Melt the butter in a large frying pan. Add the peach slices, then sprinkle with the brandy and sugar. Cook for about 4 minutes, shaking the pan frequently until the sugar has dissolved and the peaches are tender. Set the pan aside to cool.

3 Cut the pastry into two pieces, one slightly larger than the other, and roll out. Cut the larger piece of pastry into a 30cm/12in circle and the smaller one into a 28cm/11in circle. Place the circles on separate baking sheets lined with parchment, cover with clear film (plastic wrap) and chill for 30 minutes.

4 Preheat the oven to 200°C/400°F/Gas 6. Spoon the peaches into the middle of the larger pastry round and spread them out to within about 2cm/1in of the edge. Place the smaller round on top, shaping it in a mound over the peaches. Brush the edge of the larger pastry round with water, then fold this over the top and press to seal. Twist the edges together to make a pattern all the way round.

5 Make the glaze by mixing the egg and water together in a cup. Lightly brush it over the pastry and sprinkle over the granulated sugar, spreading it evenly over the pastry. Make five or six small crescent-shaped slashes on the top of the pastry, radiating from the centre towards the edge.

6 Bake the pie for about 45 minutes, or until the pastry is risen and golden brown. Serve warm in slices with vanilla ice cream.

Nutritional information per portion: Energy 343kcal/1437kJ; Protein 5.2g; Carbohydrate 39.2g, of which sugars 19.1g; Fat 18.7g, of which saturates 2.8g; Cholesterol 34mg; Calcium 50mg; Fibre 1.7g; Sodium 215mg.

Pear tarte tatin with cardamom

Cardamom is a spice that is equally at home in sweet and savoury dishes. It is delicious with pears, and brings out their flavour beautifully in this simple tart.

SERVES 4–6

50g/2oz/¼ cup butter, softened
50g/2oz/¼ cup caster (superfine) sugar
seeds from 10 green cardamom pods
225g/8oz puff pastry
3 ripe, large round pears
cream, to serve

1 Preheat the oven to 220°C/425°F/Gas 7. Spread the butter over the base of an 18cm/7in heavy ovenproof omelette pan. Sprinkle with sugar, then sprinkle the cardamom over. Roll out the pastry to a circle slightly larger than the pan. Prick the pastry all over with a fork, place on a baking sheet and chill.

2 Peel the pears, cut in half lengthways and remove the cores. Arrange, rounded side down, in the pan. Heat until the sugar melts and begins to bubble with the pear juice. Once the sugar has caramelized remove the pan from the heat. Place the pastry on top, tucking in the edges with a knife. Bake for 25 minutes.

3 Leave the tart in the pan until the juices have stopped bubbling. Invert a serving plate over the pan then, wearing oven gloves to protect your hands, hold the pan and plate together and quickly turn over, gently shaking it to release the tart. It may be necessary to slide a spatula underneath the pears to loosen them. Serve the tart warm, with cream.

Nutritional information per portion: Energy 265kcal/1106kJ; Protein 2.5g; Carbohydrate 30.1g, of which sugars 16.8g; Fat 16.1g, of which saturates 4.3g; Cholesterol 18mg; Calcium 36mg; Fibre 1.7g; Sodium 170mg.

Strawberry tart

This tart is best assembled just before serving, but you can bake the pastry case early in the day. Make the filling ahead of time and put it together in a few minutes.

SERVES 6

350g/12oz rough puff or puff pastry
225g/8oz/1 cup cream cheese
grated rind of ¹/₂ orange
30ml/2 tbsp orange liqueur or
    orange juice
45–60ml/3–4 tbsp icing (confectioners')
    sugar, plus extra for dusting (optional)
450g/1lb/4 cups strawberries, hulled

1 Roll out the pastry on a lightly floured surface to a thickness of about 3mm/¹/₈in and use to line a 28 x 10cm/11 x 4in tranche tin (pan). Trim the edges of the pastry neatly with a knife, then chill for 30 minutes. Preheat the oven to 200°C/400°F/Gas 6.

2 Prick the base of the pastry all over with a fork. Line the pastry case with foil, fill with baking beans and bake for 15 minutes. Remove the foil and beans and bake for 10 minutes more until the pastry is browned. Gently press down on the pastry base to deflate it, then leave to cool on a wire rack.

3 Using a hand-held electric whisk or food processor, beat together well the cream cheese, orange rind, liqueur or orange juice and icing sugar. Spread the cheese filling in the pastry case. Halve the strawberries and arrange them on top of the cheese filling. Dust with icing sugar, if you like.

Nutritional information per portion: Energy 434kcal/1805kJ; Protein 5.2g; Carbohydrate 34.4g, of which sugars 13.5g; Fat 32.2g, of which saturates 11.1g; Cholesterol 36mg; Calcium 87mg; Fibre 0.8g; Sodium 299mg.

Apple, raisin and maple pies

Calvados accentuates the apple flavour of these individual puff pastry pies. Serve them with whipped cream, flavoured with orange liqueur, for a delectable dinner party dessert.

SERVES 4

350g/12oz puff pastry

beaten egg or milk, to glaze

whipped cream, flavoured with orange
   liqueur and sprinkled with grated
   orange rind, to serve

FOR THE FILLING

75g/3oz/scant ¹/₂ cup soft light
   brown sugar

30ml/2 tbsp lemon juice

45ml/3 tbsp maple syrup

150ml/¹/₄ pint/²/₃ cup water

45ml/3 tbsp Calvados

6 small eating apples, halved, peeled
   and cored

75g/3oz/¹/₂ cup raisins

1 To make the filling, heat the sugar, lemon juice, maple syrup and water in a pan until the sugar has dissolved. Bring to the boil and cook until reduced by half. Stir in the Calvados.

2 Cut four of the apples into eight even segments. Add the apple pieces to the syrup. Simmer for 5–8 minutes until just tender. Lift out using a slotted spoon. Set aside. Chop the remaining apples. Add to the syrup with the raisins, simmer until the mixture is thick, then cool. Preheat the oven to 200°C/400°F/Gas 6.

3 Roll out the pastry and stamp out eight 15cm/6in rounds with a fluted cutter. Use half the pastry to line four 10cm/4in individual flan tins (pans). Spoon in the raisin mixture and level the surface. Arrange the apple segments on top of the raisin mixture. Brush the edge of the cases with egg and cover with a pastry lid. Trim, seal and flute the edges.

4 Cut shapes from the pastry trimmings and use to decorate the pies. Brush with beaten egg or milk. Bake for 30–35 minutes. Serve hot with the flavoured cream.

Nutritional information per portion: Energy 545kcal/2294kJ; Protein 5.8g; Carbohydrate 82.8g, of which sugars 51.6g; Fat 21.6g, of which saturates 0g; Cholesterol 0mg; Calcium 75mg; Fibre 2g; Sodium 316mg.

Tarte tatin

This classic French upside-down tart can be made either with pâte sucrée or, more simply, with puff pastry, as it is here. It can also be made with apricots, peaches or plums.

SERVES 6

3 eating apples, which will hold their
   shape after cooking
juice of ½ lemon
50g/2oz/¼ cup butter, softened
75g/3oz/6 tbsp caster
   (superfine) sugar
250g/9oz puff pastry
single (light) cream, to serve

1 Preheat the oven to 220°C/425°F/Gas 7. Cut the apples in quarters and remove the cores. Toss them in the lemon juice to prevent discolouring.

2 Spread the butter over the base of a 20cm/8in heavy ovenproof omelette pan. Sprinkle the caster sugar over the base of the pan and add the apple wedges, skin side down. Cook over a medium heat for about 15 minutes, or until the sugar and butter have melted and the apples are golden.

3 Roll out the pastry and cut it into a 25cm/10in round. Gently place it over the apples, then tuck in the edges with a knife. Bake for 15–20 minutes, or until the pastry is golden.

4 Remove from the oven and loosen the edge with the knife. Invert the serving plate on the omelette pan, then, protecting your hands with oven gloves, hold the pan and plate together and quickly turn over. Lift off the pan. Cool slightly before serving with cream.

Nutritional information per portion: Energy 162Kcal/675kJ; Protein 13.1g; Carbohydrate 8.5g, of which sugars 7g; Fat 8.6g, of which saturates 3.8g; Cholesterol 44mg; Calcium 42mg; Fibre 3g; Sodium 55mg.

Coffee cream profiteroles

Crisp-textured coffee choux pastry puffs are filled with cream and drizzled with a white chocolate sauce. For those with a sweet tooth, there is plenty of extra sauce.

SERVES 6

50g/2oz/¼ cup sugar
100ml/3¾ fl oz/scant ½ cup water
150g/5oz good quality white chocolate
25g/1oz/2 tbsp butter
300ml/½ pint/1¼ cups double
   (heavy) cream
30ml/2 tbsp coffee liqueur

FOR THE PASTRY

65g/2½oz/9 tbsp plain (all-purpose) flour
pinch of salt
50g/2oz/¼ cup butter, diced
150ml/¼ pint/⅔ cup freshly made coffee
2 eggs, lightly beaten

1 Preheat the oven to 220°C/425°F/Gas 7. To make the pastry, sift the flour and salt on to a sheet of baking parchment and set aside. Put the butter into a pan with the coffee. Bring to a rolling boil, then remove the pan from the heat and tip in all the flour. Beat vigorously with a wooden spoon until the mixture forms a ball and comes away from the sides of the pan. Leave to cool for 2 minutes.

2 Gradually add the beaten eggs to the flour mixture, beating thoroughly after each addition, until they are fully incorporated and you have a smooth consistency. Spoon the mixture into a piping (pastry) bag fitted with a 1cm/½in plain nozzle.

3 Pipe about 24 small buns on to a dampened baking sheet. Bake for about 20 minutes, then transfer to a wire rack. Pierce each bun with a knife to let out the steam. Leave the buns to cool.

4 To make the sauce, put the sugar and water in a pan and heat gently until the sugar has dissolved. Bring to the boil, then simmer for about 3 minutes. Remove the pan from the heat and add the chocolate and butter, stirring until smooth. Stir in 45ml/3 tbsp of the cream and the coffee liqueur. Keep warm or cool to room temperature.

5 To assemble, whip the remaining cream in a small bowl until soft peaks form. Spoon the cream into a piping bag and use to fill the buns through the slits in the sides. Pile on a large plate and pour a little sauce over. Serve the remaining sauce separately.

Nutritional information per portion: Energy 579kcal/2401kJ; Protein 6g; Carbohydrate 32.6g, of which sugars 24.4g; Fat 46.8g, of which saturates 28.4g; Cholesterol 159mg; Calcium 123mg; Fibre 0.3g; Sodium 138mg.

Gâteau Saint-Honoré

Named after the patron saint of bakers, this spectacular dessert has a puff pastry base topped with caramel-coated choux puffs and filled with crème pâtissière.

SERVES 10

175g/6oz puff pastry

FOR THE CHOUX PASTRY
300ml/½ pint/1¼ cups water
115g/4oz/½ cup butter, diced
130g/4½oz/scant 1¼ cups plain
    (all-purpose) flour, sifted
2.5ml/½ tsp salt
4 eggs, lightly beaten
beaten egg, to glaze

FOR THE CRÈME PÂTISSIÈRE
3 egg yolks
50g/2oz/¼ cup caster (superfine) sugar
30ml/2 tbsp plain (all-purpose) flour
30ml/2 tbsp cornflour (cornstarch)
300ml/½ pint/1¼ cups milk
150ml/¼ pint/⅔ cup double (heavy) cream
30ml/2 tbsp orange liqueur, e.g. Grand Marnier

FOR THE CARAMEL
225g/8oz/1 cup sugar
120ml/4fl oz/½ cup water

1 Roll out the puff pastry and cut out a 20cm/8in circle, using an upturned plate as your guide. Place the pastry round on a baking sheet lined with baking parchment, prick all over with a fork and chill.

2 To make the choux pastry, put the water and butter in a large pan. Heat until the butter has melted, then bring to the boil. Quickly tip in all the flour with the salt, remove the pan from the heat and beat well until the mixture leaves the sides of the pan. Beat in the eggs, a little at a time, to form a paste.

3 Preheat the oven to 200°C/400°F/Gas 6. Spoon the choux pastry into a piping (pastry) bag fitted with a 1cm/½in plain nozzle. Pipe a spiral of choux on to the puff pastry base, starting at the edge and working to the centre.

4 Pipe 16 small choux buns on to a lined baking sheet with the remaining choux pastry. Glaze with egg. Bake the small buns for 20 minutes and the choux-topped puff pastry on the shelf below for 35 minutes, or until well risen. Pierce several holes in the top and sides of the spiral, and pierce one hole in the side of each bun. Return to the oven for 5 minutes to dry out, then cool on a wire rack.

5 To make the filling, whisk the egg yolks and caster sugar until light and creamy. Whisk in the flour and cornflour. Bring the milk to the boil in a pan and pour over the egg mixture, whisking. Return to the cleaned pan and cook for 2–3 minutes, until thick and smooth. Cover with damp baking parchment and leave to cool.

6 Whip the cream lightly and fold into the crème pâtissière with the orange liqueur. Spoon half into a piping bag fitted with a small plain nozzle and use to fill the choux buns.

7 To make the caramel, heat the sugar and water in a pan until completely dissolved, stirring occasionally. Bring to the boil and cook until it turns a rich golden colour. Remove from the heat and set over a large bowl half-filled with just boiled water to keep the caramel liquid.

8 Dip the bases of the choux buns, one at a time, into the caramel and arrange in a ring around the edge of the pastry case. Pipe the remaining crème pâtissière into the centre. Drizzle the top with the remaining caramel and leave to set. Set aside in a cool place for up to 2 hours before serving.

Nutritional information per portion: Energy 466kcal/1952kJ; Protein 7.3g; Carbohydrate 51.9g, of which sugars 30.9g; Fat 26.5g, of which saturates 12.5g; Cholesterol 186mg; Calcium 139mg; Fibre 0.5g; Sodium 221mg.

Bakewell tart

Although the pastry base makes this a tart, in the English village of Bakewell in Derbyshire, where it originated, it is traditionally called Bakewell pudding.

SERVES 4

225g/8oz puff pastry
30ml/2 tbsp raspberry
   or apricot jam
2 eggs, plus 2 egg yolks
115g/4oz/¹/₂ cup caster
   (superfine) sugar
115g/4oz/¹/₂ cup butter, melted
50g/2oz/²/₃ cup ground almonds
a few drops of almond extract
icing (confectioners') sugar, for dusting

1 Preheat the oven to 200°C/400°F/ Gas 6. Roll out the pastry on a lightly floured surface and use to line an 18cm/7in pie plate. Trim the edge.

2 Re-roll the pastry trimmings and cut out wide strips of pastry. Use these to decorate the edge of the pastry case by gently twisting them around the rim, joining the strips together as necessary. Prick the pastry case all over, then spread the jam over the base.

3 Whisk the eggs, egg yolks and sugar together in a bowl until the mixture is thick and pale.

4 Gently stir the melted butter, ground almonds and almond extract into the whisked egg mixture.

5 Pour the mixture into the pastry case and bake for 30 minutes, or until the filling is just set and is lightly browned. Dust with icing sugar before serving hot, warm or cold.

Nutritional information per portion: Energy 700kcal/2919kJ; Protein 10.8g; Carbohydrate 57.1g, of which sugars 36.7g; Fat 49.9g, of which saturates 17.1g; Cholesterol 257mg; Calcium 110mg; Fibre 0.9g; Sodium 394mg.

Apple strudel

This classic recipe is usually made with strudel dough, which is wonderful, but can be tricky and time-consuming, especially for a novice. Filo pastry makes a good shortcut.

SERVES 8–10

**500g/1¼lb filo pastry, thawed
if frozen**
**115g/4oz/½ cup unsalted
butter, melted**
**icing (confectioners') sugar,
for dusting**

FOR THE FILLING
**1kg/2¼lb cooking apples, peeled,
cored and sliced**
**115g/4oz/2 cups fresh
white breadcrumbs**
150g/5oz/¾ cup sugar
5ml/1 tsp cinnamon
75g/3oz/generous 1½ cups raisins
finely grated rind of 1 lemon
50g/2oz/¼ cup butter

1 Preheat the oven to 180°C/350°F/ Gas 4. To make the filling, place the sliced apples in a large mixing bowl. Add the breadcrumbs, sugar, cinnamon, raisins and grated lemon rind and mix well. Melt the butter in a pan, then stir it in to the mixture.

2 Lay a sheet of filo pastry on a floured work surface and brush with melted butter. Place another sheet on top. Brush with melted butter as before. Continue stacking the sheets and brushing with the butter until there are four or five layers in all.

3 Spoon the filling into the centre of the pastry, leaving a 2.5cm/1in border all round. Fold in the two shorter sides, then roll up from one long side, Swiss-roll (jelly-roll) style. Place the strudel on a lightly buttered baking sheet, seam side down. Brush the pastry with the remaining melted butter. Bake for 30–40 minutes, or until golden.

4 Remove the strudel from the oven and place on a wire rack to cool. Dust with icing sugar before cutting into slices for serving.

Nutritional information per portion: Energy 162Kcal/675kJ; Protein 13.1g; Carbohydrate 8.5g, of which sugars 7g; Fat 8.6g, of which saturates 3.8g; Cholesterol 44mg; Calcium 42mg; Fibre 3g; Sodium 55mg.

Fresh cherry and hazelnut strudel

Serve this wonderful old-world treat as a warm dessert with crème fraîche or allow to cool and offer as a delicious accompaniment to coffee or afternoon tea.

SERVES 6–8

75g/3oz/6 tbsp butter

90ml/6 tbsp light muscovado (brown) sugar

3 egg yolks

grated rind of 1 lemon

1.5ml/¼ tsp grated nutmeg

250g/9oz/generous 1 cup ricotta cheese

8 large sheets of filo pastry, thawed if frozen

75g/3oz ratafia biscuits (almond macaroons), crushed

450g/1lb/2½ cups cherries, pitted

30ml/2 tbsp chopped hazelnuts

icing (confectioners') sugar, for dusting

cream, to serve

1 Preheat the oven to 190°C/375°F/Gas 5. Beat 15g/½oz/1 tbsp of the butter with the sugar and egg yolks in a mixing bowl until light and fluffy. Beat in the lemon rind, grated nutmeg and ricotta cheese.

2 Melt the remaining butter in a small pan. Place a sheet of filo on a clean dish towel and brush it generously with melted butter. Place a second sheet on top and repeat the process. Continue until all the sheets of filo have been used, reserving some of the butter.

3 Sprinkle the crushed ratafias over the top of the filo, leaving a 5cm/2in border all round. Spoon the ricotta mixture over the ratafia biscuits, spread it lightly to cover, then sprinkle over the cherries.

4 Fold in the filo pastry border on all four sides, then using the dish towel to help you, roll up the strudel, Swiss-roll (jelly-roll) style, beginning from one of the long sides of the pastry and rolling away from you. Grease a large baking sheet with a little of the remaining melted butter.

5 Place the strudel, seam side down, on the baking sheet, brush with the remaining melted butter, and sprinkle the hazelnuts over the surface.

6 Bake for 35–40 minutes, or until golden and crisp. Dust with icing sugar and serve with cream.

Nutritional information per portion: Energy 317kcal/1326kJ; Protein 6.5g; Carbohydrate 34.2g, of which sugars 22.9g; Fat 18.1g, of which saturates 9.1g; Cholesterol 109mg; Calcium 54mg; Fibre 1.2g; Sodium 93mg.

Mango and amaretti strudel

Fresh mango and crushed amaretti wrapped in wafer-thin filo pastry make a special treat. It looks remarkably impressive, but takes very little time to assemble and bake.

SERVES 4

1 large mango
grated rind of 1 lemon
2 amaretti
25g/1oz/3 tbsp demerara
   (raw) sugar
60ml/4 tbsp wholemeal
   (whole-wheat) breadcrumbs
2 sheets of filo pastry, each measuring
   48 x 28cm/19 x 11in, thawed if frozen
25g/1oz/2 tbsp butter or 20g/³⁄₄oz/4 tsp
   soft margarine, melted
15ml/1 tbsp chopped almonds
icing (confectioners') sugar, for dusting

1 Preheat the oven to 190°C/375°F/Gas 5. Lightly grease a baking sheet. Cut the flesh from the mango and chop it into small cubes. Place in a bowl and sprinkle with the grated lemon rind. Crush the amaretti busicuits and mix them with the sugar and breadcrumbs.

2 Lay one sheet of filo pastry on a flat surface and brush with a quarter of the melted butter or margarine. Top with the second sheet, brush with one-third of the remaining butter, then fold both sheets over, if necessary, to make a rectangle measuring 28 x 24cm/11 x 9¹⁄₂in. Brush with half the remaining butter.

3 Sprinkle the filo with the amaretti mixture, leaving a border on each long side. Arrange the mango over the top. Roll up the filo from one long side, Swiss-roll (jelly-roll) fashion.

4 Lift the strudel on to the baking sheet, seam-side down. Brush with the remaining melted fat and sprinkle with the chopped almonds. Bake for 20–25 minutes until golden brown, then transfer to a board. Dust with the icing sugar, slice diagonally and serve warm.

Nutritional information per portion: Energy 190kcal/803kJ; Protein 3.4g; Carbohydrate 35.2g, of which sugars 13.2g; Fat 4.9g, of which saturates 0.2g; Cholesterol 0mg; Calcium 48mg; Fibre 1.7g; Sodium 164mg.

Moroccan serpent cake

This is perhaps the most famous of all Moroccan pastries, filled with lightly fragrant almond paste, and dusted with icing sugar and cinnamon.

SERVES 8

8 sheets of filo pastry, thawed
     if frozen
50g/2oz/¼ cup butter, melted
1 egg, beaten
5ml/1 tsp ground cinnamon
icing (confectioners') sugar, for dusting

FOR THE ALMOND PASTE
about 50g/2oz/¼ cup butter, melted
225g/8oz/2⅔ cups ground almonds
2.5ml/½ tsp almond extract
50g/2oz/½ cup icing
     (confectioners') sugar
1 egg yolk, beaten
15ml/1 tbsp rose water or orange
     flower water

1 To make the almond paste, mix the melted butter in a bowl with the ground almonds and almond extract. Add the sugar, egg yolk and rose or orange water, mix well and knead until pliable. Chill for 10 minutes.

2 Break the paste into ten even-sized balls and, with your hands, roll them into 10cm/4in sausages. Chill again. Preheat the oven to 180°C/350°F/Gas 4.

3 Overlap two sheets of filo to form a rectangle 18 x 56cm/7 x 22in. Secure the edges with butter, then brush butter all over. Cover with two more sheets and brush them with butter. Place five almond paste sausages along the lower edge of the filo sheet and roll up tightly, tucking in the ends. Repeat to make two rolls. Shape the first into a loose coil. Transfer to a baking sheet brushed with butter. Attach the second and continue coiling into a snake. Tuck the end under.

4 Beat the egg with half the cinnamon. Brush over the pastry. Bake for 25 minutes. Invert the snake on to another baking sheet. Bake for 5–10 minutes more. Transfer to a plate and dust with icing sugar and the remaining cinnamon.

Nutritional information per portion: Energy 162Kcal/675kJ; Protein 13.1g; Carbohydrate 8.5g, of which sugars 7g; Fat 8.6g, of which saturates 3.8g; Cholesterol 44mg; Calcium 42mg; Fibre 3g; Sodium 55mg.

Chocolate, date and almond filo coil

Experience the allure of the Middle East with this delectable dessert. Crisp filo pastry conceals a chocolate and rose water filling studded with dates and almonds.

SERVES 6

275g/10oz thawed filo pastry
50g/2oz/¼ cup butter, melted
icing (confectioners') sugar, unsweetened
    cocoa powder and ground cinnamon,
      for dusting

FOR THE FILLING

75g/3oz/6 tbsp butter
115g/4oz dark (bittersweet) chocolate,
    broken into pieces
115g/4oz/1⅓ cup ground almonds
115g/4oz/⅔ cup chopped dates
75g/3oz/¾ cup icing (confectioners') sugar
10ml/2 tsp rose water
2.5ml/½ tsp ground cinnamon

1 Preheat the oven to 180°C/350°F/Gas 4. Grease a 22cm/8½in round cake tin (pan). To make the filling, melt the butter with the chocolate in a heatproof bowl set over a pan of barely simmering water, then remove from the heat and stir in the remaining ingredients to make a thick paste. Leave to cool.

2 Lay one sheet of filo on a clean, flat surface. Brush with melted butter, then lay a second sheet on top and brush with more butter.

3 Roll a handful of the chocolate and almond mixture into a long sausage shape and place along one long edge of the layered filo. Roll up the pastry tightly around the filling to make a roll.

4 Fit the filo roll in the cake tin, so that it sits snugly against the outer edge. Make more filo rolls in the same way, adding them to the tin from the outside towards the centre, until the coil fills it.

5 Brush the coil with the remaining melted butter. Bake for 30–35 minutes until the pastry is golden and crisp. Transfer to a serving plate. Serve warm, dusted with icing sugar, cocoa powder and cinnamon.

COOK'S TIP
Filo pastry dries out quickly, so remove one sheet at a time from the pile and cover the rest with a damp dish towel.

Nutritional information per portion: Energy 543kcal/2267kJ; Protein 8.2g; Carbohydrate 55.4g, of which sugars 32.4g; Fat 33.6g, of which saturates 15g; Cholesterol 46mg; Calcium 108mg; Fibre 3.2g; Sodium 133mg.

Filo-topped apple pie

Scrunched up filo pastry, brushed with a little melted butter, is the very easiest way to top a pie. A light dusting of icing sugar gives it an attractive finish.

SERVES 6

900g/2lb cooking apples
75g/3oz/6 tbsp caster (superfine) sugar
grated rind of 1 lemon
15ml/1 tbsp lemon juice
75g/3oz/½ cup sultanas (golden raisins)
2.5ml/½ tsp ground cinnamon
4 large sheets of filo pastry, thawed
**   if frozen**
25g/1oz/2 tbsp butter, melted
icing (confectioners') sugar, for dusting
custard, to serve

1 Peel, core and dice the apples. Place them in a pan with the caster sugar and lemon rind. Drizzle the lemon juice over. Bring to the boil, stir well, then cook for 5 minutes or until the apples are soft. Stir in the sultanas and cinnamon.

2 Pour the mixture into a 1.2 litre/2 pint/5 cup pie dish and level the top with a spoon. Leave to cool.

3 Preheat the oven to 180°C/350°F/Gas 4. Place a pie funnel in the centre of the fruit to allow steam to escape. Brush each sheet of filo with a little melted butter. Scrunch up the sheets loosely and place on the fruit to cover it.

4 Bake for 20–30 minutes until the filo is golden. Dust the pie with icing sugar. Serve with custard, if you like.

Nutritional information per portion: Energy 198kcal/843kJ; Protein 2.2g; Carbohydrate 44.8g, of which sugars 35.3g; Fat 2.4g, of which saturates 0.6g; Cholesterol 0mg; Calcium 38mg; Fibre 3g; Sodium 44mg.

Fresh fig filo tart

Desserts don't come much easier than this – fresh figs in crisp filo pastry, with a creamy almond batter. The tart tastes wonderful served with cream or yogurt.

SERVES 6–8

5 sheets of filo pastry, each measuring 35 x 25cm/14 x 10in, thawed if frozen

25g/1oz/2 tbsp butter, melted

6 fresh figs, cut into wedges

75g/3oz/³⁄₄ cup plain (all-purpose) flour

75g/3oz/6 tbsp caster (superfine) sugar

4 eggs

450ml/³⁄₄ pint/scant 2 cups creamy milk

2.5ml/¹⁄₂ tsp almond extract

15ml/1 tbsp icing (confectioners') sugar, for dusting

whipped cream or Greek (US strained plain) yogurt, to serve

1 Preheat the oven to 190°C/375°F/Gas 5. Grease a 25 x 16cm/10 x 6¹⁄₄in baking tin (pan) with butter. Brush each filo sheet in turn with melted butter and use to line the prepared tin. Trim the excess pastry, leaving a little overhanging the edge. Arrange the figs over the base of the tart.

2 Sift the flour into a bowl and stir in the caster sugar. Add the eggs and a little milk and whisk until smooth.

3 Gradually whisk in the remaining milk and the almond extract. Pour the batter over the figs.

4 Bake for 1 hour or until the batter has set and is golden. Remove the tart from the oven and allow it to cool in the tin on a wire rack for 10 minutes.

5 Dust with the icing sugar and serve with whipped cream or Greek yogurt.

Nutritional information per portion: Energy 304kcal/1286kJ; Protein 9.9g; Carbohydrate 49.2g, of which sugars 30.2g; Fat 9.1g, of which saturates 4.1g; Cholesterol 140mg; Calcium 203mg; Fibre 2.3g; Sodium 118mg.

The art of pastry making

Making pastry is, as the old adage goes, as 'easy as pie', so long as you follow a few simple rules. Any good pastry cook knows that practice really does make perfect. You don't need fancy equipment: a bowl, a set of scales or measuring cups and a rolling pin are perfectly adequate, plus one or two pie plates or dishes in sizes to suit your style of cooking. As you become more proficient and discover how creative making pastry can be, you may want to expand your range of utensils, but remember, cool, competent hands are the cook's most valuable assets.

Pastry making equipment

Using the right baking equipment simplifies and enhances the art of pastry making. Few specialist items are essential but, as with all things, having the correct tool for the job makes it considerably easier.

BASIC EQUIPMENT

Most of the basic items you will probably already possess, such as accurate weighing scales or calibrated measuring cups and jug (pitcher), a good-size mixing bowl, measuring spoons, a fine sieve (strainer) or sifter, heavy pans for making choux or hot water crust pastry, and a few sharp knives.

Among the specialist equipment available, there is much that you may find very handy, particularly as you start to make more elaborate dishes.

Timers

You may already have a timer on your stove; otherwise a timer with a rotating dial registering time between one and 60 minutes is ideal.

Pastry boards

These should be as large as you can accommodate and completely flat and smooth. Marble is considered the most suitable material for pastry making as it is cool to the touch. Nowadays, however, Formica work surfaces have a very smooth finish. These are a good alternative.

Baking sheets

Heavy baking sheets and trays are used as a base for small individual tartlets and choux pastries, as well as for large 'free-form' pies not cooked in tins (pans), such as jalousies and vol-au-vents. They are also handy as trays for quiches and flans to help lift them in and out of the oven. When choosing one, make sure the metal is thick enough so that it won't develop hot spots or buckle and twist in the oven at high temperatures; if it does, liquid fillings in open pies may tip out.

Rolling pins

A thick, heavy, wooden rolling pin is best for rolling out pastry. You may choose one without handles made from a single piece of wood or one with a fixed handle at either end. You can also get 'cool' rolling pins. Some of these are made from marble, while others are hollow and designed to be filled with chilled water. These have no advantage over the traditional wooden pin as long as you chill your pastry thoroughly before starting to roll it out on a lightly floured surface.

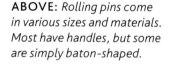

ABOVE: *Rolling pins come in various sizes and materials. Most have handles, but some are simply baton-shaped.*

ABOVE: *Balloon whisk*

Whisks

An electric whisk or hand-held balloon whisk is useful for whisking sauces, fillings and toppings.

Baking beans

To ensure pastry cases cook through and become crisp, they are usually lined with foil or baking parchment and weighed down with baking beans, and baked blind. You can buy ceramic or aluminium beans that last for ever in any good cook shop, but dried beans or pulses are a very good alternative.

Pastry brush

An essential item for brushing egg or glazes on pastry. The best are made from natural bristles set in a wooden handle (although nylon bristles are considered more hygienic). Rinse brushes that have been used for egg glazing in cold water before washing in warm soapy water.

Pastry wheel

This makes cutting pastry quick and easy. It has a zig-zag edge that patterns the pastry.

Wire rack

Used for cooling pastries. It allows air to circulate, preventing trapped warmth turning to moisture, and making the pastry base soggy.

Lattice cutter

This easy-to-use tool has a series of wheels that cut a pattern of broken lines on rolled-out pastry. You gently ease the pastry open, starting from the middle and working your way outwards to form a net-like lattice.

Palette knife

This wide, round-bladed metal spatula is used for mixing pastry dough and for smoothing fillings in flans and tartlets. It is also useful for removing small or delicate items from their tins (pans).

Piping nozzles and bags

Plain or fluted nozzles are used in a piping (pastry) bag to pipe cream and add meringue toppings to pies. Large plain ones, about 1cm/½in in diameter, are ideal for piping choux pastries and filling them after baking.

Pie funnels

When making a pie with a lid, a ceramic pie funnel can be used. The hollow funnel pokes up through the lid like a chimney, letting out steam, which might otherwise make the pastry soggy and prevent it from rising properly. The shoulders of the funnel give further support to the pastry. Made of porcelain, pie funnels usually have semi-circular holes cut out of the base so the juices of the filling can mingle freely.

RIGHT: Pie funnel with small holes cut out of its base to allow sauces to mix.

Pastry blender

This is used to cut fat into flour in the same way as you would rub it in with your fingers.

Pastry prickers

Also known as dockers, these consist of a large number of spikes set in a roller, or six or more prongs at the end of a wooden handle. Used to make tiny holes in the bases of tarts and flans before baking, they're handy if you've got a lot of pastry to prick.

Pastry cutters

Available in a wide range of sizes and shapes, these are ideal for small pastries and decorating the tops of larger ones.

Cornet moulds

These metal cones, just over 10cm/4in long, are used to shape pastry horns. Pastry is wrapped around, then baked.

Cannoli forms

These 10cm/4in metal cylinders are used to shape and bake pastry.

PIE DISHES, TINS AND MOULDS

Pie dishes can be oval, round, square or rectangular and made from earthenware, glass or metal. The rim is wide and flat, so that the pastry crust can be attached easily.

Springform tins are round and straight-sided, with a removable base and side clip to release the pie. They are very useful for deep pies.

ABOVE: Sets of graduated fluted and plain pastry cutters, star pastry cutter, cannoli forms and cornet moulds.

Raised pie moulds are hinged on one side, to simplify removing raised meat and game pies. They vary in size and shape. They often have patterned sides, to give pies an embossed look.

Wooden pie moulds are cylinders, used to shape raised pies.

Pie plates have a wide rim and are usually made of metal to conduct the heat to the pastry. They are used to bake shallow, lidded pies or open tarts with decorated edges.

FLAN TINS AND RINGS

Metal flan tins (pans) come in all shapes and sizes. The commonest is the fluted round. The best flan tins have loose bases, which make turning out fragile tarts simple. Fluted sides are easy to line and add strength to the pastry cases.

Flan rings come without bases to be set directly on a baking sheet.

Tranche tins are long rectangular tins with fluted edges.

Porcelain flan dishes have unglazed bases. They are best used as a serving dish.

Tartlet tins come in many shapes and sizes.

Making pastry

This section contains recipes for classic shortcrust and its variations; flaky, rough puff and puff pastries; choux; and strudel. There are also traditional pastries and others with a more modern twist, such as olive oil pastry.

SHORTCRUST PASTRY

Perfect shortcrust needs a cool light hand, as over-handling will develop the gluten, making it heavy and hard. The following makes enough for a 25cm/ 10in flan tin (pan) or ten 7.5cm/3in tartlet tins (muffin pans).

MAKES ABOUT 375G/13OZ

225g/8oz/2 cups plain (all-purpose) flour
pinch of salt
115g/4oz/¹/₂ cup chilled butter, diced, or half
   butter/half lard or white vegetable fat
45–60ml/3–4 tbsp chilled water

1 Sift the flour and salt into a mixing bowl. Cut in the fat using a pastry blender or use your fingertips. Shake the bowl a little to bring any large pieces of fat to the top. Blend until it resembles fine breadcrumbs.

2 Sprinkle 45ml/3 tbsp of the water evenly over the mixture and mix lightly with a round-bladed knife or fork until the dough comes together. Add a little more water if the mixture is still too dry; it should just begin to hold together.

3 Using one hand, gather the dough together and press to form a ball. Incorporate any loose pieces of the rubbed-in mixture. Knead on a lightly floured surface for a few seconds until smooth.

4 Wrap the dough in clear film (plastic wrap), and chill for about 30 minutes, or until it is firm but not too stiff to roll out on a lightly floured surface. The shortcrust pastry is now ready to use.

RICH SHORTCRUST PASTRY

Also known as pâte brisée, this is a richer version of shortcrust pastry which has a higher proportion of fat. It is usually made with an egg yolk and chilled water, but a whole egg may be used. This quantity makes enough for a 25cm/10in flan tin (pan) or ten 7.5cm/3in tartlet tins (muffin pans).

MAKES ABOUT 400G/14OZ

225g/8oz/2 cups plain (all-purpose) flour
pinch of salt
150g/5oz/10 tbsp chilled butter, diced
1 egg yolk
30ml/2 tbsp chilled water

1 Sift the flour and salt into a large mixing bowl, getting as much air in as possible. Rub or cut the butter into the flour until the mixture resembles fine breadcrumbs.

2 Mix the egg yolk and water together in a bowl or jug. Sprinkle over the dry ingredients and mix in lightly to form a soft dough.

3 Gather the dough together into a ball. Knead on a lightly floured work surface until it is smooth. Wrap the pastry in clear film (plastic wrap) and chill in the refrigerator for 30 minutes before using.

MAKING SHORTCRUST PASTRY IN A FOOD PROCESSOR

This method of making pastry is good for rich shortcrust, especially where the higher proportion of fat and sugar may make it harder to handle. If you have hot hands, or the weather is warm, the food processor ensures that the dough stays cool.

1 Put the dry ingredients into the food processor. Process for 4–5 seconds. Scatter the fat, then process for 10–12 seconds only, or until the mixture resembles fine breadcrumbs.

2 Sprinkle the water or other liquid (such as egg and water) over the flour. Use the pulse button to process until it starts to hold together. Pinch together with your thumb and finger. If the dough is too dry and crumbly, add a little more water and process for just 1–2 seconds more. Do not allow the pastry to form a ball.

3 Remove the mixture from the food processor and form into a ball. Lightly knead the pastry on a floured surface for just a few seconds until smooth, then wrap in clear film (plastic wrap) and chill for 30 minutes.

Steps to shortcrust success

• It is best to make shortcrust pastry as and when you need it.
• If you need a large amount, make in batches.

• Sift flour before using to remove lumps and incorporate air.
• Store flour in a cool, dry place, preferably in an airtight container. Keep an eye on the use-by date.
• Use fat that is cool but not hard.
• The fat may be all butter – which makes the best-flavoured pastry – or a combination of butter and white vegetable fat. This makes pastry with a much shorter (crumblier) texture.
• Use chilled water when mixing the rubbed-in fat and flour together, so that it will not soften or melt the fat.
• Always sprinkle water evenly over the rubbed-in mixture, then toss with a fork to moisten, before gathering the mixture into a ball.
• Take care when adding water. If the pastry is too wet, it will be sticky to handle and tough when cooked; if too dry, it will crumble and be difficult to roll out. Always add the minimum amount suggested, then add a little more as necessary until the correct consistency is met.

• When kneading pastry, use your fingertips or the heel of your hand.
• If using the heel of your hand, knead lightly and for a few seconds only before wrapping and chilling.
• Roll out pastry in short gentle strokes. Avoid stretching it.
• Always chill shortcrust pastry before rolling, even if only for a short time, and again after rolling and before baking. This allows the gluten to 'relax' and helps prevent the pastry from shrinking when it is cooked.
• After chilling the pastry, if your kitchen is fairly cool and airy, leave the pastry at room temperature for 10 minutes before rolling out. On a warm day, leave for 2 minutes to stop the pastry becoming too warm.

Using ready-made shortcrust

Although there is nothing quite as satisfying as making your own pastry at home, good quality, ready-made shortcrust pastry is available.
• It can be bought either frozen in blocks, 'fresh' in the chilled cabinet of the supermarket or as a ready-rolled sheet. Simply unroll and use.
• Usually, brands of ready-made shortcrust pastry are available in two sizes: the 375g/13oz packet is roughly equivalent to home-made shortcrust or rich shortcrust pastry made with 225g/8oz/2 cups flour; a 450g/1lb packet is the equivalent of shortcrust pastry made with 275g/10oz/2½ cups flour.
• Bought shortcrust should be left at room temperature for 20 minutes before rolling or it will crack.

FRENCH FLAN PASTRY

This pastry is traditionally used for lining flan tins (pans) and tartlet cases. It is always made with all butter to ensure a good flavour. It has a high proportion of fat, so it needs to be chilled before use. Care must be taken when rolling out. After making, the pastry is kneaded by a process known as fresage. The following makes enough for a 25cm/10in flan tin or ten 7.5cm/3in tartlet tins (muffin pans).

MAKES ABOUT 300G/11OZ

200g/7oz/1³/₄ cups plain
   (all-purpose) flour
1.5ml/¹/₄ tsp salt
115g/4oz/¹/₂ cup chilled butter, diced
1 egg yolk
1.5ml/¹/₄ tsp lemon juice
30–45ml/2–3 tbsp chilled water

1 Sift the plain flour and salt into a mixing bowl. Rub or cut in the butter until the resulting mixture resembles fine breadcrumbs.

2 Whisk the egg yolk, lemon juice and 30ml/2 tbsp of the water together in a bowl. Sprinkle over the dry ingredients. Stir in carefully with a fork to mix.

3 Shape the moistened ingredients into a ball with your hand. Add the remaining water if too dry.

4 With the heel of your hand, lightly knead the dough for 1 minute on a lightly floured surface, pushing small portions of dough away from you and smearing them on the surface until the dough is smooth and pliable.

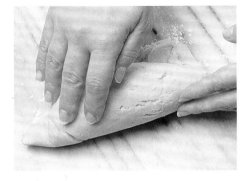

5 Shape the dough into a ball, then flatten into a round. Wrap in clear film (plastic wrap) and chill for an hour.

French flan pastry variations

These simple recipes add texture and flavour and can be used for savoury or sweet dishes.

Light nut crust Nuts such as walnuts go particularly well with savoury cheese quiches and flans. Use chopped toasted almonds or hazelnuts in fruit flans. Stir in 40g/11/2oz/1/3 cup finely chopped nuts to the basic French flan flour mixture before adding any liquid.

Rich flan pastry This pastry has an extra egg yolk and more butter. It is ideal for lining larger flan and tranche tins (pans). Use 200g/7oz/ 13/4 cups plain (all-purpose) flour, 2.5ml/1/2 tsp salt, 150g/5oz/10 tbsp chilled butter, diced, 2 egg yolks and 15–30ml/1–2 tbsp water.

Sweet flan pastry This sweetened pastry is perfect for fruit-, nut- or frangipane-filled tartlets. To make, sift 200g/7oz/13/4 cups plain (all-purpose) flour with a pinch of salt and add 15g/1/2oz/1 tbsp caster (superfine) sugar. Rub or cut in 150g/5oz/10 tbsp butter and add 2 egg yolks mixed with 15–30ml/ 1–2 tbsp water and 2.5ml/1/2 tsp vanilla extract.

PÂTE SUCRÉE

This rich and crisp sweet pastry is used mainly for making flan and tartlet cases, as it holds its shape well during cooking. It has a high proportion of sugar, so is much softer than shortcrust and needs to be chilled for 1 hour before using. It is made with icing (confectioners') sugar. You can use caster (superfine) sugar too. It is kneaded using the heel of the hand. Mix the pastry in a bowl or on a marble slab or other cold surface. This is enough for a 23cm/9in flan tin (pan) or eight 7.5cm/3in tartlet tins (muffin pans).

MAKES ABOUT 275G/10OZ

150g/5oz/1¼ cups plain (all-purpose) flour
pinch of salt
75g/3oz/6 tbsp chilled butter, diced
25g/1oz/¼ cup icing (confectioners')
   sugar, sifted
2 egg yolks

1 Sift the flour and salt together into a mound on a cold work surface. Make a well in the centre and put in the butter and sugar. Place the yolks on top.

2 Using a pecking action with your fingertips, work the butter, yolks and sugar together. Pull in a little of the surrounding flour to prevent the mixture from becoming too sticky.

3 When the mixture begins to form a smooth paste, pull in more of the flour to make a rough dough, gradually working in all the flour. Work quickly, using just your fingertips, so that the butter does not become oily. If the pastry is slightly crumbly at this stage, you can remedy this by working in a small amount of egg white.

4 Lightly knead the dough with just the heel of your hand for 1 minute, pushing small portions of dough away from you and smearing them on the surface until smooth and pliable.

5 Shape the dough into a ball, then flatten slightly into a flat round – this makes it easier when you start rolling it out. Wrap in cling film (plastic wrap) to prevent the pastry from drying out and chill in a refrigerator for about 1 hour before using.

Top tips for making and baking pâte sucrée
• Allow at least 1 hour for the pastry to chill in the refrigerator.
• If the pastry has been chilled for more than 1 hour, allow it to soften at room temperature for about 10 minutes before using, or it may crack when you roll it out.

• If your pâte sucrée is difficult to handle, roll it between sheets of clear film (plastic wrap) or press it into the tin with your fingers.

• Although pâte sucrée is slightly trickier to handle, it is much easier to patch; just press any small tears together with your fingers.
• Sweet pastry pies should be taken out of the oven as soon as they are golden brown and crisp, or they will burn very quickly.

WHOLEMEAL PASTRY

Pastry made with all wholemeal flour can be heavy in both taste and texture. A mixture of flours together with a little fat gives lighter results. This is enough for a 25cm/10in flan tin (pan).

MAKES ABOUT 400G/14OZ

115g/4oz/1 cup wholemeal
    (whole-wheat) flour
115g/4oz/1 cup plain
    (all-purpose) flour
pinch of salt
pinch of mustard powder
115g/4oz/$^{1}/_{2}$cup chilled butter, diced
25g/1oz/2 tbsp white vegetable
    fat or lard
1 egg yolk
30ml/2 tbsp chilled water

1 Sift the flours, salt and mustard powder into a mixing bowl. Rub or cut in the butter and fat until the mixture resembles breadcrumbs. Mix the egg yolk with the water and sprinkle over the dry ingredients. Mix to a dough.

2 Knead on a lightly floured work surface for a few seconds until smooth. Wrap the dough in clear film (plastic wrap) and chill for about 20 minutes.

OLIVE OIL PASTRY

Choose a well-flavoured olive oil for this crisp pastry. It is best used for savoury tarts and complements vegetable fillings especially well. This quantity is enough for a 23cm/9in flan tin (pan).

MAKES ABOUT 275G/10OZ

225g/8oz/2 cups plain
    (all-purpose) flour
pinch of salt
1 egg
60ml/4 tbsp olive oil
30ml/2 tbsp lukewarm water

1 Sift the flour and salt into a bowl. In a separate bowl, use a fork to whisk the egg, olive oil and water together.

2 Make a well in the centre of the flour and salt, add the egg mixture and stir with a fork, gradually incorporating the surrounding flour until all the liquid has been worked in and a dough is formed.

3 Knead on a lightly floured surface for a few seconds until smooth, then cover with a damp dish towel and leave to rest for 30 minutes before using. Knead only until smooth and do not overwork, or the pastry will be tough.

SUET PASTRY

This pastry can be used for both sweet and savoury steamed puddings and has a light, spongy texture. It is wonderfully easy to make as there is no rubbing-in. Because suet is a heavy fat, self-raising (self-rising) flour is always used for this recipe. Lower-fat or vegetarian suet may also be used. This quantity is enough for a 1.75 litre/ 3 pint/7$^{1}/_{2}$ cup ovenproof bowl.

MAKES ABOUT 500G/1$^{1}/_{4}$LB

275g/10oz/2$^{1}/_{2}$ cups self-raising
    (self-rising) flour
2.5ml/$^{1}/_{2}$ tsp salt
150g/5oz/1 cup shredded suet
    (US chilled, grated shortening)
175ml/6fl oz/$^{3}/_{4}$ cup chilled water

1 Sift the flour and salt into a large mixing bowl.

2 Stir in the shredded suet, followed by most of the chilled water and mix with a fork to form a soft dough.

3 Knead on a lightly floured work surface for a few seconds until smooth. Roll out the suet pastry and use straight away. Don't be tempted to roll the pastry too thinly or it will break up. It needs to be about 1cm/$^{1}/_{2}$in thick.

POTATO PASTRY

This substantial pastry has a crumbly texture when baked. It's rolled out more thickly than shortcrust pastry and is ideal as a topping for meat or other savoury pies. This makes enough for a 25cm/10in pie crust.

MAKES ABOUT 450G/1LB

115g/4oz floury potatoes, diced
225g/8oz/2 cups plain
    (all-purpose) flour
115g/4oz/1/2 cup chilled butter, diced
1/2 beaten egg
10ml/2 tsp chilled water

1 Cook the diced potatoes in a pan of salted boiling water until tender. Drain well and mash until smooth.

2 Sift the flour into a mixing bowl. Rub or cut in the butter until the mixture resembles breadcrumbs.

3 Mix together the beaten egg and water in a mixing bowl, and stir into the mashed potato. Add to the flour mixture and stir with a round-bladed knife to mix to a smooth, pliable dough. Wrap the dough in clear film (plastic wrap) and chill for about 30 minutes in the refrigerator before using.

CORNMEAL PASTRY

This pastry can be used in savoury or sweet dishes. It is particularly good in fruit pies, especially apple or pear. The yellow cornmeal gives the pastry an attractive colour. Use the following in a 25cm/10in flan tin (pan).

MAKES ABOUT 350G/12OZ

115g/4oz/1 cup plain
    (all-purpose) flour
75g/3oz/3/4 cup fine yellow cornmeal
5ml/1 tsp salt
5ml/1 tsp soft dark brown sugar
90g/31/2oz/7 tbsp chilled butter, diced
1 egg yolk
30ml/2 tbsp chilled water

1 Sift the flour with the cornmeal and salt into a large mixing bowl. Stir in the sugar. Rub or cut in the butter until the mixture resembles fine breadcrumbs.

2 Mix the egg yolk with the chilled water, add to the dry ingredients and mix to a dough, adding a little more water if needed. Gather the dough into a ball, then flatten slightly into a flat round, to make it easier to roll out. Wrap in clear film (plastic wrap) and chill for 30–40 minutes before using.

CREAM CHEESE PASTRY

This moist, flaky pastry is very easy to make and use, provided it is well chilled before being rolled out. It is perfect for tiny tartlets with rich fillings and also makes a wonderful shoofly pie. This quantity is enough for a 25cm/10in flan tin (pan) or ten 5–7.5cm/2–3in tartlet tins (muffin pans).

MAKES ABOUT 375G/13OZ

150g/5oz/11/4 cups plain (all-purpose) flour
pinch of salt
5ml/1 tsp caster (superfine) sugar
115g/4oz/1/2 cup full-fat cream cheese,
    at room temperature
115g/4oz/1/2 cup butter, at room
    temperature, diced

1 Sift the flour, salt and caster sugar into a mixing bowl. Add the cream cheese and diced butter to the bowl.

2 Mix the butter and cream cheese into the flour, using the back of a fork, to make a soft, smooth dough. Then form the dough into a smooth ball and flatten slightly to make rolling out easier. Wrap the dough in clear film (plastic wrap) and chill for about 1 hour in the refrigerator before using.

CHOCOLATE PASTRY

This rich, dark pastry is ideal for tarts or flans with creamy fillings or fruit such as pears or mixed soft summer berries. This quantity is enough to line a 23cm/9in flan tin (pan).

MAKES ABOUT 300G/11OZ

115g/4oz/1 cup plain (all-purpose) flour
25g/1oz/¹/₄ cup icing
   (confectioners') sugar
25g/1oz/¹/₄ cup unsweetened
   cocoa powder
75g/3oz/6 tbsp chilled butter, diced
2 eggs
2.5ml/¹/₂ tsp vanilla extract

1 Sift the flour, icing sugar and cocoa powder into a mixing bowl. Rub or cut in the butter until the mixture resembles fine breadcrumbs.

2 Mix the eggs with the vanilla extract in a small bowl. Add to the dry ingredients and mix to a dough with a round-bladed knife.

3 Knead the dough on a lightly floured surface until smooth. Form into a ball, then wrap in clear film (plastic wrap) and chill for 20 minutes in the refrigerator before using.

ALMOND PASTRY

This dough resembles pâte sucrée and is especially good with fruits such as apples and cherries. The addition of ground almonds makes it fairly soft to handle, so it must be well chilled before using. This quantity is sufficient to line a 23cm/9in flan tin (pan).

MAKES ABOUT 350G/12OZ

150g/5oz/1¹/₄ cups plain
   (all-purpose) flour
pinch of salt
25g/1oz/2 tbsp caster (superfine) sugar
50g/2oz/¹/₂ cup ground almonds
90g/3¹/₂oz/7 tbsp chilled butter, diced
1 egg
1–2 drops almond extract

1 Sift the plain flour and salt into a large mixing bowl. Stir in the caster sugar and ground almonds. Rub or cut in the butter until the mixture resembles fine breadcrumbs.

2 Beat the egg and almond extract together in a small bowl. Stir into the dry ingredients to make a soft dough. Wrap in clear film (plastic wrap) and chill for 40 minutes in the refrigerator until firm, before using.

SPICED ORANGE PASTRY

This spicy pastry works well with winter fruit fillings. The following is enough to line a 23cm/9in flan tin (pan).

MAKES ABOUT 275G/10OZ

175g/6oz/1¹/₂ cups plain
   (all-purpose) flour
pinch of salt
75g/3oz/6 tbsp chilled butter, diced
4 green cardamom pods
pinch of ground cloves
finely grated rind of 1 orange
25g/1oz/2 tbsp caster (superfine) sugar
2 egg yolks
10ml/2 tsp fresh orange juice

1 Sift the flour and salt into a large mixing bowl. Rub or cut in the butter until the mixture resembles fine breadcrumbs.

2 Using a pestle and mortar, crush the black seeds from the cardamom pods to a powder. Stir them into the flour with the cloves, orange rind and sugar.

3 Mix the egg yolks with the orange juice. Add to the bowl and mix to a dough. Knead until smooth, then wrap and chill for 40 minutes before using.

PUFF PASTRY

Rich and light, puff pastry contains an equal amount of butter to flour. Air is trapped between the layers of dough and this, together with the steam created as the water heats, makes the pastry rise up when baked.

It is essential that everything be kept cold. The water should be chilled and the butter cold, but not so cold that it will break up and tear the dough; before commencing let the butter stand at room temperature for 10 minutes. Never make puff pastry on a hot day. This is enough for two single-crusts in 1.5 litre/2^1/$_2$ pint/6^1/$_4$ cup pie dishes or fifteen 8.5cm/3^1/$_2$ in vol-au-vents.

MAKES ABOUT 500G/1¼LB

**225g/8oz/2 cups strong
 white bread flour
pinch of salt
225g/8oz/1 cup chilled butter
15ml/1 tbsp lemon juice
150ml/^{1}/$_4$ pint/^{2}/$_3$ cup chilled water**

1 Sift the flour and salt into a bowl. Rub 25g/1oz/2 tbsp of the butter into the flour until it resembles fine breadcrumbs. Place the remaining butter between two sheets of clear film (plastic wrap). Beat it out into a 15cm/6in flat square.

2 Make a well in the centre of the dry ingredients. Stir the lemon juice into the water and add most of it to the bowl. Mix with a round-bladed knife, adding a little more water if necessary to make a soft, but not sticky, dough.

3 Using a floured rolling pin, roll out the dough on a lightly floured surface to a 25cm/10in square. The dough may look a little lumpy at this stage, but don't knead it. Place the butter diagonally in the centre of the dough, so that it looks like a diamond. Bring each corner of the dough to the centre of the butter to enclose it completely.

4 Roll out the dough to a 40 x 15cm/ 16 x 6in rectangle. Fold the lower third of the pastry over the centre third, and the top third of the pastry down over that. Seal the edges with the rolling pin. Brush off excess flour with a dry pastry brush. Wrap the pastry in film and chill for 30 minutes.

5 Roll out the pastry to the same size again, with the sealed edges at the top and bottom. Fold up and chill as before. Repeat the rolling, folding and chilling process five more times. After this, the pastry is ready to be used.

Puff pastry perfection

• Strong white bread flour is often used to make puff pastry as it contains extra gluten to strengthen the dough. However, plain (all-purpose) flour will give good results too. You can use a mixture of the two.

• Lemon juice softens the gluten in the flour and makes the dough supple. Measure it carefully; too much will make the pastry difficult to handle.

• When chilling the pastry between rollings, do not leave for longer than 30 minutes or it may break up when rolling out. If you do chill it for longer, leave it at room temperature for 10 minutes to soften before re-rolling.

• Mark the pastry each time you roll it out by pressing it with the appropriate number of fingertips.

• Allow the pastry to stand for 15 minutes at room temperature before rolling it out for use.

• Always roll out puff pastry at least 5mm/^{1}/$_4$in thick. If it is too thin, it won't rise sufficiently.

• If you are not going to use the pastry straightaway, wrap it in clear film (plastic wrap), then in foil. It will keep in the refrigerator for up to three days.

SHORT-CUT PUFF PASTRY

This quick version of puff pastry forms light flaky layers. It uses a mixture of half butter, for flavour, and half white vegetable fat or lard, to give it a crisper texture as compensation for the reduced rolling-out and resting time. It is crucial that all the ingredients are kept cold, so mix the initial dough together quickly. This is enough for two single-crusts in 1.5 litre/2½ pint/6¼ cup pie dishes.

MAKES ABOUT 500G/1¼LB

115g/4oz/½ cup butter
115g/4oz/½ cup white vegetable fat/lard
225g/8oz/2 cups plain
    (all-purpose) flour
pinch of salt
10ml/2 tsp lemon juice
150ml/¼ pint/⅔ cup chilled water

1 Cut up both the fats into small cubes. Spread out on a plate and freeze for 10 minutes.

2 Sift the flour and salt into a mixing bowl. Add the diced fat and stir to coat in flour. Make a well in the centre. Stir the lemon juice into the water and add to the dry ingredients. Mix together with a round-bladed knife to make a dough.

3 Gently shape into a block on a floured work surface, then roll out to a 35 x 20cm/14 x 8in rectangle. Fold the lower third of the pastry over the centre third, then fold the top third over that. Press the edges firmly with the rolling pin to seal. Wrap in clear film (plastic wrap). Chill for 10 minutes.

4 Roll out the pastry to the same size again, with the sealed edges at the top and bottom. Fold up and chill as before. Repeat the rolling, folding and chilling three more times. Wrap in clear film. Chill for at least 3 hours, but preferably overnight, before using.

ROUGH PUFF PASTRY

This is far less time-consuming to make than puff pastry, and has a lower proportion of fat to flour. You will get lovely flaky results, but not a good rise. Use it for flan crusts and sweet and savoury pies. This makes enough for two single-crust pies in 1.5 litre/2½ pint/6¼ cup dishes.

MAKES ABOUT 500G/1¼LB

250g/9oz/2¼ cups plain (all-purpose) flour
pinch of salt
175g/6oz/¾ cup chilled butter, diced
5ml/1 tsp lemon juice
120ml/4fl oz/½ cup chilled water

1 Sift the flour and salt into a bowl. Add the butter. Mix together with your fingertips. Stir the lemon juice into the water, then add to the dry ingredients and mix in with a round-bladed knife. Don't worry if the dough is slightly lumpy.

2 Put the dough on to a lightly floured surface and knead for a few seconds to bring it together.

3 Roll out the pastry to a 30 x 10cm/ 12 x 4in rectangle. Fold the lower third over the centre and the top third over that. Seal the edges. Wrap in clear film (plastic wrap) and chill for 15 minutes.

4 Place the pastry on a lightly floured surface with the sealed edges at the top and bottom. Roll, fold and chill, as before, four more times until you are ready to use it.

FLAKY PASTRY

When baked, this pastry looks a little like puff pastry, but has fewer layers. Instead of adding the fat at the start, it is incorporated by dotting it over the rolled-out dough. This creates pockets of air and helps to separate the layers. Half white vegetable fat or lard and half butter can be used for an even flakier texture. This makes enough for two single-crusts in 1.2 litre/2 pint/5 cup pie dishes.

MAKES ABOUT 450G/1LB

225g/8oz/2 cups strong white
    bread flour
pinch of salt
175g/6oz/³⁄4 cup chilled butter
150ml/¹⁄4 pint/²⁄3 cup chilled water

1 Sift the flour and salt into a mixing bowl. Rub or cut in 40g/1¹⁄2oz/3 tbsp of the butter until the mixture resembles fine breadcrumbs. Pour over 120ml/4fl oz/¹⁄2 cup of the water and, using a round-bladed knife, mix to a soft dough, adding more water if needed.

Using bought puff pastry

If you do not have the time to make your own pastry, ready-made chilled and frozen puff pastry can be bought instead, usually in two sizes: 375g/13oz and 450g/1lb. Ready-rolled puff pastry is also available; check the packet first to make sure it will be large enough for your needs. All-butter varieties are worth searching out as these are richer in flavour and particularly good.

2 Place the dough on a lightly floured clean work surface and gently knead it until it is smooth and pliable. Then wrap it in clear film (plastic wrap) and chill for 15 minutes in the refrigerator.

3 Roll the dough out to a 30 x 10cm/ 12 x 4in rectangle. Cut another 40g/ 1¹⁄2oz/3 tbsp of the remaining butter into small pieces and dot them evenly all over the top two-thirds of the pastry, leaving a 1cm/¹⁄2in margin at the edge.

4 Fold the lower third of the pastry up and over the centre third, and fold the buttered third down over that. Press the edges together to seal. Wrap in clear film (plastic wrap) and chill in the refrigerator for 10 minutes.

5 Repeat the rolling out and folding process (without adding any more of the butter) once more. Roll out the pastry two more times, with the folded edges at the sides, using 40g/ 1¹⁄2oz/3 tbsp of the butter each time. Roll it out and fold one more time, this time without adding any fat. Chill the finished pastry for at least 1 hour in the refrigerator before using.

SHORT-CUT FLAKY PASTRY

In this version, instead of dotting the dough with the fat, the butter is chilled and grated or shredded into the flour. This pastry has the same buttery flavour and crispness of flaky pastry, but it isn't as light. This makes enough for two single-crusts in 1.2 litre/2 pint/5 cup pie dishes.

MAKES ABOUT 450G/1LB

175g/6oz/³⁄4 cup chilled butter
225g/8oz/2 cups plain (all-purpose) flour
pinch of salt
90ml/6 tbsp chilled water

1 Put the butter into the freezer for 40 minutes, or until very hard. Sift the flour and salt into a mixing bowl and chill while the butter is hardening.

2 Holding the butter in a piece of foil, coarsely grate it into the flour, working quickly. Stir in the butter with a round-bladed knife. Sprinkle the water over the mixture and stir to make a dough, adding a little more water if needed.

3 Bring the dough together with your hands. Wrap it up in clear film (plastic wrap) and chill for 40 minutes before using.

CHOUX PASTRY

Choux pastry puffs up during baking to at least double its original size, creating a hollow centre, perfect for both sweet and savoury fillings.

Choux is one of the easiest pastries to make. Unlike other pastries, where the fat is rubbed into the flour, choux is made on the hob (stovetop). The butter is melted with water then brought to the boil before adding the flour. Beating the mixture over a low heat partially cooks the flour. Finally, eggs are gradually incorporated to make a thick glossy paste, ready for spooning or piping into puffs and éclairs, or for making an impressive gâteau (layer cake). This quantity is sufficient for 20 small puffs, 14 large puffs or 12 éclairs.

MAKES ABOUT 150G/5OZ

65g/2¹/₂oz/9 tbsp plain (all-purpose) flour
pinch of salt
50g/2oz/¹/₄ cup butter, diced
150ml/¹/₄ pint/²/₃ cup water
2 eggs, lightly beaten

1 Preheat the oven to 200°C/400°F/ Gas 6. Sift the flour and salt on to a piece of baking parchment. Heat the butter and water in a pan until the butter melts.

2 Increase the heat and bring to a rolling boil. Remove the pan from the heat and immediately tip in all the flour and beat vigorously until the flour is mixed into the liquid.

3 Return the pan to a low heat and beat the mixture until it begins to form a ball and leave the sides of the pan. This will take about 1 minute. Remove the pan from the heat again and allow to cool for 2–3 minutes.

4 Add the beaten eggs a little at a time, beating well between each addition, until you have a very smooth shiny paste, thick enough to hold its shape. (You may not have to add all the egg.)

5 Spoon or pipe the pastry on to a baking sheet dampened or lined with baking parchment. Space well apart.

Top choux pastry tips

• As the choux pastry cooks, the water in the dough turns to steam and puffs up the pastry so, when making, don't let the water boil before the butter fully melts or some of this essential water will evaporate and be lost.

• When adding flour, beat only until the paste begins to leave the sides of the pan; over-beating makes it oily.
• Eggs lighten the pastry and should be added a little at a time. The mixture will be slightly lumpy at first, but beat vigorously after each addition until the egg and paste are thoroughly mixed. This will ensure you have a smooth and glossy texture.

• Spoon or pipe choux pastry into the required shapes while it is still warm. For the best results, bake immediately.
• If short of time, you can make choux with a hand-held electric mixer.

STRUDEL PASTRY

Strudel is one pastry that doesn't need gentle handling; the more you bash the pastry dough, the more flexible it will be. It does require careful rolling-out on a very large surface until almost transparent. This makes enough for one large strudel.

MAKES ABOUT 275G/10OZ

225g/8oz/2 cups strong white bread flour
2.5ml/^{1}/$_2$ tsp salt
1 egg, lightly beaten
10ml/2 tsp sunflower oil
150ml/^{1}/$_4$ pint/^{2}/$_3$ cup slightly warm water

1 Sift the flour and salt into a bowl. Make a well in the centre. Stir the egg and oil into the water, add to the flour and mix to form a sticky dough.

2 'Beat' the dough by lifting it and slapping it down on to a lightly floured surface until it no longer sticks to your fingers, then knead for 5 minutes until smooth and elastic. Shape into a ball, place on a dish towel and cover. Leave to rest in a warm place for 30 minutes.

3 Lightly flour a very large clean cloth, such as a tablecloth, and roll out the dough as thinly as possible, lifting frequently to prevent it from sticking.

4 Stretch the dough with your hands spread out underneath it. Work around it, stretching until it is paper thin and forms a square 65cm/26in. Trim off the edges with scissors.

HOT WATER CRUST PASTRY

This traditional British pastry is used for cold meat and game pies. The following is enough for a 20cm/8in raised pie mould or loose-based cake tin (pan) or a 25 x 7.5cm/10 x 3in raised pie mould.

MAKES ABOUT 450G/1LB

275g/10oz/2^1/$_2$ cups plain (all-purpose) flour
1.5ml/^{1}/$_4$ tsp salt
65g/2^1/$_2$oz/5 tbsp lard or white vegetable fat
150ml/^{1}/$_4$ pint/^{2}/$_3$ cup water

1 Sift the flour and salt into a bowl. Make a well in the centre. Gently heat the fat and water in a pan until the fat melts. Increase the heat and bring to the boil. Pour the hot liquid into the dry ingredients. Mix to a soft dough.

2 Knead in the bowl for a few seconds until smooth. Wrap the dough in clear film (plastic wrap) and leave to rest in a warm place for 10 minutes until it feels firmer. Use while still warm.

PÂTE A PÂTE

This is a rich, buttery pastry that is the French equivalent of hot water crust pastry. The following makes enough for a 20cm/8in raised pie mould or loose-based tin (pan) or a 25 x 7.5cm/10 x 3in raised pie mould.

MAKES ABOUT 450G/1LB

225g/8oz/2 cups plain (all-purpose) flour
2.5ml/^{1}/$_2$ tsp salt
165g/5^1/$_2$oz/11 tbsp butter, softened
2 egg yolks
30–45ml/2–3 tbsp chilled water

1 Sift the flour and salt together to make a mound on a cool surface. Make a well in the centre. Add the butter. Place the egg yolks on top.

2 Using a light pecking action with your fingertips only, work the butter and yolks together. Pull in a little of the surrounding flour to prevent the mixture getting too sticky. Add a little of the water. Gradually work in all the flour, adding more water if necessary.

3 Knead for 30 seconds until the dough is smooth and soft. Wrap in clear film (plastic wrap). Chill for 30 minutes in the refrigerator.

Making flans and pies

Once the shortcrust, puff or filo pastry is prepared, you are ready to roll and line or cut and layer it into flans, pies or tartlets. Then there's any number of decorative ideas, from simple edgings to lattice tops, pastry cut-outs and glazes.

ROLLING OUT PASTRY

It is not difficult to roll out pastry properly. Try and ensure a cool and airy kitchen, keep the work surface and rolling pin lightly floured, and the dough well chilled. Dust the work surface and the rolling pin with flour as needed; never flour the pastry.

1 Roll out the pastry evenly in one direction, rolling from the centre to the far edge, but not over the edge. Always roll away from you and rotate the pastry frequently. When rolling out a round, turn the pastry 45 degrees each time to keep an even shape and thickness. (If rolling out to a square or a rectangle, rotate the pastry by 90 degrees each time.)

2 Once or twice during rolling out, push in the edges of the dough with your cupped palms, to keep the dough in shape. Avoid pulling the pastry as you roll it, or it will shrink during cooking.

LINING A FLAN TIN

A traditional flan tin (pan) has straight sides – either fluted or plain – and no rim. Most come with removable bases, making it easy to remove the flan without disturbing the base of it.

Less commonly used is a flan ring, which is a straight-sided metal ring that is set directly on a heavy baking sheet. They are often used by professional pastry cooks, and are a little more tricky to line with pastry.

When lining a very deep-sided flan tin, roll the pastry large enough to cover the base and sides of the tin, then fold it in half, then in half again. Lift the dough into the tin with the point in the centre, then unfold it to the edges of the tin.

1 Remove the chilled pastry from the refrigerator. If it has been chilled for longer than 1 hour, let it stand at room temperature for 15 minutes.

2 On a lightly floured surface, roll out the pastry to a thickness of 3mm/$\frac{1}{8}$in, and to a round about 5–7.5cm/2–3in larger than the flan tin, depending on the depth of the tin.

3 To transfer the pastry to the flan tin, fold the edge over the rolling pin. Roll the pastry loosely around the pin.

4 Hold the edge of the pastry round and rolling pin over the far edge of the flan tin and carefully unroll the pastry towards yourself, letting it settle easily into the tin without being stretched.

5 Lift the outside edge of the pastry and gently ease it into the base and sides of the tin. Gently press the pastry against the side of the tin so there are no gaps between the pastry and the tin.

6 Roll the rolling pin over the top of the tin to neatly cut off the excess dough. Prick the base all over with a fork, to stop it rising up during baking.

7 Cover the pastry case with clear film (plastic wrap) and chill in the refrigerator for at least 30 minutes to rest the pastry. This will prevent shrinking during cooking.

LINING PIE DISHES

There are three main ways to make a pie. The first is to line the tin with pastry and then fill it; the second is to have a single piece of pastry covering the pie (single-crust); and the third is to enclose the filling between two layers of pastry (double-crust).

You can use any of the shortcrust-type pastries when simply lining the tin, though French flan pastry is especially ideal. For single- and double-crust pies, plain or a rich shortcrust pastry is best.

Puff pastry also makes a good pie covering. Use the same techniques as for shortcrust pastry, but roll the dough slightly thicker, so it rises well.

Making a pastry base for a pie

Roll out the pastry until it is 5cm/2in larger all round than the pie dish. If using shortcrust or one of its variations, the pastry should be 3mm/$\frac{1}{8}$in thick.

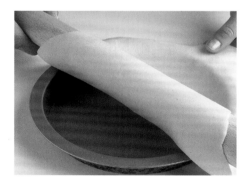

1 Wrap the pastry loosely around the rolling pin. Holding the rolling pin over the pie dish, gently unroll the pastry away from you so that it gently drapes into the dish, centring it as much as possible.

2 With floured fingertips, press the pastry over the base and up the sides. Trim off the excess with a sharp knife.

Making a single-crust pie

Roll out the pastry on a work surface until it is 3mm/$\frac{1}{8}$in thick and 5cm/2in larger all round than the dish.

1 Place the pie funnel in the dish, if using. Cut a 2cm/$\frac{3}{4}$in strip from the rolled out pastry. Brush the rim of the dish with water and place the pastry strip around the rim, pressing it down. Brush with water, then add the filling.

2 Using a rolling pin, place the pastry over the filling, using the pie funnel to support it. If you are not using a funnel, make a dome of filling, then cover with the pastry. Seal the edges.

3 Trim off the excess and finish the edge. Glaze and make steam holes.

Making a double-crust pie

Cut the pastry in half. Roll out one half on a floured surface to 3mm/$\frac{1}{8}$in thick, and 5cm/2in larger all round than the dish. Keep the other half wrapped in clear film (plastic wrap).

1 Lift the rolled out pastry into the pie dish using a rolling pin, without stretching it.

2 Spoon the filling into the case in a dome. Brush the edge with water to moisten it. Roll out the remaining pastry to a round larger than the top of the pie. Roll it up around the rolling pin and unroll over the pie. Press the edges together.

3 Hold the pie dish in one hand and cut off the excess pastry with a knife, holding the blade at a slight angle. Reserve the trimmings for use as decorations on the top or edge. Glaze, then make steam holes and bake.

Quantity guide for flans and tarts
These pastry weights are a guide only, and refer to shortcrust pastry and its variations only. Figures given are the combined weight of ingredients.

Tin (pan) size	Pastry weight
18cm/7in	200g/7oz
20cm/8in	275g/10oz
23cm/9in	350g/12oz
25cm/10in	400g/14oz
4 x 10cm/4in	250g/9oz
6 x 7.5cm/3in	250g/9oz

LINING TARTLET TINS

Use pâte sucrée, chocolate or almond pastry for sweet tarts, and rich shortcrust or French flan pastry for savoury ones.

1 When lining tartlet tins (muffin pans) that are less than 5cm/2in in diameter, put the tins together. Roll out the pastry until it is about 3mm/^{1}/₈in thick and able to cover all the tins. Wrap the pastry around the rolling pin, then drape it over the tins.

2 Using a floured thumb, press the pastry into the tins. Roll over the top with a rolling pin to trim the edges.

Lining a tin with fragile pastry
If your pastry is too fragile to roll out and lift into a loose-based flan tin (pan) with a rolling pin, remove the loose base and dredge it lightly with flour. Put the pastry on top then roll it out, so that it overhangs the base by 5cm/2in all round. Fold in the overhanging pastry then place the base back in the tin. Unfold the pastry over the edge of the tin, gently pressing into the sides of the tin to fit. Roll a rolling pin over the top to trim the edges.

LINING A HEATPROOF BOWL OR PUDDING BASIN WITH SUET PASTRY

This spongy pastry is normally used for steamed puddings but it can also be used as a single-crust topping for a baked pie. Its texture makes it easy to shape, but because it is made with self-raising (self-rising) flour it must be rolled out and used immediately.

1 Roll out three-quarters of the suet (US chilled, grated shortening) dough on a floured surface to a thick round, large enough to line the bowl or basin. Lift it into the bowl, overlapping the edge by 1cm/^{1}/₂in. Press out the folds with your fingers.

2 Spoon the filling into the bowl, so it nearly comes to the top. Lightly brush the pastry edge with cold water. Roll out the remaining pastry to make a lid. Place it on top of the filling, pressing down with your fingertips to seal the edges. Trim off the excess pastry with a sharp knife.

3 Cover the bowl or basin with a pleated, double layer of baking parchment, securing it under the rim with string. Top with pleated foil – the pleats will expand to allow the pastry to rise.

LINING A TIN WITH FILO PASTRY

Before lining the tin (pan), remove the filo from the refrigerator. Leave in its wrapper for 15 minutes at room temperature. Unwrap and unroll and place the filo stack on a board, covering it with a damp dish towel.

1 Lightly brush a sheet of filo pastry with cooled melted butter or oil, then line the base and sides of the tin. There is no need to grease the tin if it is shallow, but when lining a deep tin it is easier to position the first sheet of pastry if the tin is lightly greased.

2 Brush a second sheet of pastry with butter or oil and place on top of the first. Layer the pastry to the desired thickness: four or five sheets are usually enough. Neaten the edges by trimming with a pair of scissors. If the filo pastry only slightly overhangs the edge of the tin, it will look attractive if left a little jagged.

3 If the sheets of filo pastry aren't large enough to completely cover a tin, such as a tranche tin, layer up the pastry by covering each end, and overlapping it slightly in the middle to make the base wider.

MAKING FILO PASTRY PIES

Filo can be used to make all manner of pies. Use the melted butter sparingly, so that the finished pastry is crisp and golden.

Making simple filo toppings

For an incredibly quick and easy way to make a pie, top with either smooth or crumpled sheets of buttered or oiled filo. The filling should require little cooking as the pastry will be crisp and brown in about 30 minutes.

One-crust topping A savoury or sweet filling can be spooned into a pie dish and covered with a smooth filo pastry topping. You will need six sheets of filo, slightly larger than your pie dish – you can use the upturned dish as a guide. Spoon the filling into the dish. Place the sheets of filo on top, lightly buttering between the layers and neatly tucking them down the sides of the dish to fit smoothly.

Scrunch topping Loosely crumple sheets of buttered or oiled filo. Use five to six sheets of filo, placed buttered-side up, to cover the filling. The filling must not be too wet, or steam will spoil the crisp texture of the filo.

Making a free-form pie

Filo pastry can be used to make a free-form pie without using a dish or tin (pan). Pies can be any size you choose.

1 Melt and cool 50g/2oz/¼ cup butter. Take eight large sheets of filo pastry. Lay the first sheet on a damp dish towel or baking sheet. Brush with melted butter.

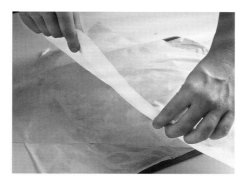

2 Cover with a second sheet of pastry at a slightly different angle and brush with a little butter. Add three more sheets in the same way, brushing with butter as you go.

3 Put the filling into the centre. Cover with the remaining sheets, brushing each layer with butter. Draw up the pastry edges around the filling, twisting and scrunching them to seal. Brush with the remaining butter before baking.

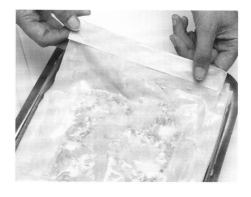

Double-crust filo pies

A single sheet of filo can be draped over the base and sides of a tin, and folded over to enclose the filling.

Brush the tin with melted butter. Fit a square sheet of filo pastry into each tin, draping it so that it hangs over the sides. Brush with butter. Add another sheet at right angles to the first. Spoon in the filling. Draw the overhanging edges together and scrunch to cover the filling. Brush with melted butter before baking.

Working with filo

Filo comes stacked into sheets, factory-rolled to a thinness that only a pastry chef could achieve.
• Keep the stack covered with a damp dish towel and peel off only the sheets that you're working with. It can be cut, folded or layered into shape for quick and easy results.
• To add flavour and to make the pastry light and crisp, lightly brush sheets of bought filo with melted butter or oil, as you layer them.
• Bought pastry is available in various sizes; smaller sheets are about 30 x 18cm/12 x 7in and larger ones are about 50 x 24cm/20 x 9½in.

CREATING DECORATIVE EDGES

For some patterns, most pastries will be thick enough around the edge, but shortcrust and rich shortcrust need a double thickness. If the pie only has a single pastry layer on the rim, leave an overhang of pastry when trimming that can be tucked under the edge to create a double thickness.

Knocking up

After trimming, finish by holding the blunt edge of a knife horizontally against the pastry edge. Tap to seal and make indentations all the way round.

Crimped edges

Leave an overhang of 1cm/½in all round. Fold under. Push your forefinger into the rim and, using the thumb and forefinger of the other hand, pinch the pastry to form 'V' shapes. Work the pattern all around.

Ruffled edges

Leave an overhang of about 1cm/½in all the way around the dish and fold under. Place your thumb and forefinger inside the pastry's edge and use the forefinger of the other hand to pull the dough between them to the edge of the rim. Continue all the way around.

Scalloped edges

Instead of using your thumb and forefinger to decorate the crust, a knife can be used very effectively to finish the edge of the pie. Trim the pastry with a knife to leave an overhang of 1cm/½in all the way around the dish and fold it under the rim. Press your forefinger and middle finger on the edge of the pastry. Pressing the blunt edge of a small knife between them, mark a regular pattern around the edge of the rim at 2.5cm/1in intervals.

Gabled edges

Trim the pastry to the rim of the dish. Use a knife to make an even number of cuts about 1cm/½in apart all the way around. Using your forefinger, fold alternate pieces of pastry inwards around the entire other edge of the pie. Use on dishes with a rim of more than 1cm/½in.

Ribbon edges

To create a ribbon edge for a pie, trim the pastry even with the rim of the pie dish. Cut long strips of pastry about 2cm/¾in wide with a sharp knife. Moisten the edge of the rim with a little water, taking care not to make it too wet. Carefully twist a pastry strip and attach it to the rim with gentle pressure, twisting and attaching as you go. Add in another pastry strip, if necessary, to cover the entire outer edge of the pie. Press the ends together to seal.

Cut-out edges

Trim the pastry even with the rim. Using a small pastry cutter, stamp out shapes from the trimmings. Moisten the rim with water and attach the shapes.

Braided edges

Cut three narrow strips. Pinch the ends together. Take the right hand strip and lay it over the centre strip. Take the left strip and lay over the new centre piece.

Twisted edges

Twist together two sausage shapes. Seal the ends. Attach to the moistened rim.

DECORATING A PIE WITH A LATTICE TOP

Roll out half the pastry dough, using either shortcrust or a variation. Line the pie dish. Trim to leave a 1cm/½in overhang all round. Add the filling.

1 Roll out the remaining pastry to a round that is 5cm/ 2in larger all round than the dish. Cut strips 1cm/½in wide.

2 Lay half the strips across the pie, evenly spaced and parallel.

3 Fold back to the centre every other strip. Lay another strip across, on the flat strips, at right angles to them. Lay the folded strips flat again.

4 Next, fold back those strips that were not folded the first time. Lay another strip across those now flat, spacing this new strip evenly from the centre strip.

5 Continue until half of the lattice is completed. Now repeat the entire process on the other side.

6 Trim the ends of the lattice strips even with the rim of the dish. Moisten the edge of the case with a little water, taking care not to make it too wet. Press the strips gently on to it to seal the edges. Decorate the rim of the pie as wished.

How to bake flans and pies

When you are ready to bake your flan or pie, there are a few simple rules that will ensure perfect cooking.

Always preheat the oven for about 15 minutes to reach the required temperature. Bake pastry on the middle shelf or just above the middle of the oven, unless otherwise stated.When blind-baking or cooking a double-crust pie, heat a heavy baking sheet in the oven. The hot sheet will give the base of the pie a blast of heat to help make the bottom of the pastry crisp.

Baking times may vary depending on your oven and how chilled the pie was. Check the pie at least 5 minutes before the end of the suggested cooking time. Don't keep opening the oven door though, or the temperature will drop, and the pastry will be less crisp.

BAKING SHORTCRUST PASTRY

Shortcrust pastry and its variations should be well chilled before baking to minimize shrinkage. Between 30 and 60 minutes is adequate for a flan or pie that is filled prior to baking. If a flan case is to be blind-baked or filled just before baking, chill for an hour uncovered, or cover with clear film (plastic wrap) and chill overnight.

Shortcrust-type pastries are usually baked at 200°C/400°F/Gas 6, but often the temperature is reduced part-way through baking to allow the filling to cook sufficiently. Pastries that contain added sugar need to be removed from the oven as soon as the pastry is golden brown, or they can burn very quickly.

Don't cook foods that release a lot of steam at the same time as the shortcrust is cooking. This could stop the pastry from becoming crisp.

BAKING BLIND

This process is used to partly cook an empty pastry case so that it does not become soggy when the filling is added. It is also used to completely bake a case when the filling cooks in a short time and you need to ensure that the pastry is fully cooked, and when the case is to contain a filling that does not require any cooking.

Lining the pastry case with baking parchment or foil and filling it with baking beans stops the pastry from rising up during cooking.

1 Cut out a round of baking parchment or foil about 7.5cm/3in larger than the tin. Prick the base of the case all over with a fork.

2 Press the baking parchment or foil smoothly over the base of the case and up the sides.

3 Evenly spread commercially made ceramic baking beans, or dried beans, over the base of the case.

4 To partially bake, place in a preheated oven at 200°C/400°F/Gas 6 for 15 minutes until the pastry is set and the rim is dry and golden. Lift out the paper and beans. Bake for a further 5 minutes. The pastry case can now be filled and the baking completed.

5 For fully baked pastry, bake at 200°C/400°F/Gas 6 for 15 minutes, then remove the paper and beans and return to the oven. Bake for a further 5–10 minutes, or until golden brown. Cool completely before filling.

6 Allow 6–8 minutes for partial baking of tartlets, and 12–15 minutes for fully baked pastry.

Planning ahead
Fully baked pastry cases may be baked up to two days ahead if carefully stored in airtight containers. Interleave them with greaseproof (waxed) paper, or use baking parchment, if you are keeping several, and always make sure that they are cooled before storing.

BAKING PUFF PASTRY

Puff pastry should be chilled before baking, and shaped puff pastries should be chilled for at least an hour. Take great care when brushing with egg glaze; any that runs down the sides of the pastry will make the layers stick together and prevent the pastry from rising well and evenly.

Layered pastries must be cooked in a preheated hot oven, so that the air trapped within the layers expands and, together with the steam produced by the water, lifts up the pastry. If the oven is too cool the butter will melt before the dough has a chance to cook, preventing the pastry from rising well. The oven temperature is usually 230°C/450°F/Gas 8, but small pastries are sometimes cooked at 220°C/425°F/Gas 7. Reduce the temperature after about 15 minutes, to give the filling enough time to cook through.

When baking single- and double-crust pies, up to three slits or holes should be made in the pastry top to allow the steam from the filling to escape. Don't make too many steam holes though, or too much air will be lost and the pastry won't rise well. After baking, cover steam holes with cooked pastry decorations.

Unlike shortcrust pastries, a steamy atmosphere helps the pastry to rise. Put a dish of hot water on the lowest shelf when preheating the oven. Remove it for the last few minutes of cooking. If the pastry starts to sink after cooking, it hasn't cooked sufficiently and should be returned to the oven for a little longer.

BAKING FILO PASTRY

Filo pastry does not require chilling before baking, but it must never dry out, or it will become brittle and hard to fold and shape. Keep the sheets you are not working with covered with a damp dish towel. It may also crumble if it is too cold so, before using, remove from the refrigerator and allow to stand for 1 hour.

Filo must always be lightly brushed with melted butter before baking to give it a shiny glaze — unsalted butter is perfect because it has a lower water content, or oil can also be used. Choose a flavoursome oil, such as groundnut (peanut) or sunflower oil, or try olive oil when making savoury pastries. It should be brushed as thinly and evenly as possible to create light, crisp layers. Never brush with egg or milk as this will make it soggy.

The usual temperature for baking filo pastry is 200°C/400°F/Gas 6, although it can be cooked at a slightly lower temperature without its crisp texture being affected. It colours quickly, so check the oven often towards the end of cooking. If it has browned sufficiently before the filling is done, cover it with foil, then remove it again for the last few minutes of cooking to make sure the top of the pie is dry and crisp.

Wrap any unused filo in clear film (plastic wrap) and return it to the refrigerator. It will keep for seven to ten days. It is possible to re-freeze filo, but don't do this more than once. To thaw, allow 4 hours at room temperature, or leave overnight in the refrigerator.

Shortcrust baking tips for success

• Repair any holes in a cooked pastry case by brushing with a beaten egg, then returning the case to the oven for 2–3 minutes to seal. Larger holes can be repaired by pressing a little raw pastry in the gap, brushing with egg, then returning to the oven.
• If the pastry starts to bubble up during baking, remove the case from the oven, prick again with a fork to release trapped air and return to the oven. If it has bubbled up when you take it out after cooking, make a very small slit in the case with a knife and leave it to shrink back on its own.

• If pastry fully browns before the filling is cooked, protect it with foil. Cover single- or double-crust pies completely, making a steam hole in the top. On open flans, just cover the pastry edge.

Shaping and baking choux pastry

This thick, smooth and glossy paste can be piped or spooned into a variety of shapes. It can also be fried to make churros and French aigrettes, which are crunchy on the outside and soft in the centre. It is made on the hob (stovetop). Shape it while warm for best results.

PIPING CHOUX PASTRY

Before piping, draw guidelines on the baking parchment, then place the paper pencil-side down on the baking sheet. **Rounds** Use a piping (pastry) bag with a 1cm/$\frac{1}{2}$in nozzle for small puffs, or, for large puffs, a 2.5cm/1in nozzle. Use a wet knife to cut off the pastry.

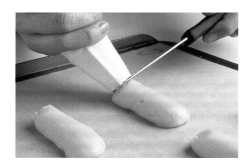

Eclairs Spoon into a piping bag with a 2.5cm/1in plain nozzle. Pipe 10cm/4in lengths on to parchment. Use a wet knife to cut off the pastry.
Ring Draw an 18cm/7in circle on parchment. Place pencil-side down on a baking sheet. Spoon the choux into a piping bag with a 1cm/$\frac{1}{2}$in nozzle and pipe a ring using the pencil guide.

SHAPING CHOUX PUFFS

Whether spooned or piped, these balls of choux will rise to about three times their original size, creating a hollow centre for filling. Small ones are perfect for profiteroles and larger ones can be turned into cream buns.

Small and large puffs

To make small puffs, use two small spoons dipped in water. Drop the paste in 2.5cm/1in balls on a greased or lined baking sheet. Leave a 4cm/1$\frac{1}{2}$in space between each. For large puffs, make balls 5cm/2in wide.

FRYING PIPED CHOUX PASTRY

Choux pastry can be deep-fried in hot oil, to give a crisp, golden outside and a soft, light centre.

Spoon into a piping bag with a large star nozzle. Pipe four or five 7.5cm/3in lengths at a time into hot oil, using scissors to snip off each length. Fry for 3 minutes until crisp, then drain.

BAKING CHOUX PASTRY

No matter what shape or size, choux pastry should be dark golden and crisp on the outside and cooked sufficiently so that it holds its shape when removed from the oven. For this reason, choux is usually baked at a higher temperature first, to cook the outside, then at a lower one to firm and dry the pastry. Bake small puffs in a preheated oven at 200°C/400°F/Gas 6 for 15–20 minutes; large puffs, eclairs and rings will take 25–30 minutes. Turn down the oven to 180°C/350°F/Gas 4, remove from the oven, make small slits in the sides of the pastries, then return and bake small puffs for a further 5 minutes; large puffs, eclairs and rings for a further 8–12 minutes.

It is important not to open the oven during the first 15 minutes of baking or the choux may collapse. When you remove the pastries to make slits in them, check that they are fully cooked and set first.

The more steam in the oven at the start of baking, the more successfully the pastry will rise. Try dampening the baking sheet by sprinkling it with cold water before piping the pastry, or place an ovenproof dish of water on the lowest shelf of the oven. Remove for the last 5 minutes of cooking to allow the pastries to become properly crisp.

Choux pastries are best freshly made, but will keep for a day or two in an airtight container. To regain their crispness, place in a medium oven for 3–4 minutes. Once filled, serve them as soon as possible.

Shaping and baking hot water crust pastry

This pastry is used for traditional cold meat and game pies as it holds its shape and can withstand long cooking.

MOULDING HOT WATER CRUST PASTRY

Keep this pastry warm while moulding; if the lard starts to set, it may crack.

1 Make a basic quantity of dough, and cut off one-third. Wrap it in clear film (plastic wrap) and leave in a warm place. Shape the remaining two-thirds into a ball. Grease and flour the outside of an empty 900g/2lb jam jar. Turn it upside-down and mould the dough over the base and two-thirds down the sides.

2 Cover with clear film (plastic wrap) and chill for 20 minutes. Invert the case and jar on to a baking sheet and ease out the jam jar. Spoon the filling into the mould, packing it firmly. Roll out the reserved pastry to make a lid.

3 Wrap the trimmings and set aside. Dampen the edges, place the lid on top, and crimp to seal. Make a hole in the top of the pie with a 1cm/½in plain pastry cutter. Attach pastry trimmings, if you wish. Secure a double layer of baking parchment around the pie with paper clips to keep the pastry in shape during cooking.

LINING A TIN WITH HOT WATER CRUST PASTRY

To line a 15cm/6in round cake tin (pan), you need to use 350g/12oz/3 cups plain (all-purpose) flour, 1.5ml/¼ tsp of salt, 75g/3oz/6 tbsp fat and 190ml/6½fl oz/ generous ¾ cup warm water. To line a 23cm/9in long pointed oval pie tin, or a 20cm/8in round springform tin, use the following: 450g/1lb/4 cups plain flour, 2.5ml/½ tsp salt, 115g/4oz/½ cup fat and 250ml/8fl oz/1 cup water.

1 Make the pastry as before. Cut off slightly less than a third, wrap in clear film (plastic wrap) and set aside in a warm place. Roll out the remaining pastry to a round large enough to line the tin. Lift the pastry in, allowing the edges to hang over. Mould the pastry into place with your fingers, then spoon in and pack down the filling.

2 Trim off the overhanging pastry, angling the knife outwards. Wrap the pastry trimmings and set them aside.

3 Roll out the reserved pastry to make a lid slightly larger than the top of the tin. Brush the edges with water and place the lid over the pie. Press the edges together to seal, then crimp to give it a fluted edge.

BAKING HOT WATER CRUST PASTRY

Hot water crust pies are usually cooked at 200°C/400°F/Gas 6 for the first 20–30 minutes, then at 180°C/350°F/Gas 4 or lower for the remaining cooking time.

1 Use a small cutter to make a steam hole in the middle of the lid, or cut a cross in the lid and fold back the corners. Make decorations with the leftover pastry trimmings and attach them to the crust to cook with a little water, or bake them separately.

2 After baking put a funnel through the hole in the lid and pour in jelly or aspic until it reaches the level of the lid. Replace or add the cooked pastry decorations and then chill until set. If the jelly leaks through a crack, seal it by filling with butter.

Making parcels and shaped pastries

Without the restrictions of tins and pie dishes, there are an infinite number of ways to shape pastry packages. Shortcrust and puff pastries and their variations, as well as filo, can all be simply and easily used to create delicious parcels in a range of sizes.

SHAPING SHORTCRUST PASTRY

Rounds, strips, crescents and squares of shortcrust pastry provide the perfect packages for sweet and savoury fillings. Mini baked circles of pastry also serve as delightful bases to toppings of fresh fruit and cream.

Making round parcels

This little round pastry parcel is ideal for sweet fillings of thinly sliced raw fruit such as apples and pears tossed in a little sugar, or cooked, then drained, fruits such as gooseberries. The hole in the top allows the filling to be seen and provides a steam hole.

1 Roll out 450g/1lb shortcrust pastry to a thickness of 3mm/1 1/8in. Cut four 10cm/4in rounds and four slightly larger rounds, about 13cm/5in in diameter. Use a small pastry cutter to stamp a hole in the centre of the larger rounds. Spoon a small heap of filling on the smaller rounds.

2 Brush the edges of the filled rounds with water, cover with the larger rounds and crimp the edges together. Bake for 20 minutes at 200°C/400°F/Gas 6 for a cooked filling, or at a lower temperature for longer if uncooked.

Making pasties

In these traditional single-serving pies, shortcrust pastry completely encloses the filling, which is usually a mixture of either raw or cooked minced (ground) meat and vegetables.

1 Roll out 450g/1lb shortcrust pastry to a thickness of 5mm/1/4in and cut into four 20cm/8in rounds. Spoon the filling into the centre of each round and brush the edges with water. Bring the edges together to seal, then flute.

2 Transfer to a baking sheet, brush with egg and make a steam hole in the top. For uncooked filling, bake at 220°C/425°F/Gas 7 for 15 minutes, then lower the heat to 160°C/325°F/Gas 3. Bake for 1 hour. For cooked filling, bake at 200°C/400°F/Gas 6 for 20–25 minutes.

3 To cook pasties on their side, spoon the filling on to one half of each circle. Brush the edges with water. Fold over the other pastry half. Press to seal. Finish and bake as before.

Making turnovers

These triangular-shaped pastries are usually made with a pre-cooked filling such as apple. Savoury vegetable and meat mixtures are also popular.

1 Roll out 300g/11oz rich shortcrust pastry to a 25cm/10in square 3mm/1/8in thick. Cut into four squares. Place the filling on one side of a diagonal centre line, brush with water, then fold over.

2 Press the edges to seal and mark a pattern with a fork. Brush with beaten egg and make a slit in the top to allow steam to escape. Bake at 200°C/400°F/Gas 6 for 25 minutes.

Making crescents

Rich shortcrust pastry is used to make these crescent-shaped pastries as it is a flexible pastry. They are ideal for richer fillings, such as cream or curd cheese with dried fruits.

Roll out 450g/1lb pastry to a thickness of 3mm/1/8in and stamp out nine rounds, using a plain or fluted 7.5cm/3in cutter. Place the filling on one side of each. Brush with a little milk, then fold over and press the edges together to seal. Make a steam hole in each and bake at 200°C/400°F/Gas 6 for 18–20 minutes.

Making fruit dumplings

Whole peeled and cored fresh fruit is delicious wrapped in pastry and then baked. Choose firm ripe fruit which won't disintegrate during cooking.

1 Roll out 400g/14oz rich shortcrust pastry to a 35cm/14in square and cut into four squares of the same size. Place a small apple or a squat pear on each pastry square – the hollowed-out centre of the fruit can be stuffed if you like.

2 Brush the edges with egg and pull up the four corners to meet at the top. Press the edges together to seal, then flute with your forefinger and thumb. Chill for 40 minutes before brushing with egg and baking at 220°C/425°F/Gas 7 for 30 minutes. Reduce the oven to 180°C/350°F/ Gas 4 and bake for 20 minutes more until the pastry is golden and the fruit is tender when pierced with a skewer.

3 Alternatively, you can encase whole fruit in strips of pastry. Cut the rolled out pastry into 1cm/½in strips and wind them around the prepared fruit from the base to the stalk end, slightly overlapping the edges and dampening with a little water to hold together. Chill, then bake them as before.

Wrapping larger fillings

Known as en croûte, wrapping meat in pastry keeps it succulent. These dishes can be prepared up to a day before cooking, providing the meat or fish is very fresh, as the pastry stops the meat from drying out. Cover with clear film (plastic wrap) and chill until needed, but allow to stand at room temperature for 25 minutes before baking.

Brown the outside of larger cuts such as beef and lamb, then cool; this isn't necessary for smaller pieces of meat or fish. Use about 450g/1lb rich shortcrust pastry or puff pastry for a 1.3kg/3lb fillet (tenderloin) of beef and 800g/1¾lb for a leg of lamb or medium-sized salmon.

1 Roll out the pastry to the appropriate shape, large enough to fully enclose the meat or fish. Wrap the meat or fish in the pastry. Seal the edges with a little water, then put seam side down on a baking sheet.

2 Use a tiny round cutter to stamp two or three steam holes out of the pastry. Bake at 200°C/400°F/Gas 6 for the first 15 minutes, then lower the temperature to 180°C/350°F/Gas 4, using a meat thermometer to check if the meat is cooked.

Making pastry tubes

Little cannoli cylinders, 10cm/4in long, are used as moulds to shape and bake pastry. The pastry tubes can then be filled with flavoured whipped cream or ricotta cheese, nuts and candied fruit, and dusted with sugar.

1 Roll out 7.5cm/3in rounds of pâte sucrée into ovals the same length as the cannoli moulds. About 350g/12oz pastry will make eight tubes. Wrap each oval lengthways around a mould, sealing the join with egg white. Chill for 30 minutes.

2 Deep-fry in sunflower oil heated to 180°C/350°F until golden brown. Drain on kitchen paper and remove from the moulds while still hot.

Making galettes

The name of these round flat pastries comes from the French word for a flat weather-worn pebble. They are made from sweet pastries such as pâte brisée or pâte sucrée, and are topped with fruit and cream. Roll out the pastry to a thickness of 5mm/¼in and stamp out 6cm/2½in rounds. Place the rounds on a baking sheet, prick all over and chill. Bake at 200°C/400°F/Gas 6 for 10 minutes until golden brown.

SHAPING PUFF PASTRY

Although puff pastry rises, it holds its shape well and is used for well-known pastry gateaux (layer cakes) such as mille-feuilles, as well as smaller sweet and savoury puff pastries, such as palmiers and mini vol-au-vents.

Making puff pastry envelopes

Puff pastry is more flexible than shortcrust, and less likely to tear when making a parcel. It works well with partially or fully cooked fillings, such as chopped cooked chicken and vegetables in a white sauce.

1 Roll out 350g/12oz puff pastry to a 30cm/12in square. Pile the filling into the middle of the square to form a 14cm/5$^1/_2$in square at right angles to the pastry (so that it looks like a diamond).

2 Bring the corners of the dough to the centre and gently crimp the edges together. Make a small steam hole. Chill for 30 minutes before brushing with beaten egg. Bake in a preheated oven at 230°C/450°F/Gas 8 for 15 minutes, then reduce the heat to 190°C/375°F/Gas 5 for 15 minutes more until crisp and golden.

Making puff pastry cases

Known as vol-au-vents, these cases can be made in different sizes and can be stuffed with all sorts of fillings, from hot garlic mushrooms to prawns (shrimp) in mayonnaise. When baked, the scored inner circle makes a lid that can be lifted out and the outer circle forms the walls of the vol-au-vent.

1 Roll out 500g/1$^1/_4$lb puff pastry to a 23cm/9in round. Put a dinner plate on top and cut round with a knife. Lift the pastry round on to a baking sheet.

2 Put a side plate in the middle of the round pastry and, holding it firmly, score the pastry around it, but do not cut all the way through the pastry.

3 Knock up the pastry edges with the back of a knife. Chill for 30 minutes, then bake in a preheated oven at 230°C/450°F/Gas 8 for 25 minutes.

4 Cut around the pastry lid with a small sharp knife, and carefully lift the lid out in one piece. Set the lid aside. Scrape any soft pastry out of the middle of the vol-au-vent, then return it to the oven for about 4 minutes to dry out. Spoon filling into the vol-au-vent, then replace the lid.

Making bouchées

These vol-au-vents are made quite tiny, and are usually served as finger food. They are cooked at a slightly lower temperature so the pastry becomes really dry and crisp. Make fillings thick without too much sauce, so that they can be easily picked up.

Unbaked cases can be cooked from frozen. 450g/1lb puff pastry will yield about 25 bouchées.

1 Roll out the pastry to a thickness of 5mm/$^1/_4$in. Stamp out rounds using a floured 4cm/1$^1/_2$in cutter. Transfer the rounds to a baking sheet. Brush the tops with beaten egg.

2 To make the lid, cut halfway through the depth of each round using a slightly smaller cutter. Chill, then bake in a preheated oven at 220°C/425°F/Gas 7 for 12–15 minutes until golden brown. When cooked, ease off the lid. Scoop out any soft pastry and discard. Spoon in the filling. Replace the lids and serve.

Planning ahead
Puff pastry cases are best eaten on the day they are baked, but they can be made up to a day ahead and stored in an airtight container.

Varying vol-au-vent depth and shape

Puff pastry cases can be made deeper by placing a ring of pastry on top of the pastry round, making it possible to add more filling. Different shaped cases are also possible.

1 To make individual deep round vol-au-vents, roll out the pastry to 5mm/¼in thick and stamp out rounds using a floured 10cm/4in cutter. Cut rings from half the pastry rounds, using a 7.5cm/3in cutter and discard the centres.

2 Place the large rounds on a baking sheet. Brush the edges with egg, then place a ring on top of each. Chill, brush the rings with egg, and bake at 220°C/425°F/Gas 7 for 15–18 minutes. Discard the centres, or use as lids.

Mini rectangular cases can be made by rolling the puff pastry out to 7.5 x 10cm/3½ x 4in rectangles, about 5mm/¼in thick. Cut an inner rectangle 2.5cm/1in from the edge, scoring halfway through. Mark criss-cross lines on the inner rectangle, brush with egg and bake in a preheated oven at 220°C/425°F/Gas 7 for 12–15 minutes. Use the notched rectangles for lids.

Making a slatted-top pie

Also known as a jalousie, a slatted-top pie was originally a simple pastry filled with jam. Today, various fillings are used.

1 Roll out 500g/1¼lb puff pastry to a 30cm/12in square. Trim the edges. Cut in half to make two rectangles. Put one on a baking sheet and chill. Spread the pastry on the baking sheet with 225g/8oz/¾ cup jam, leaving a 2.5cm/1in border all round. Dampen the edges with a little water or milk.

2 Fold the second piece of pastry in half lengthways. Make cuts 1cm/½in apart along the folded edge to within 2.5cm/1in of the outer edge.

3 Without unfolding, carefully place the folded piece of pastry on top of one side of the jam-covered pastry, so that the corners and edges match, then unfold the slatted pastry to cover the other half.

4 Press the edges of the pastry together to seal, then knock them up with the back of a knife. Chill for 30 minutes before baking in a preheated oven at 230°C/450°F/Gas 8 for 25 minutes. Cut the jalousie in crossways slices to serve.

Gateau Pithiviers

This scored-top pastry originates from the town of the same name, near Paris. It has a rum-flavoured almond filling and is recognized by the spiral pattern on the pastry lid.

1 Roll out two 25cm/10in rounds from 500g/1¼lb puff pastry. Place one on a baking sheet. Mix 50g/2oz/¼ cup butter, 115g/4oz/1 cup sifted icing (confectioners') sugar, 115g/4oz/1 cup ground almonds, 2 egg yolks and 30ml/2 tbsp rum in a bowl, and spread over the pastry round leaving a border of 2.5cm/1in all round.

2 Brush the border with water and top with the second pastry round, pressing to seal the edges. Knock up and scallop the edge.

3 With a knife, mark curved lines 5mm/¼in apart, from the centre to the edge of the pie, and cutting only halfway through the pastry. Cover the pie with clear film (plastic wrap) and chill in the refrigerator for about 30 minutes. Glaze, then bake in a preheated oven at 230°C/450°F/Gas 8 for 25 minutes.

Making puff pastry layers

Mille-feuille is the classic example of a layered puff pastry dessert and means a thousand leaves. After baking, the rectangles of pastry are sandwiched together, usually with fruit and cream.

1 Roll 500g/1¼lb puff pastry to a 30 x 20cm/12 x 8in rectangle. Cut into three pieces, each 10 x 20cm/4 x 8in.

2 Place on a baking sheet, cover and chill for 30 minutes. Brush with egg, prick each piece, then bake in a preheated oven at 230°C/450°F/Gas 8 for 8–10 minutes. Cool and sandwich the layers together with the filling.

Making feuilletées

These are a simple form of mille-feuille. Small rectangles of puff pastry are baked then split in half to form two layers. A filling such as whipped cream and fruit is added, then the layers are sandwiched back together.

Roll out 350g/12oz puff pastry and cut into four 10 x 6cm/4 x 2½in rectangles, 1cm/½in thick. Chill for 20 minutes, then brush with beaten egg and bake in a preheated oven at 220°C/425°F/Gas 7 for 12–15 minutes.

Shaping palmiers

These pastries are a Parisian speciality. They are often simply rolled in sugar, or may have a nut filling of finely chopped almonds, walnuts or hazelnuts mixed with ground cinnamon and sugar.

1 Lightly sprinkle the work surface with caster sugar and roll out 225g/8oz puff or rough puff pastry to a 50 x 20cm/20 x 8in rectangle.

2 Brush with beaten egg, then sprinkle evenly with half the nut mixture.

3 Fold in the long edges of the pastry to meet in the centre and flatten with the rolling pin. Brush the top with egg and sprinkle with three-quarters of the nut mixture. Fold in the edges again to meet in the centre, brush with egg and sprinkle with the remaining nut mixture. Fold half the pastry over the other half.

4 Cut crossways into 2cm/¾in thick slices and place, cut side down, about 2.5cm/1in apart on greased baking sheets. Slightly open up the pastries.

5 Bake in a preheated oven at 220°C/425°F/Gas 7 for 8–10 minutes until golden, turning the palmiers over halfway through the cooking time.

Making coiled puff pastry cones

Strips of puff pastry are coiled around metal cornet moulds then baked to make cones ready to be filled with flavoured whipped cream. To make a savoury version, prepare the cones without the sugar coating, and fill with a mixture of pâté and butter.

1 Roll out 225g/8oz puff pastry to a 56 x 15cm/22 x 6in rectangle. Starting at one short end, roll up tightly. Cut the roll into 1cm/½in coiled slices.

2 Unroll each coil and dampen the ends of each strip with water. Wrap the pastry around a lightly greased metal cornet mould in a spiral, starting at the pointed end and overlapping it slightly. At the end, press the strip firmly to secure.

3 Chill on a baking sheet, finished ends underneath, for 30 minutes. Brush with egg. Sprinkle with caster (superfine) sugar. Bake in a preheated oven at 220°C/425°F/Gas 7 for 8–10 minutes.

4 Cool the pastries on the baking sheet for 5 minutes, then carefully remove from the moulds. Allow to cool completely, before piping in flavoured whipped cream.

SHAPING FILO PASTRY

This paper-thin pastry is incredibly easy to shape and can be simply cut to the required size with a normal pair of scissors.

Making a filo pastry roll

This is an easy way to use filo pastry. It combines well with sweet and spicy fruit fillings. Use 675g/1¹/₂lb of mixed apples, dried fruit, sugar and spices.

1 Carefully separate six sheets from a large packet of filo pastry. Lay one sheet of filo on a dish towel, lightly brush it with melted butter, then place a second sheet on top. Continue to layer the filo, brushing butter between each layer.

2 Spoon the filling over the filo pastry leaving a 2.5cm/1in margin around the edges. Turn in the short pastry side edges.

3 With the help of the clean dish towel, roll up the pastry from a long edge to completely enclose the filling. Transfer the filo roll to a greased baking sheet and brush with a little melted butter before baking in a preheated oven at 180°C/350°F/ Gas 4 for 30–40 minutes until crisp and golden brown.

Making layered filo pastries

The Middle East, Turkey and Greece all have their own version of baklava, where layers of buttery filo are filled with nuts, sugar and spices, and sometimes slices of fruit, before being baked and coated in a syrup. Lemon, cinnamon or cardamom and scents such as rose water or orange flower water may be used in the syrup. This very sweet and sticky pastry is usually cut into small diamonds and served with cups of strong black coffee.

1 Cut 16 sheets of filo pastry to snugly fit an 18 x 25cm/10 x 7in baking tin (pan). Put a sheet of filo pastry in the base of the tin. Brush with melted butter and top with another sheet. Repeat until there are eight layered sheets.

2 Sprinkle half of the filling over, then place two sheets of filo on top, brushing each with more melted butter as before. Sprinkle over the rest of the filling.

3 Layer the remaining sheets of filo on top, buttering each one, including the final layer. Mark a diamond pattern, cutting through to the base. Bake in a preheated oven at 160°C/325°F/Gas 3 for 50 minutes until golden.

4 Remove the baklava from the oven, and pour over a spicy sugar syrup. Leave in the tin until cold, then serve cut into diamonds. Store in an airtight container and eat within three days.

Making filo baskets

Crisp filo cups can be made by layering up buttered squares of pastry on top of small metal moulds, then baking. Fresh berries make a delicious filling, and rich seafood is a good savoury option. When cool, they can be stored in an airtight container for up to two days, but, once filled, serve them within an hour or so.

Invert ramekins on a baking sheet and grease with a little unsalted butter. Cut the filo pastry sheets into 13cm/5in squares, and brush each with a little melted butter. Drape four or five filo squares at different angles over each mould. Bake in a preheated oven at 180°C/350°F/Gas 4 for 12 minutes until golden and crisp. Cool, then fill.

Making a spiced sugar syrup
This sweet spicy syrup is ideal for pouring over baklava or drizzling over fruit in baskets. To make, put the pared rind and juice of ¹/₂ lemon in a pan with 150g/5oz/³/₄ cup caster (superfine) sugar, 60ml/4 tbsp water and a cinnamon stick. Heat until the sugar dissolves, then simmer for about 2 minutes. Cover and infuse (steep) for 10 minutes. Strain and stir in 10ml/2 tsp rose water or orange flower water.

Making braided filo parcels

These parcels are an attractive way of presenting individual portions. They can be used for either savoury or sweet fillings.

1 Use sheets of filo about 30 x 18cm/ 12 x 7in and fold in half widthways. Put the filling in the middle and fold the sides over to make a neat parcel. This will stop the mixture from seeping out through the braided filo during cooking.

2 Brush a second sheet of folded filo with cooled melted butter and place the parcel, seam side down, in its centre. Make six cuts in the pastry, an equal distance apart, on either side of the parcel, stopping just short of the edges. Fold the top and bottom edges over the ends of the parcel.

3 Fold the pastry strips over the parcel, alternating sides to achieve a braided effect. Place the parcel on a baking tray and brush with melted butter over the braided ends, to fix securely in place. Bake in a preheated oven at 190°C/350°F/ Gas 5 for 20 minutes, or until the pastry is lightly browned and crisp.

Making filo cocktail snacks

Filo pastry can be stacked in layers with a filling and baked before being cut to the required shape and size. Strong flavours, such as goat's cheese and olives, work well.

These are meant to be eaten with fingers, so it's important that they hold together when the pastries are picked up. Chop the ingredients finely before mixing together and spread them thinly; this will help to make the pastries easier to cut when baked.

1 Layer three sheets of filo, brushing each layer with a little cooled melted butter or oil. Thinly spread with full-fat cream cheese blended with plenty of chopped fresh herbs. Top with three more layers of filo, each brushed with a little melted butter or oil. If you like, add flavourings to the butter or oil – chopped fresh herbs such as parsley, mint or oregano would all work well, or try chopped red and green chillies.

2 Mark squares across the pastry with a knife. Bake in a preheated oven at 180°C/350°F/Gas 4 for about 20 minutes until golden and crisp. Cut into bitesize pieces along the scored lines and serve hot or cold.

Making filo purses

Sometimes called money or swag bags, these parcels are made by drawing the edges together and pinching the neck. Choose a richly flavoured filling to contrast with the generous serving of filo pastry. A mixture of lightly cooked leeks with Roquefort cheese would be delicious, as would a rich tomato filling, given a fillip with the addition of anchovies. The more robust the filling, the better.

1 Cut filo pastry into 13cm/5in squares. Lay three squares on top of each other, each at a slight angle to the others to make a 12-pointed star. Brush each layer with melted butter or oil. Flavoured oils such as garlic or sesame may be used, first blended with a milder oil such as sunflower so that the flavour isn't overpowering.

2 Spoon in the filling – a heaped teaspoon will be plenty – then pull the corners of the pastry up round it and pinch firmly to seal and make a neat purse shape.

3 Place on a baking sheet and brush with melted butter or oil. Bake in a preheated oven at 190°C/375°F/Gas 5 for 15 minutes until golden brown.

Making coiled filo pastries

In Morocco and the Middle East coiled filo pastries often contain a sweet rather than savoury filling, and rich-scented almond paste is a popular choice. These coiled pastries are simple to make: you will need about 200g/7oz almond paste.

1 Use eight sheets of filo, each measuring 30 x 18cm/12 x 7in. Place two on a work surface, overlapping them slightly to form a 56 x 18cm/ 22 x 7in rectangle. Brush the overlapping pastry with melted butter to secure, then brush the whole sheet sparingly with more melted butter.

2 Shape one-quarter of the almond paste into a long sausage, place along the edge of the filo sheet and roll up tightly. Repeat with the rest of the paste and filo to make four lengths.

3 Shape the first roll into a coil. Attach the remaining rolls by brushing with melted butter, making a large coil. Brush with butter. Bake on a baking sheet in a preheated oven at 180°C/ 350°F/Gas 4 for 25 minutes. Invert on to another baking sheet and brush with butter. Bake for 5–10 minutes more.

Making filo triangles

Traditional Indian pasties, or samosas, consist of small deep-fried or baked filo triangles, which are usually filled with a pre-cooked spiced minced (ground) meat or potato and vegetable filling. These triangles can be used to enclose other fillings, however, such as chopped spring onions (scallions) softened in butter and mixed with cooked prawns (shrimp). Six sheets of filo will make 12 triangles.

1 Fold the filo sheets, each measuring 30 x 18cm/12 x 7in, in half lengthways. Cut in half widthways. Brush with a little melted butter if baking in the oven; if deep-frying the triangles, this step is not necessary.

2 Place a spoonful of filling on the filo, 5cm/2in from the end. Turn over one corner to make a triangle. Fold the triangle over on itself, down the length of the filo, to fully enclose the filling. Seal the ends with oil.

3 Deep-fry the triangles in vegetable oil heated to 190°C/375°F for 4–5 minutes, turning them so they brown evenly. Drain on kitchen paper. Alternatively, bake in the oven at 190°C/375°F/Gas 5 for 20 minutes.

Making filo spring rolls

Spring roll wrappers are usually used, but filo works very well too, and is more readily available. Brushing the edges with a little beaten egg stops the rolls from unravelling during frying. Keep the wrapping thin, so that you can just see the filling inside. Suitable fillings include ingredients such as beansprouts, water chestnuts, bamboo shoots and soaked dried mushrooms, with chopped prawns (shrimp) or finely minced (ground) pork.

1 Cut the filo pastry into 13cm/5in squares and brush them lightly with oil. Place the filling in a strip about 2.5cm/1in from one side of the square, leaving a 2cm/3/4in margin at both ends.

2 Fold the sides of the square over the filling, then roll up the pastry to enclose the filling completely, carefully sealing all the loose edge with a little beaten egg.

3 Deep-fry the spring rolls, a few at a time, in oil heated to 180°C/350°F, for 4–5 minutes. Drain on kitchen paper to get rid of the excess oil and serve warm.

Index